STEPHEN WALSH

Drools JBoss Rules 5.X Developer's Guide

D1373001

Define and execute your business rules with Drools

Michal Bali

[PACKT] PUBLISHING

open source
community experience distilled

BIRMINGHAM - MUMBAI

Drools JBoss Rules 5.X Developer's Guide

Copyright © 2013 Packt Publishing

All rights reserved. No part of this book may be reproduced, stored in a retrieval system, or transmitted in any form or by any means, without the prior written permission of the publisher, except in the case of brief quotations embedded in critical articles or reviews.

Every effort has been made in the preparation of this book to ensure the accuracy of the information presented. However, the information contained in this book is sold without warranty, either express or implied. Neither the author, nor Packt Publishing, and its dealers and distributors will be held liable for any damages caused or alleged to be caused directly or indirectly by this book.

Packt Publishing has endeavored to provide trademark information about all of the companies and products mentioned in this book by the appropriate use of capitals. However, Packt Publishing cannot guarantee the accuracy of this information.

First published: May 2013

Production Reference: 1170513

Published by Packt Publishing Ltd.
Livery Place
35 Livery Street
Birmingham B3 2PB, UK.

ISBN 978-1-78216-126-4

www.packtpub.com

Cover Image by Suresh Mogre (suresh.mogre.99@gmail.com)

Credits

Author

Michal Bali

Reviewers

Alaa Abed

Mario Fusco

Acquisition Editor

Kunal Parikh

Lead Technical Editor

Joel Noronha

Technical Editors

Kaustubh S. Mayekar

Sharvari Baet

Project Coordinator

Arshad Sopariwala

Proofreader

Jonathan Todd

Indexer

Rekha Nair

Graphics

Ronak Dhruv

Production Coordinator

Melwyn D'sa

Nilesh R. Mohite

Cover Work

Nilesh R. Mohite

About the Author

Michal Bali, freelance software developer, has more than 8 years of experience working with Drools and has an extensive knowledge of Java, JEE. He designed and implemented several systems for a major dental insurance company. He is an active member of the Drools community and can be contacted at michalbali@gmail.com.

I'd like to thank Drools lead Mark Proctor and his team that consists of Edson Tirelli, Mario Fusco, Kris Verlaenen, and other contributors for giving me something to write about. They were of great help while I was writing the book.

I'd also like to thank all the reviewers and the whole editorial team for their patience and help while I was writing this book and in particular, Sarah Cullington, Suchi Singhal, Anish Ramchandani, Joanna Finchen, Mario Fusco, and other anonymous reviewers.

Finally, I thank my wife Michala for supporting me and putting up with me while I wrote.

About the Reviewers

Alaa Abed is a die-hard open source philosophy advocate. In 1995, after having his Masters degree in automation, he started his career in software engineering. His early projects involved writing assembly language and C/C++ device drivers, TCP/IP stack implementation, and Unix terminal emulation tools.

His passion with Java started in 1998 when he designed and implemented a content management system for mobile content syndication. Since then, he has been working with a diverse set of clients across various industries such as financial, energy, health, and many ISVs.

For the past several years he enjoyed designing Java frameworks for ORM, MVC-based presentation, analytics and reporting and enabling rapid development for rich web applications.

He currently is a Senior Architect working on enterprise integration, multichannel delivery, and business intelligence solutions.

I'd like to thank Sara and Nadia for making my life worth living.

Mario Fusco is a senior software engineer at Red Hat working at the development of the core of Drools, the JBoss rule engine. He has huge experience as a Java developer, having been involved in (and often leading) many enterprise-level projects in several industries ranging from media companies to the financial sector. Among his interests, there are also functional programming and domain-specific languages. By leveraging these two passions, he also created the open source library lambdaj with the purposes of providing an internal Java DSL for manipulating collections and allowing a bit of functional programming in Java.

www.PacktPub.com

Support files, eBooks, discount offers and more

You might want to visit www.PacktPub.com for support files and downloads related to your book.

Did you know that Packt offers eBook versions of every book published, with PDF and ePub files available? You can upgrade to the eBook version at www.PacktPub.com and as a print book customer, you are entitled to a discount on the eBook copy. Get in touch with us at service@packtpub.com for more details.

At www.PacktPub.com, you can also read a collection of free technical articles, sign up for a range of free newsletters and receive exclusive discounts and offers on Packt books and eBooks.

http://PacktLib.PacktPub.com

Do you need instant solutions to your IT questions? PacktLib is Packt's online digital book library. Here, you can access, read and search across Packt's entire library of books.

Why Subscribe?
- Fully searchable across every book published by Packt
- Copy and paste, print and bookmark content
- On demand and accessible via web browser

Free Access for Packt account holders

If you have an account with Packt at www.PacktPub.com, you can use this to access PacktLib today and view nine entirely free books. Simply use your login credentials for immediate access.

For Matilda.

Table of Contents

Preface

Business rules and processes can help your business by providing a level of agility and flexibility. As a developer, you will be largely responsible for implementing these business rules and processes effectively, but implementing them systematically can often be difficult due to their complexity. Drools makes the process of implementing these rules and processes quicker and handles the complexity, making your life a lot easier!

This book guides you through various features of Drools, such as rules, processes, decision tables, complex event processing, Drools Rete implementation with various optimizations, and others. It will help you to set up the Drools platform and start creating your own business. It's easy to start developing with Drools if you follow our real-world examples that are intended to make your life easier.

Starting with an introduction to the basic syntax that is essential for writing rules, the book will guide you through validation and human-readable rules that define, maintain, and support your business agility. As a developer, you will be expected to represent policies, procedures, and constraints regarding how an enterprise conducts its business; this book makes it easier by showing you the ways in which it can be done.

A real-life example of a banking domain allows you to see how the internal workings of the rules engine operate. A loan approval process example shows the support of processes within Drools. Parts of a banking fraud detection system are implemented with the Drools Fusion module, which is the complex event processing part of Drools. This, in turn, will help developers to work on preventing fraudulent users from accessing systems in an illegal way.

Finally, more technical details are shown on the inner workings of Drools, the implementation of the ReteOO algorithm, indexing, and node sharing.

What this book covers

Chapter 1, Programming Declaratively, introduces the reader into the domain of business rules and business processes. It talks about why standard solutions fail at implementing complex business logic. We will also see a possible solution in the form of a declarative programming model. The chapter talks about its advantages and disadvantages. A brief history of Drools is also mentioned.

Chapter 2, Writing Basic Rules, shows us the basics of working with the Drools rule engine, Drools Expert. It starts with a simple example that is explained step-by-step. It begins with the development environment setup, writing a simple rule and then executing it. The chapter goes through some necessary keywords and concepts that are needed for more complex examples.

Chapter 3, Validating, introduces the reader to a banking domain that will be the basis for examples later in this book. The chapter then goes through an implementation of a decision service for validating this banking domain. A reporting model is designed that holds reports generated by this service.

Chapter 4, Transforming Data, shows how Drools can be used for doing complex data transformation tasks. It starts with writing some rules to load the data, continues with the implementation of various transformation rules, and finally, puts together the results of this transformation. The chapter shows how we can work with a generic data structure such as a map in Drools.

Chapter 5, Creating Human-readable Rules, focuses on rules that are easy to read and change. Starting with domain-specific languages, the chapter shows how to create a data transformation-specific language. Next, it focuses on decision tables as another more user friendly way of representing business rules. An interest rate calculation example is shown, and finally, the chapter introduces the reader to jBPM as a way of managing the rule execution order.

Chapter 6, Working with Stateful Session, talks about executing the validation decision service in a stateful manner. The validation results are accumulated between service calls. This shows another way of interacting with a rule engine. Logical assertions are used to keep the report up-to-date. Moreover, various ways to serialize a stateful session are discussed.

Chapter 7, Complex Event Processing, goes through various features such as events, type declarations, temporal operators, sliding windows, and others. Drools Fusion, another cornerstone of the Drools platform, is about writing rules that react to various events. The power of Drools Fusion is shown on a banking fraud detection system.

Chapter 8, Defining Processes with jBPM, goes into more detail about the workflow aspect of the Drools platform. It is shown on a loan approval service that demonstrates the use of various nodes in a flow. Among other things, the chapter talks about implementing a custom work item, human task, and a subflow.

Chapter 9, Building a Sample Application, shows you how to integrate Drools in a real web application. We'll go through the design and implementation of persistence, business logic, and presentation layers. All examples written so far will be integrated into this sample application.

Chapter 10, Testing, aims to give you an idea of various ways of how to test your business logic. Starting with unit testing, integration testing through acceptance testing will be shown on the business rules management server (Guvnor). The chapter provides useful advice on various troubleshooting techniques.

Chapter 11, Integrating, shows integration with the Spring framework. It describes how we can make changes to rules and processes while the application runs. It shows how to use an external build tool such as Ant to compile rules and processes. It talks about the rule execution server that allows us to execute rules remotely. It also briefly mentions support of various standards.

Chapter 12, Learning about Performance, takes us under the hood of the Drools rule engine. By understanding how the technology works, you'll be able to write more efficient rules and processes. It talks about the ReteOO algorithm, node sharing, node indexing, and left/right unlinking.

Appendix A, Setting Up the Development Environment, lists the various steps required to get you up and running with Drools.

Appendix B, Creating Custom Operator, shows an implementation of a custom operator that can be used to simplify our rules.

Appendix C, Dependencies of Sample Application, lists various dependencies used by the sample application.

What you need for this book

In order to learn Drools and run the examples in this book, you'll need a computer with any operating system (Windows, Mac, or Linux), Java Development Kit (JDK) Version 1.5 or later, Drools binary distribution, some IDE—preferably Eclipse IDE for Java EE developers, Drools and jBPM plugins for Eclipse, and some third-party libraries that will be specified per chapter. All the mentioned software is freely available on the Internet under a business friendly license.

You can download some additional support material from `http://code.google.com/p/droolsbook/`.

Who this book is for

The book is for Java developers who want to create rules-based business logic using the Drools platform. Basic knowledge of Java is essential.

Conventions

In this book, you will find a number of styles of text that distinguish between different kinds of information. Here are some examples of these styles, and an explanation of their meaning.

Code words in text are shown as follows: "Let's say that we have the `Account` bean that has one property called `balance`."

A block of code will be set as follows:

```
if (customer.getLevel() == Level.Gold) {
  // do something for Gold customer
} else if (customer.getLevel() == Level.Silver) {
  if (customer.getAccounts() == null) {
    // do something else for Silver customer with no accounts
  } else {
    for (Account account : customer.getAccounts()) {
      if (account.getBalance < 0) {
        // do something for Silver Customer that has
        // account with negative balance
      }
    }
  }
}
```

New terms and **important words** are shown in bold. Words that you see on the screen, in menus or dialog boxes for example, appear in the text like this: "Clicking on the **Next** button moves you to the next screen".

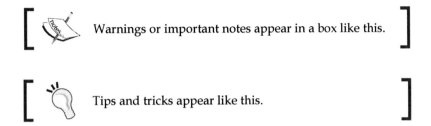

Warnings or important notes appear in a box like this.

Tips and tricks appear like this.

Reader feedback

Feedback from our readers is always welcome. Let us know what you think about this book—what you liked or may have disliked. Reader feedback is important for us to develop titles that you really get the most out of.

To send us general feedback, simply send an e-mail to feedback@packtpub.com, and mention the book title via the subject of your message.

If there is a topic that you have expertise in and you are interested in either writing or contributing to a book, see our author guide on www.packtpub.com/authors.

Customer support

Now that you are the proud owner of a Packt book, we have a number of things to help you to get the most from your purchase.

Downloading the example code

You can download the example code files for all Packt books you have purchased from your account at http://www.packtpub.com. If you purchased this book elsewhere, you can visit http://www.packtpub.com/support and register to have the files e-mailed directly to you.

Errata

Although we have taken every care to ensure the accuracy of our content, mistakes do happen. If you find a mistake in one of our books—maybe a mistake in the text or the code—we would be grateful if you would report this to us. By doing so, you can save other readers from frustration and help us improve subsequent versions of this book. If you find any errata, please report them by visiting http://www.packtpub.com/submit-errata, selecting your book, clicking on the **erratasubmissionform** link, and entering the details of your errata. Once your errata are verified, your submission will be accepted and the errata will be uploaded on our website, or added to any list of existing errata, under the Errata section of that title. Any existing errata can be viewed by selecting your title from http://www.packtpub.com/support.

Piracy

Piracy of copyright material on the Internet is an ongoing problem across all media. At Packt, we take the protection of our copyright and licenses very seriously. If you come across any illegal copies of our works, in any form, on the Internet, please provide us with the location address or website name immediately so that we can pursue a remedy.

Please contact us at copyright@packtpub.com with a link to the suspected pirated material.

We appreciate your help in protecting our authors, and our ability to bring you valuable content.

Questions

You can contact us at questions@packtpub.com if you are having a problem with any aspect of the book, and we will do our best to address it.

1
Programming Declaratively

The need to build more and more complex systems is increasing. We're trying to automate all kinds of business processes and implement complex business decisions (for example, insurance-claim adjudication, subscriber enrollment, retail-pricing, promotion, banking-mortgage application, and fraud detection). However, these processes and decisions may not be represented well using traditional programming languages, such as Java or C#. Instead, we should use a specialized technology, such as the Drools platform.

In this chapter we'll look at why there is a need for a platform such as Drools, what advantages and disadvantages it brings, and when or not to use it. We'll briefly look at its history and what modules it consists of.

Problems with traditional approaches

There is no well-defined way to represent the business logic in Java or C#. What usually happens is that every application represents business logic differently.

For example, consider this code that does some checking on customer level, customer accounts, and account balance:

```
if (customer.getLevel() == Level.Gold) {
  // do something for Gold customer
} else if (customer.getLevel() == Level.Silver) {
  if (customer.getAccounts() == null) {
    // do something else for Silver customer with no accounts
  } else {
    for (Account account : customer.getAccounts()) {
      if (account.getBalance < 0) {
```

```
        // do something for Silver Customer that has
        // account with negative balance
      }
    }
  }
}
```

Code listing 1: Code written in standard Java (or any imperative-style language)

First, the code checks if the customer's level is `Gold` and does something, then it checks if the customer's level is `Silver`, and if so, it checks if this customer has no accounts and does something in this case. If the customer has accounts, the code performs some logic for each account that has a negative balance.

The point of this Java "spaghetti code" is to give you an idea about what we are trying to prevent. You may think that it doesn't look that bad; however, after a couple of changes in requirements and developers who are maintaining the code, it can get much worse. It is usually the case that if you fix one bug, you are more likely to introduce several new bugs. Lots of requirements are literally packed into few lines of code. This code is hard to maintain or change to accommodate new requirements.

It is not only difficult to represent business logic in an imperative programming style language, but it is also hard to differentiate between code that represents the business logic and the infrastructure code that supports it.

For developers, it is hard to change the business logic. For the domain experts, it is impossible to verify the business logic and even harder to change it.

There is a need for a different paradigm for representing the business logic.

The solution

The problem is that with an imperative-style language, we are implementing both: what needs to be done (business requirements) and how it needs to be done (algorithm). Let's look at declarative-style programming, for example, the SQL in relational databases. The SQL describes what we want to search; it doesn't say anything about how the database should find the data. This is exactly what we need for our business requirements.

A rule engine provides an alternative computation model. We declare rules in pretty much the same way as the business analyst does requirements, that is, as a group of if-then statements. The rule engine can then take these rules and execute them over our data in the most efficient way. Rules that have all their conditions true have their then part evaluated. This is different to imperative-style programming languages where the developer has to explicitly specify how it needs to be done (with sequence of conditionals and loops).

If we rewrite code from *Code listing 1* in a declarative manner, it might look something like this:

```
if Customer( level == Level.Gold )
then do something else for Gold customer

if Customer( level == Level.Silver )
and no Account( )
then do something for Silver customer who has no accounts

if Customer( level == Level.Silver)
and Account( balance < 0, customer.accounts contains account )
then do something for Silver Customer that has account with negative
balance
```

Code listing 2: Rules from Code listing 1 written using declarative style

Each rule represents one requirement. This is more readable and maps to business requirements more naturally.

It is also useful to note that in an imperative program, the piece of code evaluating the customer's level in the first example needs to be explicitly invoked, passing to it a specific customer. In a declarative program you cannot invoke a given rule directly; do not decide on which data you want to run it, because the customer instance is actually taken from a working memory (this will be described later).

Advantages

The following is a summary of the various advantages of a declarative-style solution that Drools brings:

- **Easier to understand**: Rules are easier to understand for a business analyst or a new developer than a program written in Java or other imperative-style language. It is more likely for a technically skilled business analyst to verify or change rules than a Java program.

- **Improved maintainability**: Since rules are easier to understand, a developer can spend more time solving the actual problem.

- **Dealing with evolving complexity**: It is much easier to add new, modify, or remove existing rules than to change, for example, a Java program. The impact this has on other rules is minimal in comparison with an imperative-style implementation.

- **Flexibility**: It deals better with changes to the requirements or changes to the data model. Changing or rewriting an application is never an easy task. However, thanks to the formalism that rules bring, it is much easier to change rules than to change a Java program.

- **Reasonable performance**: Thanks to the Rete algorithm that is behind Drools; in theory, the performance of the system doesn't depend on the number of rules. With every release of Drools, the performance of the engine is getting better by adding various optimizations such as Rete node sharing, node indexing, parallel execution, and so on. All this benefits new as well as old rules.

- **Translating requirements into rules**: The representation of business rules is consistent. For example, let's take some business rule and implement it in Java. Developers, depending on their experience, tend to use different ways to solve a problem. We'll find out that the possible solutions will vary greatly. Whereas with rules, this diversification becomes less apparent. It is simply because we are expressing "what" instead of "how". As a result the code is much easier to read even by new developers.

- **Ability to apply enterprise management to our rules**: This builds on the previous advantage of consistent representation. If we have consistent representation, it is much easier to introduce new features that apply across all our rules (for example, auditing, logging, reporting, or performance optimizations).

- **Reusability**: The rules are kept in one place (separation of business logic from the rest of the system), which means easier reusability. For example, imagine you've written some validation rules for your application and later on there is a need to do some batch imports of data, so you could simply reuse the validation rules in your batch import application.

- **Modeling the application closely**: Rules model the application invariants more closely. The imperative-style solutions tend to impose arbitrary and often unnecessary ordering on operations, depending on the algorithm chosen. This then hides the original invariants of the application.

- **Unifying**: The Drools platform brings unification of rules and processes. It is easy to call rules from a process or vice versa.

- **Redeploying**: It is possible to change/redeploy rules and processes without even stopping the whole application.

Disadvantages

On the other side don't think of Drools as the silver bullet. Writing systems that make complex decisions is never an easy task; Drools just helps to make it a bit easier. You'll have to invest in the training of developers. Failing to do so can result in inefficient rules and seemingly unpredictable results. The developers need to adopt a different way of thinking to write business rules declaratively. It may look difficult at first, but once we master this, then the rules will be much easier and faster to write.

You may be thinking that since we don't specify how the business rules should be implemented, we just specify what needs to happen, and so it may be difficult to troubleshoot. This is a valid point, and to resolve this, Drools comes with a variety of tools that greatly help you with troubleshooting.

When you are debugging a program written in Java, you can easily step through the program flow and find out what is going on. The debugging of rules can be more difficult without an understanding of how the underlying system works. Rule engines have many advantages, but on the other side, they can be dangerous if you don't know exactly what's going on. And in this book you'll learn just that.

Another disadvantage of a rule engine is its memory consumption. This is a price a rule has to pay for being efficient. Lots of calculations are being cached to avoid processing them again. However, since the memory is so cheap nowadays, this is no longer a problem.

The interaction of rules can be quite complex, especially when some rules modify data that other rules depend on, which can easily cause recursion. The Drools platform provides many ways to prevent this from happening.

When not to use a rule engine

You probably don't need a rule engine:

- If your project is small, possibly with less than 20 rules then a rule engine would probably be an overkill. However, think twice before making a decision, because many systems start small, but as more requirements are implemented, it suddenly becomes unmanageable.

- If your business logic is well-defined or static and doesn't change often; you don't need to change rules at runtime.

- If your rules are simple, self-contained, usually spanning only a single object (for example, a check that a user's age is less than 21). You don't need a rule engine if in pseudocode, you don't have more than two nested `if-then` statements. Again, consider this carefully because every system grows in complexity overtime.

- If the performance is your primary concern. Are you implementing some algorithm where you want to have precise control over its execution? For example, it is not a good idea to write a video codec in a rule engine. Do you have a memory-constrained environment?

- If your project is a one-shot effort and it will never be used again or maintained over time.

- If you don't have the time and money to train your developers to use a rule engine. If developers have no prior experience with declarative programming, you need to include it in your time planning. It can take few weeks to get used to the syntax and start to write rules.

If you answered yes to any of these questions, you probably shouldn't use a rule engine.

Drools

Drools is a **Business Logic integration Platform (BLiP)**. It is written in Java. It is an open source project that is backed by JBoss and Red Hat, Inc. It is licensed under the Apache License, Version 2.0 (`http://www.apache.org/licenses/LICENSE-2.0.html`). This book will focus on Version 5.5 of this platform that was released in November 2012.

Work on Drools (the rule engine) began in 2001. From its beginning Drools underwent many changes. Drools 1.0 started with a brute force linear search. It was then rewritten in Version 2.0, which was based on the Rete algorithm. The Rete algorithm boosted Drools' performance. Rules were written mainly in XML. The next Version 3.0 introduced a new `.drl` format. This is a domain-specific language specially crafted for writing rules. It proved to be a great success and it became the main format for writing rules. Version 4.0 of the rule engine had some major performance improvements together with first release of **Business Rules Management System (BRMS)**. This formed the base for the next big release 5.0, where Drools became a BLiP. The platform consists of four main modules:

- **Drools Expert**: This is a rule engine itself.

- **Drools Fusion**: This is a **complex event processing** (CEP) module. It is will be covered in *Chapter 7, Complex Event Processing*.

- **jBPM**: Workflow combines rules and processes together. It will be introduced at the end of *Chapter 5, Creating Human-readable Rules* and then fully covered in *Chapter 8, Defining Processes with jBPM*.

- **Drools Guvnor**: This is a BRMS. It won't be covered in this book except for testing and rule analysis in *Chapter 10, Testing*.

Drools has several optional modules. For example, OptaPlanner for solving planning problems or Drools Chance that adds uncertainty support. Another very important part of Drools is its Eclipse plugin.

Drools has a very active and friendly community. It is growing with every year. You can get in touch by visiting the Drools blog, wiki, or the mailing lists. For more information please visit the Drools website at `http://www.jboss.org/drools/`.

Summary

We've learned why there is a need for a business logic integration platform such as Drools. What problems it is trying to solve and in what ways it is trying to solve them. We've seen advantages and disadvantages of this solution.

In the following chapter we're going to look at how to set up the development environment before starting with some basics needed to write and execute rules in Drools.

2
Writing Basic Rules

In this chapter we'll start writing our first rules in Drools. We'll go through some basics needed to write and execute rules. We'll learn the necessary keywords of the Drools rule language.

But before all this we have to set up our development environment. If you haven't already done so, please refer to *Appendix A, Setting up the Development Environment*, on development environment setup.

Rule basics

We'll now write our first Drools rule. Let's say that we have the `Account` bean that has one property called `balance`. For every `Account` bean whose balance is less than 100, we want to write a message to the standard output:

```
package droolsbook;

rule "basic rule"
  when
    Account( balance < 100 ) // condition
  then
    System.out.println("Account balance is " +
      "less than 100"); // consequence
end
```

Code listing 1: Basic rule file (basic.drl)

The rule file mentioned earlier starts with a package name. The package acts as a namespace for rules. The rule names within a package must be unique. This concept is similar to Java's packages (classes within a Java package must have different names). After the package definition comes the rule definition. It starts with the rule name, following with the conditions and consequence sections. `rule`, `when`, `then`, and `end` are the Drools keywords. This rule is triggered for every bean instance of type `Account`, whose balance is less than 100. The rule prints a message to `System.out`. As we're used to in Java, `//` denotes a comment.

Very simply said: the condition section defines patterns that the rule matches with. The consequence is a block of code that is executed when all patterns within the condition are matched. Note that condition is sometimes referred to as **left-hand side (LHS)** and consequence as **right-hand side (RHS)**.

`Account` bean/**Plain Old Java Object (POJO)** is straightforward; one field with getter and setter:

```
package droolsbook;

import org.apache.commons.lang.builder.EqualsBuilder;
import org.apache.commons.lang.builder.HashCodeBuilder;
import org.apache.commons.lang.builder.ToStringBuilder;

public class Account {
  private long balance;

  public long getBalance() {
    return balance;
  }

  public void setBalance(long balance) {
    this.balance = balance;
  }

  @Override
  public boolean equals(final Object other) {
    if (this == other)
      return true;
    if (!(other instanceof Account))
      return false;
    Account castOther = (Account) other;
    return new EqualsBuilder().append(balance,
        castOther.balance).isEquals();
  }
```

```
@Override
  public int hashCode() {
    return new HashCodeBuilder(1450207409, -1692382659)
      .append(balance).toHashCode();
  }

  @Override
  public String toString() {
    return new ToStringBuilder(this)
      .append("balance", balance).toString();
  }
}
```

Code listing 2: Account bean/POJO

Drools can access the balance property directly (if it is public) or through a getter method, getBalance(). Please note that the rule and the Account bean are in the same package; this means that we don't have to import anything in our rule file.

The Account bean overrides the equals, hashCode, and toString methods. The first two are necessary for Drools to work correctly. Drools needs to know when two different objects are logically equal (whether they represent the same thing). The Apache Commons Lang library was used to simplify the implementation of these methods. It follows rules laid out in Effective Java by Joshua Bloch. This library can be downloaded from http://commons.apache.org/lang/download_lang.cgi. If we didn't override these methods, they would inherit the default implementation from the Object class. The equals method by default returns true if the input parameter is the same object instance/reference. The hashCode method by default returns different values for different object instances. This is not the logical equality check that we're after.

Executing rules

We have written a rule and a POJO. Now is the time to write an application to execute our rule. The application will create a session and will insert one instance of the Account POJO object into the session and execute the rule. The session represents our interaction with the Drools engine:

```
public class BasicRulesApp {
  public static final void main(String[] args) {
    KnowledgeBase knowledgeBase = createKnowledgeBase();
    StatefulKnowledgeSession session = knowledgeBase
      .newStatefulKnowledgeSession();
    try {
Account account = new Account();
```

```
        account.setBalance(50);
        session.insert(account);
        session.fireAllRules();
    } finally {
        session.dispose();
    }
}
```

Code listing 3: Simple application for executing Drools (part 1 of 2)

Please note that most of the time the code listings in this book won't contain Java import statements. Use the autoimport feature of your favorite editor to import the correct Java type. We'll be using classes from the standard Java library. In the case of a third-party library, the correct package will be explicitly mentioned. Drools has some classes with the same names in different packages. Luckily, they are located in separate modules. Always prefer classes from the knowledge-API module. In fact the classes from the knowledge-API module represent the only public and stable API of Drools.

The first part of *Code listing 3* shows the creation of a KnowledgeBase object. It is created by calling the createKnowledgeBase method.

org.drools.KnowledgeBase

This is an interface that manages a collection of rules, processes, and internal types. In Drools these are commonly referred to as knowledge definitions or knowledge. The knowledge definitions are grouped into knowledge packages. The knowledge definitions can be added or removed. The main purpose of the KnowledgeBase object is to store and reuse them, because their creation is expensive. The KnowledgeBase object provides methods for creating knowledge sessions. Their creation is very lightweight.

By default, the KnowledgeBase object maintains a reference to all created knowledge sessions. This is to accommodate updates to KnowledgeBase at runtime. Drools has one implementation of this interface. This implementation can be serialized. We can reuse the serialized KnowledgeBase object instead of creating a new one every time.

This implementation is based on the Rete (usually pronounced as reet, ree-tee, or re-tay) algorithm.

The KnowledgeBase object is then in turn used to create a stateful knowledge session. For now we won't mind whether it is stateful or not.

org.drools.runtime.StatefulKnowledgeSession

This is an interface that acts as an entry/exit point to the Drools engine. It has methods for inserting, updating, or retracting facts. The StatefulKnowledgeSessionis object is also used to set a session's global variables. Probably, the most interesting part of its API is the fireAllRules method, which is used to execute all rules. Event handlers can be registered on the KnowledgeBase object for auditing, debugging, or other purposes. When you finish working with the StatefulKnowledgeSession object, do not forget to call the dispose method, otherwise this object can't be garbage collected, as it also has a transient reference to parent KnowledgeBase.

A new Account instance is then created and its balance is set to 50. This instance is inserted into the session.

If we want to reason over an object, we have to insert it into the session. The object is also sometimes referred to as a fact.

Finally, we call the fireAllRules method to execute our basic rule and the dispose method to release resources. At this point we're done with the main method.

We'll continue with the implementation of the createKnowledgeBase method:

```
private static KnowledgeBase createKnowledgeBase() {
    KnowledgeBuilder builder = KnowledgeBuilderFactory
        .newKnowledgeBuilder();
    builder.add(ResourceFactory
        .newClassPathResource("basicRule.drl"),
        ResourceType.DRL);

    if (builder.hasErrors()) {
        throw new RuntimeException(builder.getErrors()
            .toString());
    }

    KnowledgeBase knowledgeBase = KnowledgeBaseFactory
        .newKnowledgeBase();
    knowledgeBase.addKnowledgePackages(builder
        .getKnowledgePackages());
    return knowledgeBase;
    }
}
```

Code listing 4: Simple application for executing Drools (part 2 of 2), which is a method for creating a KnowledgeBase object

A new `KnowledgeBuilder` object is created and our rule file is passed into its `add` method. The rule file is read from the classpath and translated to the `ResourceFactory.newClassPathResource` (basicRule.drl) method. Alternatively, the rule file can be loaded from ordinary URL, byte array, `Java.io.InputStream`, `Java.io.Reader` (allows you to specify encoding), or from the filesystem as a `Java.io.File` file.

org.drools.builder.KnowledgeBuilder

This interface is responsible for building `KnowledgePackages` from knowledge definitions (rules, processes, and types). The knowledge definitions can be in various formats. If there were any problems with building, the `KnowledgeBuilder` object will report errors through these two methods: `hasErrors` and `getError`. As we've learned already, `KnowledgePackages` form `KnowledgeBases`.

After the package is built it is added to the newly created `KnowledgeBase`. It can then be used to create knowledge sessions. This whole process of creating a knowledge session is shown in the following figure:

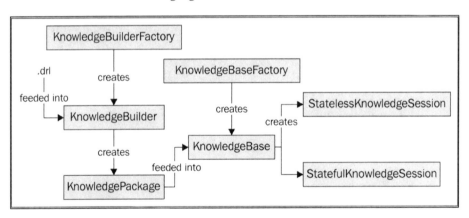

Figure 1: Process of creating a knowledge session from a rule file

When we run the application, this message should be displayed in the console:

```
Account balance is less than 100
```

This means that the rule was successfully executed. Now, we change the rule's condition to `Account ( balance > 100 )` so that it matches on an account whose balance is greater than 100. Run the application again and we won't see the message, meaning that the rule's consequence hasn't been executed this time, which is expected.

You may be wondering what did actually happen. In a nutshell Drools tries to match every fact in the knowledge session with every rule condition to see if all the rule's conditions can be satisfied. This is also sometimes called pattern matching. The condition represents the pattern that the facts are matched against. If all conditions within a rule are satisfied, the rule's consequence may be executed. In our case it is, and we can see it from the console output. If we have multiple rules and multiple facts, it would be a bit more complicated; we'll get to that shortly.

Rule syntax

The following section will provide more details on rule (.drl) syntax. It will form the basis for later examples.

Rule concepts

A rule can contain one or many conditions/patterns. For example:

```
Account( balance == 200 )
Customer( name == "John" )
```

Code listing 5: Two rule conditions, one for type Account and one for type Customer

Drools will then try to match every Account object in the session whose balance is equal to 200 with every Customer whose name is equal to John. If we have three Account objects that meet this criteria and two that don't, five Customer objects that meet this criteria and three that don't, it would create (3+2)*(5+3)=40 possible matches; however, only 3*5=15 of them valid. Meaning that a rule with these two conditions will be executed exactly 15 times.

Variables in rules

Rules can declare variables as follows:

```
$account : Account( $type : type )
```

Code listing 6: This is a simple condition and matches every Account and creates two variables: $account and $type

Downloading the example code

You can download the example code files for all Packt books you have purchased from your account at http://www.packtpub.com. If you purchased this book elsewhere, you can visit http://www.packtpub.com/support and register to have the files e-mailed directly to you.

In this example we declared the $account variable, which is of type Account. The variable name starts with the $ symbol. It is a common naming practice. $type is another variable; in this case it is mapped to a field of the Account bean. Variables can be declared upfront for later use. For example:

```
$account : Account( )
Customer( account == $account )
```

Code listing 7: These are conditions with a join and match every Customer with his/her Account

Please note that the order of fields in a condition is important. It will be incorrect to write Customer($account == account). Drools would try to find the $account field or the Customer.get$account() method, which probably doesn't exist.

Types

Drools can work with all the native Java types and more. Now let's have a look at the examples of various types that can be used in a rule condition.

The following code matches an object with the name:

```
Customer( name == "John")
```

Code listing 8: String matches every Customer with an equal name

The following code matches an object with a name starting with an uppercase:

```
Customer( name matches "[A-Z][a-z]+" )
```

Code listing 9: Regular expression matching every Customer with a name that starts with an uppercase letter followed by one or many lowercase letters

The matches operator supports any valid Java Regular Expression as defined by the Java.util.regexp API. It simply delegates to the String.matches method (regular expressions are also supported in the mvel dialect, which will be covered later):

```
Account(dateCreated> "01-Jan-2008" )
```

Code listing 10: Date matches every Account that was created after a specified date

The default date format is dd-mm-yyyy. This can be customized by changing the Java.lang.System property, drools.dateformat.

```
Transaction(isApproved == true )
```

Code listing 11: Boolean matching every approved Account

The following code demonstrates use of enums:

```
Account( type == Account.Type.SAVINGS )
```

Code listing 12: Enum matching every savings Account

The following code shows use of constants:

```
Account( balance == BigDecimal.ZERO )
```

Code listing 13: Constant matching every Account with a zero balance

The following code shows use of the free form expressions:

```
Period(endDate.isAfter(startDate) )
```

Code listing 14: Free form expressions containing a method call that returns a boolean value and matching every Period that has endDate after startDate

Comments

Comments are very useful in any programming language; this stands for rules as well. Ideally, every complex rule should be commented. It can greatly reduce the time needed to understand a rule. The declarative nature of rules helps readability a great deal, but a comment can always help. The comments can be a single line:

```
//single line comment, that can be placed anywhere in the file
```

Also, they can be multiline:

```
/* multi-line comment,
another line */
```

Package

As we already know, a package is a group of related rules. We'll go through a configuration that can be applied at the package level.

Imports

Rule imports have the same functions as standard Java imports. They allow us to use types from different Java packages by using just their simple name that consists of a single identifier (for example, `ArrayList`); otherwise, a fully qualified name would be required (for example, `java.util.ArrayList`):

```
import com.mycompany.mypackage.MyClass;
import com.mycompany.anotherPackage.*;
```

Code listing 15: Example of using an import within a rule file

For every rule package, Drools automatically imports all types from the same-named Java package. The `java.lang` package is included automatically.

Global variables

Global variables are variables assigned to a session. They can be used for various reasons:

- For input parameters (for example, constant values that can be customized from session to session)
- For output parameters (for example, for reporting a rule we could write some message to a global report variable)
- Entry points for services such as logging can be used within rules

The steps needed to use global variables:

1. Declare the global in the rule file:

   ```
   import com.mycompany.services.AccountService;
   global AccountService accountService;
   ```

   Code listing 16: Global variable declaration, whose name is accountService

   Firstly, the `AccountService` class is imported into the package, then the global variable is declared. It takes the type and an identifier. In this case it is the global variable of type `AccountService` that is accessible under the name `accountService`.

2. Set the global variable to the rule session. As a best practice, do it before inserting any objects/facts:

   ```
   AccountServiceaccountService = //..
   StatefulKnowledgeSession session =    knowledgeBase.
   newStatefulKnowledgeSession();
   session.setGlobal( "accountService", accountService );
   ```

   Code listing 17: Setting of the global variable accountService into the knowledge session

3. Use the global variable in a rule condition or consequence:

   ```
   accountService.saveAccount($account);
   ```

   Code listing 18: Use of a global variable in a rule consequence

If used in a condition, they must return a time-constant value while the rule session is active; otherwise, the results will be unpredictable. It is important to note that the rule engine doesn't track changes to global objects.

The use of global variables is generally discouraged in most programming languages. However, global variables in Drools are different because they are scoped to a session, so they are not truly global in this sense. Anyway, care should also be taken not to overuse them. Generally speaking, if you need to reason over an object (use it in a condition), you must insert it into the session rather than have it as a global variable.

Functions

Functions are a convenient feature. They can be used in conditions and consequences. Functions represent an alternative to utility/helper classes. The most common use is to remove duplicated code:

```
function double calculateSquare(double value) {
return value * value;
}
```

Code listing 19: Example of a function definition in a rule file

The following code shows how to call a function from rule's consequence:

```
long square = calculateSquare(123);
```

Code listing 20: Calling a function from a rule consequence

The following code shows how to call a function from rule's condition:

```
Rectangle( area == calculateSquare(a) )
```

Code listing 21: Calling a function from a rule condition

Type declarations

Drools provides the facility to define new types inside the .drl files. These types act like normal Java beans. They have a name and list of properties. The following is an example:

```
declare Person
   number : Long @key
   name : String @key
   salary :BigDecimal
   isStudent :boolean
end
```

Code listing 22: The Person type declaration

We've defined a `Person` type with four properties: `number`, `name`, `salary`, and `isStudent`. Their types are `Long`, `String`, `BigDecimal` (note that this type needs to be imported first), and `boolean` respectively. We can use any valid Java type and even another type declaration that was declared previously.

Type declarations can also define metadata. They can be set on the type or property level. The previously used type declaration uses the `@key` metadata on the `number` and `name` property. This annotation ensures that these two properties will be part of the `equals` and `hashCode` contracts of the generated class. If we omit the `@key` annotation, the type declaration would get the default `equals` and `hashCode` implementations.

There are lot more metadata that can be defined. Some of them will be introduced later.

The `Person` type can then be used as any other Java type:

```
rule typeDeclarations
when
  not Person( name == "John", isStudent == true )
then
  Person p = new Person();
  p.setName("John");
  p.setIsStudent(true);
  insert(p);
end
```

Code listing 23: Rule with a type declaration

We can look at type declarations as types that are private to the session. They help with decomposing problems into smaller pieces if we want to abstract some piece of information into a separate type just for the duration of the session.

Dialect

Dialect specifies the syntax used in any code expression that is in a consequence or in some cases in a condition (this applies to accumulates and evals). The default value is `java`. Drools currently supports one more dialect called `mvel`. The default dialect can be specified on the package level like this:

```
package org.mycompany.somePackage;
dialect "mvel"
```

Code listing 24: Specifying a default mvel dialect for every rule in a package

mvel

mvel is an expression language for Java-based applications. mvel supports field and method/getter access. It is based on Java syntax. More information about this language can be found at http://mvel.codehaus.org/. Some of its features include:

- **Simple property expressions**: This uses ($customer.name == "John") && (balance > 100).

- **Bean properties**: This uses $customer.address.postalCode; for example, in a rule consequence, instead of writing $customer.getAddress().setPostalCode("12345"), one can just write $customer.address.postalCode = "12345".

- **Null-safe bean navigation**: If it can happen that the customer has no address, one has to write if ($customer.address != null) { return $customer.address.postalCode }. However, with mvel, this can be simplified into $customer.?address.postalCode. Note that as of Version 5.5, it is recommended to use Drools' built-in null-safe dereferencing operator in rule conditions.

- **Last access**: This uses $customer.accounts[3].

- **Map access**: $customer.mapOfAccountNoToAccounts["000123456"].

- **Maps**: This is used to create a map of a string to account beans:
```
[
"0001" : new Account("0001"),
"0002" : new Account("0002")
 ]
```

- **Lists**: Its example includes a list of strings, ["0001", "0002", "0003"].

- **Arrays**: Its example includes an array of strings, { "0001", "0002", "0003" }.

- **Projections**: This allows us to inspect complex object models inside collections; for example, if we want to get a list of postcodes across all customers and their addresses (customer has only one address), such as listOfPostCodes = (address.postCode in $customers). Projections can be nested; for example, if the customer had many addresses, such as listOfPostCodes = (postCode in (addresses in $customers)).

- **coercion**: Let's say we have an array, array = { 1, 2, 3 }, and a Java method that takes int []; if we call this method using mvel, it will correctly coerce our array to the needed type. Internally, mvel uses untyped arrays, that is, Object [].

- **Return values**: The mvel expressions use the last value of a principle; for example, the value of the expressions, such as a = 10, b = 20; a will be 10. For better clarity, the return keyword is supported as well.

Furthermore, `mvel` supports method invocations, control flows, assignments, dynamic typing, lambda expressions, and others. It should be noted though that since `mvel` is interpreted, its performance will always be worse than pure Java, because it is compiled. Note that more and more core functionality of the Drools are being implemented using `mvel`. For example, nested accessors, free form expressions, and so on.

Rule condition

We'll look at additional Drools keywords used in conditions. Each will be demonstrated with an example.

The and element

The `and` conditional element can be implicitly used within conditions (note the comma character):

```
Customer( name == "John", age < 26 )
```

Code listing 25: Condition with multiple field constraints joined by the implicit and element

Another use is between conditions as we've seen in *Code listing 5*. Both uses are implicit.

The or element

Same as `and`, the `or` conditional element can be used within conditions:

```
Customer( name == "John" || age < 26 )
```

Code listing 26: Condition with multiple field constraints joined by the or element

The more concise form can be used if matching on a single field:

```
Customer( age < 26 || > 70 )
```

Code listing 27: Condition with multiple field constraints joined by the or element in a more concise form

More advanced conditions:

```
$customer : Customer( ( name == "John" && age < 26 ) ||
  ( name == "Peter" && age < 30 ) )
$customer : (
  Customer( name == "John", age < 26 ) or
  Customer( name == "Peter", age < 30 )
)
```

Code listing 28: Two semantically equivalent conditions, each matching a Customer object with the name John and aged less than 26 or a Customer object with the name Peter and aged less than 30

These conditions are semantically equivalent, although their performance characteristics may be different. This will be discussed in more detail in *Chapter 11, Integrating*.

The not element

The `not` element matches on the nonexistence of a fact in the session. For example, the following condition will be `true` only if there is no savings account in the session:

```
not Account( type == Account.Type.SAVINGS )
```

Code listing 29: Condition with negation

The exists element

`Exists` is the inverse of `not`. It evaluates to `true` only if the rule session contains at least one instance of a given type:

```
exists Account( type == Account.Type.SAVINGS )
```

Code listing 30: Condition that tests the existence of a savings account in the rule session

Imagine we have a rule with just one condition from the previous code listing and there are multiple savings accounts in the session. Our rule will be executed only once. However, if we remove the `exists` keyword, then the rule would execute as many times as there are savings accounts.

It is important to note that variables declared with `exists` or `not` are scoped to the local condition, and they are neither visible to subsequent conditions nor the consequence as is the usual. The following condition is illegal:

```
exists $account : Account( $number : accountNumber )
```

Code listing 31: Condition with variable declarations

In the previous example, neither the `$account` nor the `$number` object can be used in a rule consequence. It would cause a rule compilation error.

The eval element

`eval` is a catch-all solution. It allows us to execute any dialect-specific code that returns `true` or `false`. It should be used only as a last resort when all other options have failed. This is because the rule engine cannot optimize the `eval` elements. The expression is evaluated every time there is a change in the current rule's condition (a fact is added, modified, or removed). They don't have to return time-constant values. As a best practice, the `eval` elements should be the last conditions in a rule:

```
$account : Account( )
eval(accountService.isUniqueAccountNumber($account) )
```

Code listing 32: Example with eval that calls the custom service method

The return element

An example of a `return` conditional element:

```
$customer1 : Customer( )
Customer( age == $customer1.getAge() + 10 )
```

Code listing 33: Condition with a return constraint

Age is being compared to the return value of the following expression: `$customer1.getAge() + 10`. The expression must return time-constant results while the session is active, otherwise the outcome will be unpredictable. Please note that the `getAge()` method is being called explicitly in this case.

The inline eval element

The previous example can be rewritten using the inline `eval` element:

```
$customer1 : Customer( )
Customer(eval( age == $customer1.getAge() + 10) )
```

Code listing 34: Condition with an inline eval element

When comparing the inline `eval` elements with the standard `eval` elements, we can see that they both must return `true` or `false`. However, in the case of the inline `eval` elements, the expression must be a time constant. It is evaluated only once and then it is cached by Drools.

testing object identities/equalities

The following code uses the `Customer.equals` method:

```
$customer1 : Customer(  )
$customer2 : Customer( this != $customer1 )
```

*Code listing 35: Comparing two Customer instances using the Customer.
equals method*

The following code uses their object identity:

```
$customer1 : Customer(  )
$customer2 : Customer( eval( customer$2 != 
$customer1 ) )
```

*Code listing 36: Comparing two Customer instances using their object
identity (object references)*

In the later example the variable `$customer2` was used instead of `this`, because `this` cannot be used within an eval code block.

Note that the inline `eval` elements have been deprecated since Version 5.4 in favor of "free form expressions" (they will be explained in the next few paragraphs); however, the inline `eval` elements might still be needed for some expressions.

Nested accessors

The following is an example of the nested accessors:

```
$customer : Customer( )
Account( this == $customer.accounts[0]  )
```

Code listing 37: Example of nested accessors, which matches customer and first account from his/her account list

Nested accessors are internally rewritten by the rule engine as the `eval` elements of the `mvel` dialect. This allows us to use `mvel` property navigation. The expression must be time constant (as we already know it is a requirement of all the inline `eval` elements). Please note that when changing the value of a nested property, for example, changing the balance of a customer's first account, we need to notify Drools that the parent object has been updated (in this case the parent object is the `$customer` object). Nested accessors can be used on either side of the operation symbol (for example, we could use `Account(this.uuid == $customer.accounts[0].uuid ) )`.

Null-safe dereferencing operator

Many times when testing some nested property of a fact, we also need to test that the path to that property is not null, otherwise we might end up with a null pointer exception. For example, `Customer( address != null, address.postalCode == "111" )`. To simplify this we can use the null-safe dereferencing operator `Customer( address!.postalCode == "111" )`.

The keyword - this

Sometimes, inside a pattern, we need to refer to the current fact. The `this` keyword is exactly for that purpose:

```
$customer1 : Customer( )
$customer2 : Customer( this != $customer1 )
```

Code listing 38: Conditions that match on two different customers

We have to include the constraint `this != $customer1`, otherwise the same `Customer` fact could match both conditions and that is probably not what we want.

Free form expressions

In recent versions Drools started to support so-called free form expressions. This means that we don't have wrap-complex expressions in an inline `eval` element anymore. For example, *Code listing 34* can be rewritten as:

```
$customer1 : Customer( )
Customer( age == $customer1.getAge() + 10 )
```

Code listing 39: Conditions that match on two different customers

Internally, this expression is still (mostly) translated into an inline `eval` element. Other examples that are possible with free form expressions:

```
Customer(isStudent() )
```

Code listing 40: Free form expression with a boolean method, which will match all customers whose is Student method evaluates to true

Another example where we call a utility method:

```
$account : Account( number ==    AccountUtils.
normalizedNumber($account.getNumber()) )
```

Code listing 41: Free form expression with a utility method, which will match all accounts that have a normalized account number

Working with collections

Drools provides various ways to work with collections of objects. We'll now go through some of them.

The contains (Not) operator

The `contains` operator tests whether a collection has an element. Let's imagine that a customer can have multiple bank accounts. We have multiple customers with their accounts in the rule session:

```
$account : Account( )
Customer( accounts contains $account )
```

Code listing 42: Condition that matches Customer with his/her Account

```
$account : Account( )
Customer( accounts not contains $account )
```

Code listing 43: Condition that matches Customer and an Account that's not his/her

The memberOf (Not) operator

`memberOf` tests whether an element is in a collection. It is complementary to `contains`. The conditions in *Code listing 42* can be rewritten as:

```
$customer : Customer( $accounts : account )
Account( this memberOf $accounts )
```

Code listing 44: Condition that matches a Customer and his/her Account

Or more concisely, it can also be rewritten as:

```
$customer : Customer( )
Account( this memberOf $customer.accounts )
```

Code listing 45: Condition that matches a Customer and his Account

Similar to `contains`, `memberOf` can be used with `not`.

The from operator

Another very useful keyword is `from`. I can simplify our rules, especially if we use complex hierarchical models. `from` can reason over objects from nested collections. For example:

```
$customer : Customer( )
Account( ) from $customer.accounts
```

Code listing 46: Condition that matches a Customer and his/her account

The advantage this brings is that we don't have to insert the Account objects into the rule session. from accepts any mvel expression that returns a single object or a collection of them. It can reason over facts but also globals. Any service method can be called.

On the other side, from has some performance costs. Therefore, it should be avoided if possible, and we should strive to insert all objects that we want to reason over into the session.

Rule consequence

When all conditions in a rule are met, the rule becomes activated. After all rules are evaluated and some of them become activated, the rule engine will pick one activated rule and will execute its consequence. We say that a rule has fired. The activated rule is chosen based on a conflict resolution strategy. The conflict resolution strategy uses multiple criteria to decide which rule to fire. After the rule has fired, the engine re-evaluates any changes that have been made by the previous rule's consequence execution. This may activate or deactivate other rules. This process repeats again until there is no activated rule.

Consequence represents the actions that a rule will do once it fires. It can contain any valid Java or mvel code. We should try to minimize the amount of code.

 It is considered very bad practice to have conditional logic (if statements) within a rule consequence. Most of the time, a new rule should be created.

A rule condition should contain simple actions; the facts can be modified, which may cause other rules to fire. Drools comes with these convenient methods for working with the current KnowledgeSession:

- modify: This is for updating existing facts in the session. For example, a rule that adds interest for deposited money:

```
rule "interest calculation"
no-loop
  when
    $account : Account( )
  then
    modify($account) {
setBalance((long)($account.getBalance() * 1.03));
}
  end
```

Code listing 47: Rule that adds interest for an account

Note that Drools has another way to update facts in the session, the update method. However, the modify method should always be preferred, as it provides more information to the engine as to what has been updated.

- insert: This is used for inserting new facts into the session.
- retract: This is used for removing existing facts from the session.

When a fact is inserted/updated/retracted, the rule engine works with the new set of facts; rules may be activated/deactivated.

Rule attributes

Rule attributes are used to modify/enhance the standard rule behavior. All attributes are defined between the rule and when keywords. For example:

```
rule "rule attributes"
salience 100
dialect "mvel"
no-loop
  when
    //conditions
  then
    //consequence
end
```

Code listing 48: Example of a rule structure with three attributes

Shown rule attributes will be described in the following sections.

The salience (priority) attribute

The salience strategy is used by the conflict resolution strategy to decide which rule to fire. By default, it is the main criterion. We can use salience to define the order of firing rules. salience has one attribute, which takes any expression that returns a number of type int (positive as well as negative numbers are valid). The higher the value, the more likely a rule will be picked up by the conflict resolution strategy to fire:

```
salience ($account.balance * 5)
```

Code listing 49: Example of a dynamic salience expression, which can reference any bound or global variables

The default salience value is 0. We should keep this in mind when assigning salience values to some rules only.

The no-loop attribute

This attribute informs the rule engine that a rule should be activated only once per matched facts. For example, the rule in *Code listing 47* will be activated only once per each `Account` instance. If it didn't have the `no-loop` attribute, it will cause an infinite loop, because the consequence is updating the `$account` fact. Please note, however, that if other rules modify the `$account` fact, our rule will reactivate. The `no-loop` attribute has quite limited use as it prevents only the rule to active itself. A more stronger alternative is the `lock-on-active` attribute that will be described later in *Chapter 5, Creating Human-readable Rules*.

Dialect

We've already seen that dialect can be specified on a package level in *Code listing 24*. This can be overridden by specifying it on a rule level (as seen in *Code listing 48*).

Summary

In this chapter we've learned what libraries are needed to run the Drools engine, and how to write and execute simple rules. We've covered some basic package and rule components. We've touched on what happens when Drools executes. For more information, please visit the Drools documentation, which can be found at `http://www.jboss.org/drools/documentation.html`.

3
Validating

In this chapter we'll look at building a decision service for validating a domain model. By writing a set of rules we'll be separating the validation logic from the rest of the system. This set of rules can then be reused in other systems. For example, it may be used as a part of the service layer in a web application, but is also used as a part of high-performance batch application for processing large volumes of data.

Before we start with validation we'll define a simple banking domain model that will be used in examples throughout this book.

Banking domain model

The UML diagram of this model is shown in the next screenshot. It defines four entities: Customer, Address, Account, and Transaction.

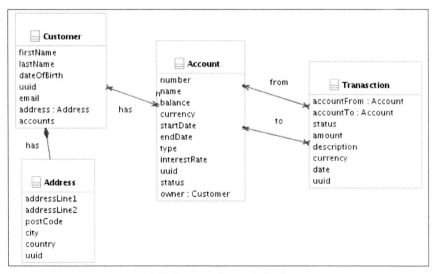

Figure 1: UML diagram of a simple banking system

Customers are pivotal for every bank. The customer information that is stored are name, date of birth, and address. For every address the model stores two address lines, postal code, city, and a country. The customer can have zero or many accounts. Each account has a number, name, actual balance, and currency. An account can be of a specific type; the following types are considered:

- **Transactional**: This is used for day-to-day banking and usually with very little interest rate.

- **Savings**: This is used as an account for saving money. Start date represents the date when the money was lodged into this account and end date represents the date when they were taken out.

- **Student**: This is designed specifically for younger customers who are price sensitive; however, they don't need more advanced services.

A bank would be useless without the ability to make transactions. Every transaction has the `accountFrom` property, which represents the source account where a sum is subtracted, and the `accountTo` property, which represents the destination account where the sum is added. Status of a transaction can have the following values: pending, completed, canceled, or refused. Transaction takes place on a certain date; it has a description, amount of money that is involved, and the currency used.

Every object in this model has a `UUID` property, which stands for Universally Unique Identifier. It will help us to easily identify an instance of an object.

This model will be enhanced, as we'll get into more complex Drools features.

The implementation of this model won't be shown in this book. All objects are simple POJOs as described in *Chapter 2, Writing Basic Rules*, where we've implemented the `Account` POJO object.

Problem definition

Imagine we have the following subset of requirements for validating a banking domain from a business analyst:

- Customer's phone number is required

- If the customer didn't provide an address, display a warning message

- Account number must be unique

- Account balance should be at least 100, otherwise display a warning message

- Only customers below 27 years of age can open a student account

We'll be validating the banking domain model, and the result of this process should be a report informing us of all problems with the input data.

Analysis

By reading the problem definition from the earlier content, it seems that each line from the list represents a single rule. The rules are simple; they include few conditions and a consequence. The consequence will report a customer who failed a validation rule. The two types of messages that will be used include an error and a warning.

We'll now define a report model that will store this information. The model might look like this:

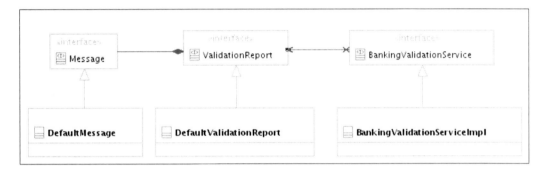

Figure 2: Validation reporting model with validation service

As can be seen in in the previous screenshot, we have the `Message` and `ValidationReport` interfaces. This validation report is then used by the `BankingValidationService` object, which represents some service that will run the validation rules and will act upon the validation report. The screenshot also shows the default implementation of these interfaces.

Design

We'll now define each interface, starting with `Message` that encapsulates one report message. Their implementations will be presented at the end of this chapter. Every message will have a type that can be an error or a warning, a key, and a context.

```java
/**
 * represents one error/warning validation message
 */
public interface Message {
  public enum Type {
    ERROR, WARNING
  }

  /**
   * @return type of this message
   */
  Type getType();

  /**
   * @return key of this message
   */
  String getMessageKey();

  /**
   * objects in the context must be ordered from the least
   * specific to most specific
   * @return list of objects in this message's context
   */
  List<Object>  getContextOrdered();
}
```

Code listing 1: Message interface

The key is used for localized message lookups. The `Message` interface also defines a context, which is of the `List` type and can contain various objects. Objects should be ordered from least specific to most specific (the `Message` interface). This may be useful for localized messages that have parameters. For example, instead of just saying "Account has negative balance", we can be more specific and say which account has the negative balance by having the account part of the context.

Next is the `ValidationReport` interface that holds all messages generated during validation. It will allow us to get all messages or to get messages of only the warnings or errors type. Messages can be added into the `ValidationReport` interface. It will have a convenient method for checking if a message exists for a particular key.

```
/**
 * represents the result of the validation process
 */
public interface ValidationReport {
  /**
   * @return all messages in this report
   */
  Set<Message> getMessages();

  /**
   * @return all messages of specified type in this report
   */
  Set<Message> getMessagesByType(Message.Type type);

  /**
   * @return true if this report contains message with
   *  specified key, false otherwise
   */
  boolean contains(String messageKey);

  /**
   * adds specified message to this report
   */
  boolean addMessage(Message message);
}
```

Code listing 2: The ValidationReport interface

As a best practice, we'll create a factory that will manage object creation for the `Message` and `ValidationReport` classes.

```
public interface ReportFactory {
  ValidationReport createValidationReport();

  Message createMessage(Message.Type type, String messageKey,
      Object... context);
}
```

Code listing 3: The ReportFactory interface

Note that the `createMessage` class accepts an array of objects as the context, for example, `Object...context`.

Validation package

Before writing our first validation rules, the domain model must be imported. The following three global objects will be used:

- Report for storing messages.

- Factory for creating messages.

- Banking inquiry service for information lookup; this object contains one method for testing if an account number is unique, `boolean isAccountNumberUnique(Account accout)`. We won't define and implement this service in this book.

We can now start creating our rule file, `validation.drl` (rules will be gradually added into this file as we'll be implementing them).

```
package droolsbook.validation;
import org.drools.runtime.rule.RuleContext;
import droolsbook.bank.model.*;
import droolsbook.bank.service.*;

global ValidationReportvalidationReport;
global ReportFactoryreportFactory;
global BankingInquiryServiceinquiryService;
import function
  droolsbook.bank.service.ValidationHelper.error;
import function
  droolsbook.bank.service.ValidationHelper.warning;
```

Code listing 4: Rule declarations in the validation.drl file

As can be seen from the previous code, we're defining the `droolsbook.validation` package, importing some classes and functions and defining already mentioned global variables.

Please note that we've decided to use the `validationReport` variable as a global variable. The individual rules will use this global variable in their consequences and they'll add error/warning messages into this validation report.

Alternatively, instead of using the `validationReport` variable as a global variable, it could be inserted into the rule session like any other fact. We could be writing rules reasoning over this report. For example, checking if the number of error messages in the report has crossed some threshold value, and in that case, stopping the validation process. The same could apply for individual report messages. If we need to reason over them, they can be added into the knowledge session as well.

The last two functions in *Code listing 4* are used for actual reporting (they create a message object and add it into the global report). They are imported from the `ValidationHelper` utility class. Please note that the method must be declared as `public static`. Internally, Drools uses a feature in Java 5 called staticimport to import these functions. Both functions can be imported in one go by using the following form:

```
import function droolsbook.bank.service.ValidationHelper.*;
```

Code listing 5: Import of multiple functions at once

The actual implementation of the error function is shown as follows:

```
public class ValidationHelper {

    /**
     * adds an error message to the global validation report
     * @param kcontext RuleContext that is accessible from
     *   rule condition
     * @param context for the message
     */
    public static void error(RuleContext kcontext,
        Object... context) {
      KnowledgeRuntime knowledgeRuntime = kcontext
          .getKnowledgeRuntime();
      ValidationReport validationReport = (ValidationReport)
          knowledgeRuntime.getGlobal("validationReport");
      ReportFactory reportFactory = (ReportFactory)
          knowledgeRuntime.getGlobal("reportFactory");

      validationReport.addMessage(reportFactory.createMessage(
          Message.Type.ERROR, kcontext.getRule().getName(),
          context));
    }
```

Code listing 6: Error reporting function that comes from the utility class ValidationHelper

Normally, you'd expect the `error` method to take the message key and the context as parameters; however, instead of a message key, the method takes the `RuleContext` class. We'll use the current rule name as the message key, and the `RuleContext` class can be used to retrieve the current rule name.

org.drools.spi.KnowledgeHelper

This shows the implementation of the `RuleContext` interface. The instance of this class is accessible from each rule consequence. It is injected into the rule consequence at runtime and can be accessed under the `kcontext` identifier. It has various convenient methods for interacting with the knowledge session, such as for inserting/updating/retracting objects and retrieval of various objects, such as current rule, tuple, activation, knowledge runtime, declaration, methods for setting the activation, focus, and others.

In the functions from *Code listing 6*, the `RuleContext` interface is also used to retrieve two global variables. Because global variables are normally not accessible inside functions, this is a simple workaround (until the Drools team implement this functionality). `reportFactory` is used to create a new message and then this message is added into the validation report. The `kcontext.getRule().getName()` code will return the current rule name, which is used as a message key. This is why we didn't need the message key as an argument for the function. Most, if not all validation rules will create only one message; however, this is a shortcut that we should be aware of. It saves us time to think about a unique message key and also time to maintain this key. If the rule name gets changed, the message key will have to be changed too.

Object required type rules

Now that all the infrastructure is in place, let's write some validation rules. Let's start with simple ones that check an object for missing fields:

```
rule "addressRequired"
 when
  Customer( address == null )
 then
  warning(kcontext );
end

rule "phoneNumberRequired"
  when
    Customer( phoneNumber == null || == "" )
 then
  error(kcontext );
end

rule "accountOwnerRequired"
 when
```

```
  $account : Account( owner == null )
  then
    error(kcontext, $account);
end
```

Code listing 7: Simple object/property's required type validation rules in the validation.drl file

The `addressRequired` rule will be activated for each customer with no address. Similarly, the `phoneNumberRequired` rule will be activated for each customer with a null or blank phone number. In each case the rule consequence simply calls the appropriate error/warning function and passes the `KnowledgeHelper` object with an optional context. The first two rules don't pass any context to the error/warning function; however, the last rule passes the `$account` fact as the context.

For the execution of these validation rules, we'll use a stateless knowledge session. It seems that it is enough to evaluate each rule only once, and there is no need to keep the state between session invocations.

org.drools.runtime.StatelessKnowledgeSession

This is a type of knowledge session that doesn't keep any state between firing rules, in other words it makes calls to the `execute` method. From the rules perspective a stateless session is no different to a stateful session; the rules look exactly the same. The benefit that statelessness brings is that the rule engine can do more optimizations. The `StatelessKnowledgeSession` session as well as a stateful session support a command interface (command design pattern).There is no need to dispose a stateless session after it's been used.

Testing

Every rule that will be written needs to be unit tested. Ideally, we should test all possible cases or at least the most important ones. Use your common sense as to how high code/rule coverage you need. JUnit Version 4 (more information about JUnit can be found at the project's homepage: `http://junit.sourceforge.net/`) will be used for this purpose. Make sure that you have this library on the classpath. Eclipse IDE provides an environment for running these tests.

The following code listing sets up a JUnit test class for testing validation rules. Each rule will be tested by at least one test method. The validation test class will define one setup method; for example, the `setupClass` method that will be run only once (we'll use the `@BeforeClass` JUnit4 annotation) per test class. It will create the `KnowledgeBase` object that will be in turn used to create the `StatelessKnowledgeSession` object. This session will then be reused for each test method. By doing this we'll avoid creating the `KnowledgeBase` object for every test method execution, because it is an expensive object to create. We can push this even further by caching the session because it is stateless. We can also cache some global variables needed by our rules, such as `BankingInquiryService` and `ReportFactory`. These objects are stateless as well. The only thing we cannot reuse is the validation report itself that will be generated. We'll worry about it shortly. The `ValidationTest` class follows:

```
public class ValidationTest {
    static StatelessKnowledgeSession session;
    static ReportFactory reportFactory;

    @BeforeClass
    public static void setUpClass() throws Exception {
        KnowledgeBuilder builder = KnowledgeBuilderFactory
            .newKnowledgeBuilder();
        builder.add(ResourceFactory.newClassPathResource(
            "validation.drl"), ResourceType.DRL);
        if (builder.hasErrors()) {
            throw new RuntimeException(builder.getErrors()
                .toString());
        }

        KnowledgeBaseConfiguration configuration =
            KnowledgeBaseFactory.newKnowledgeBaseConfiguration();
        configuration.setOption(SequentialOption.YES);

        KnowledgeBase knowledgeBase = KnowledgeBaseFactory
            .newKnowledgeBase(configuration);
        knowledgeBase.addKnowledgePackages(builder
            .getKnowledgePackages());

        BankingInquiryService inquiryService =
            new BankingInquiryServiceImpl();
        reportFactory = new DefaultReportFactory();

        session = knowledgeBase.newStatelessKnowledgeSession();
        session.setGlobal("reportFactory", reportFactory);
        session.setGlobal("inquiryService", inquiryService);
    }
```

Code listing 8: JUnit4 ValidationTest setup method

Please note that the KnowledgeBase creation process is little bit different than we've seen in *Chapter 2, Writing Basic Rules*. We're using the KnowledgeBaseConfiguration object to create a sequential knowledge base.

> In the sequential KnowledgeBase object all rules are matched and executed sequentially one by one (the ones that have satisfied all conditions). It is a single-pass process. From a rules perspective, it is more or less the same. However, as we'll be writing those rules, we should remember this. Every rule will be fired at most once.
>
> The KnowledgeBase factory takes the KnowledgeBaseConfiguration object that can contain various configuration options for the knowledge base. In this case we're setting the SequentialOption.YES object.

As can be seen at the bottom of *Code listing 8*, two global objects are inserted into the session with the setGlobal method. These globals are scoped to the session, which means they will be shared by all test methods as well. We can do this since they are immutable. The only global object that is not immutable is the validation report itself. We'll need to scope it to the session execution call, which will be done soon.

Also note that the setupClass method is static as needed by JUnit4.

Now that the test class is set up, let's write a test for the addressRequired rule. We'll validate a customer who has no address and another customer who has an address. In the first case we're expecting to see a warning message in the report, and in the second case the report should be empty:

```
@Test
public void addressRequired() throws Exception {
   Customer customer = createCustomerBasic();
   assertNull(customer.getAddress());
   assertReportContains(Message.Type.WARNING,
       "addressRequired", customer);

   customer.setAddress(new Address());
   assertNotReportContains(Message.Type.WARNING,
       "addressRequired", customer);
}
```

Code listing 9: Test for the addressRequired rule

> Note that we've used some static JUnit4 methods; for example, assertNull that have to be imported like import static org. junit.Assert.*; simply add it to the import statements section of this file.

The `addressRequired` test method creates a basic customer using the `createCustomerBasic` method, which creates an empty customer object with one empty account. The test then assumes that customer's address is null, calls the `assertReportContains` method, which runs the validation, and asserts that the report contains the `addressRequired` warning message.

Batch execution

We'll use a different way of executing the validation rules. As we already know that the knowledge session supports a command interface, two commands will be created: one that will insert a new validation report (remember, it needs to be scoped to the execution call by setting the global object this way, so we'll achieve just that), and the second command will insert all our facts into the session. Both commands will then be run and the report will be populated with messages. This `assertReportContains` method is implemented as shown:

```
void assertReportContains(Message.Type type,
    String messageKey,Customer customer,Object... context) {
  ValidationReport report =
      reportFactory.createValidationReport();
  List<Command> commands = new ArrayList<Command>();
  commands.add(CommandFactory.newSetGlobal(
      "validationReport", report));
  commands.add(CommandFactory
      .newInsertElements(getFacts(customer)));
  session.execute(CommandFactory
      .newBatchExecution(commands));

  assertTrue("Report doesn't contain message [" + messageKey
      + "]", report.contains(messageKey));
  Message message = getMessage(report, messageKey);
  assertEquals(Arrays.asList(context),
      message.getContextOrdered());
}

private Collection<Object> getFacts(Customer customer) {
  ArrayList<Object> facts = new ArrayList<Object>();
  facts.add(customer);
  facts.add(customer.getAddress());
  facts.addAll(customer.getAccounts());
  return facts;
}
```

Code listing 10: Reusable method for running validation and asserting the report contains specified objects

The command for inserting facts, `CommandFactory.newInsertElements(getFac ts(customer))`, gets passed in all the facts as returned by the `getFacts` method. We're inserting all the objects that we want to reason over into the session; it is the customer itself, customer's address, and all accounts.

Next, the `assertReportContains` method verifies that the message is in the report, `assertTrue(...)`. The message is then retrieved from the report by the `getMessage` method. It takes `messageKey` as an argument and simply iterates over all messages inside the report, and if it finds a message with such `messageKey`, it returns it. Finally, the `assertReportContains` method verifies that the message has the expected context.

If we run the `addressRequired` test, it should successfully pass.

Minimal account balance rule

The next rule that will be implemented checks the account balance. According to our original requirements, the account balance should be at least 100. As a good practice from **Test-Driven Development (TDD)**, this time we'll start with a test first (more information about TDD can be found at `http://en.wikipedia.org/wiki/Test-driven_development`):

```
@Test
public void accountBalanceAtLeast() throws Exception {
  Customer customer = createCustomerBasic();
  Account account =customer.getAccounts().iterator().next();
  assertEquals(BigDecimal.ZERO, account.getBalance());
  assertReportContains(Message.Type.WARNING,
      "accountBalanceAtLeast", customer, account);

  account.setBalance(new BigDecimal("54.00"));
  assertReportContains(Message.Type.WARNING,
      "accountBalanceAtLeast", customer, account);

  account.setBalance(new BigDecimal("122.34"));
  assertNotReportContains(Message.Type.WARNING,
      "accountBalanceAtLeast", customer);
}
```

Code listing 11: Test that checks the account balance

The test verifies that for an account balance of ZERO and 54, a warning is generated. The account balance is then increased to 122.34, which doesn't generate the warning. We can now run this test and see that it fails like it does in true TDD. Let's fix it by implementing the rule. The rule looks as follows:

```
rule "accountBalanceAtLeast"
  when
    $account : Account( balance < 100 )
  then
    warning(kcontext, $account);
end
```

Code listing 12: Rule that operates over the java.math.BigDecimal object in the validation.drl file

The rule is straightforward. Please note that the balance is of the `java.math.BigDecimal` type. When Drools evaluates this rule, it takes our hardcoded value `100` and correctly creates the `BigDecimal` instance. Then the `compareTo` method of `BigDecimal` is used to do the actual comparison.

Student account rule

The next business rule will add an error message to the report if a customer, who is 27 years old or more, has a student account. Let's write the test first:

```
@Test
public void studentAccountCustomerAgeLessThan()
    throws Exception {
  DateMidnight NOW = new DateMidnight();
  Customer customer = createCustomerBasic();
  Account account =customer.getAccounts().iterator().next();
  customer.setDateOfBirth(NOW.minusYears(40).toDate());
  assertEquals(Account.Type.TRANSACTIONAL,
      account.getType());
  assertNotReportContains(Message.Type.ERROR,
      "studentAccountCustomerAgeLessThan", customer);

  account.setType(Account.Type.STUDENT);
  assertReportContains(Message.Type.ERROR,
      "studentAccountCustomerAgeLessThan",customer,account);

  customer.setDateOfBirth(NOW.minusYears(20).toDate());
  assertNotReportContains(Message.Type.ERROR,
      "studentAccountCustomerAgeLessThan", customer);
}
```

Code listing 13: Test for the studentAccountCustomerAgeLessThan rule

The test creates a customer, sets his age to 40 years (that is, his date of birth is set to current time minus 40 years), and assumes that he has a TRANSACTIONAL account, which means that there should be no validation error. It is similar for the rest of the cases.

The org.joda.time.DateMidnight type comes from the Joda-Time library (Joda-Time library can be found at http://joda-time.sourceforge.net/). It is a very useful library for working with dates, times, periods, and so on. This library is also recommended by the Drools team when working with dates. After downloading the library from the project homepage, add the joda-time-X.X.X.jar (for example, joda-time-1.6.2.jar) file to the classpath (same as we've added the Drools libraries in *Appendix A, Setting up the Development Environment.*

Please note that depending on your circumstances, you may need to explicitly specify the time zone as well. By default, most date manipulation libraries use your local time zone when working with dates. For example, if your system will be deployed in multiple time zones and there is a potential of sharing some data between them.

Implementation of the studentAccountCustomerAgeLessThan rule might look like this:

```
rule "studentAccountCustomerAgeLessThan"
  when
    Customer( yearsPassedSince(dateOfBirth) >= 27 )
    $account : Account( type == Account.Type.STUDENT )
  then
    error(kcontext, $account);
end
```

Code listing 14: Rule for testing a student's age in the validation.drl file

This rule matches with any Customer and Account objects in the rule session that satisfies the specified constraints.

Care should be taken when doing this. It will only work if we have one customer in the rule session at a time. In the case of multiple customers, an additional check should be added that ties the Customer object to the Account object, that is, Account(owner==$customer) or Customer (accounts contains $account).

Let's look closer at the customer's age condition. `yearsPassedSince` is a function that is defined as:

```
/**
 * @return number of years between today and specified date
 */
public static int yearsPassedSince(Date date) {
  return Years.yearsBetween(new DateMidnight(date),
      new DateMidnight()).getYears();
}
```

Code listing 15: Imported function that calculates the number of years passed since a date

The main work is done by the Joda-Time library (the `Years` class is from this library as well). This static function can be added to the `ValidationHelper` class that was shown in *Code listing 6*. It can then be imported as was shown in *Code listing 4*.

 Let's step back for a second and think about the `yearsPassedSince` function. It creates a new instance of `DateMidnight` to get the current date. This might be a potential problem. The problem is that if we call this method at different times, it might return different results. This is not allowed (see *The eval element* section of *Chapter 2, Writing Basic Rules*). The more preferable solution would be to add the current date as a fact or a global, and then pass it into the `yearsPassedSince` function.

Unique account number rule

The last requirement states, `Account number must be unique`. To check the uniqueness of an account number, we'll use the `BankingInquiryService` method. For testing purposes we'll write a mock implementation, or you can use any mocking library for this purpose. The test is as follows:

```
@Test
public void accountNumberUnique() throws Exception {
  Customer customer = createCustomerBasic();
  Account account = customer.getAccounts().iterator()
      .next();
  session.setGlobal("inquiryService",
      new BankingInquiryServiceImpl() {
        @Override
        public boolean isAccountNumberUnique(
            Account accout) {
          return false;
        }
```

```
    });
  assertReportContains(Message.Type.ERROR,
    "accountNumberUnique", customer, account);
}
```

Code listing 16: Test for the accountNumberUnique rule

The test creates a customer and a new mock implementation of `BankingInquiryService` with the `isAccountNumberUnique` method that returns is always `false`. The `inquiryService` global is set. Rules are executed and the test verifies that there is an error in the report. The real test should also include an option where the account number is unique (the service method returns `true`).

The following is the implementation of the rule that checks the uniqueness of an account number:

```
rule "accountNumberUnique"
  when
    $account : Account(
      !inquiryService.isAccountNumberUnique($account))
  then
    error(kcontext, $account);
end
```

Code listing 17: Rule for checking account number uniqueness in the validation.drl file

The `accountNumberUnique` rule demonstrates the usage of a service method in a rule. Behind the scenes the method is being called through an inline eval. Similar to what we saw in the *Student account rule* section, the results from the inline eval must be constant during the session execution (if we evaluate the code block multiple times, we must get the same result). The code listing also shows that we can use any bound variable inside the code block (in this case it is the `$account` variable).

Implementation

In this section we'll define the implementation for various interfaces that we've defined in this chapter. This section is shown for completeness and can be skipped.

First, let's have a look at an implementation of the `Message` interface. The message is essentially another POJO, so it will basically have getters setters and it will also override the `equals`, the `hashCode`, and `toString` methods.

```
import org.apache.commons.lang.builder.EqualsBuilder;
import org.apache.commons.lang.builder.HashCodeBuilder;
import org.apache.commons.lang.builder.ToStringBuilder;
//... other imports
```

```java
public class DefaultMessage implements Message, Serializable {
  private Message.Type type;
  private String messageKey;
  private List<Object> context;

  public DefaultMessage(Message.Type type, String messageKey,
      List<Object> context) {
    if (type == null || messageKey == null) {
      throw new IllegalArgumentException(
          "Type and messageKey cannot be null");
    }
    this.type = type;
    this.messageKey = messageKey;
    this.context = context;
  }

  public String getMessageKey() {
    return messageKey;
  }

  public Message.Type getType() {
    return type;
  }

  public List<Object> getContextOrdered() {
    return context;
  }

  @Override
  public boolean equals(final Object other) {
    if (this == other)
      return true;
    if (!(other instanceof DefaultMessage))
      return false;
    DefaultMessage castOther = (DefaultMessage) other;
    return new EqualsBuilder().append(type, castOther.type)
        .append(messageKey, castOther.messageKey).append(
            context, castOther.context).isEquals();
  }

  @Override
  public int hashCode() {
    return new HashCodeBuilder(98587969, 810426655).append(
        type).append(messageKey).append(context).toHashCode();
  }
}
```

```
@Override
public String toString() {
  return new ToStringBuilder(this).append("type", type)
      .append("messageKey", messageKey).append("context",
          context).toString();
}
}
```

Code listing 18: Implementation of the Message interface

DefaultMessage has a constructor that takes the Message.Type and key. It guarantees that these two properties will be always set (not null); the context is optional.

Next, we'll look at the implementation of the ValidationReport interface. It will store all messages in a map. The key of this map will be the message type, and the value will be a set of messages. A set because we're not interested in the order of messages. We're interested only in unique messages (in the DefaultMessage.equals method sense). The declaration will look like this: Map<Message.Type,Set<Message>>messagesMap. Then, we only need a bunch of methods that will work on this map. The implementation of the DefaultValidationReport interface is a follows:

```
public class DefaultValidationReport implements
    ValidationReport, Serializable {
  protected Map<Message.Type, Set<Message>> messagesMap =
    new HashMap<Message.Type, Set<Message>>();

  public Set<Message> getMessages() {
    Set<Message> messagesAll = new HashSet<Message>();
    for (Collection<Message> messages : messagesMap.values()){
      messagesAll.addAll(messages);
    }
    return messagesAll;
  }

  public Set<Message> getMessagesByType(Message.Type type) {
    if (type == null)
      return Collections.emptySet();
    Set<Message> messages = messagesMap.get(type);
    if (messages == null)
      return Collections.emptySet();
    else
      return messages;
  }
```

```
    public boolean contains(String messageKey) {
      for (Message message : getMessages()) {
        if (messageKey.equals(message.getMessageKey())) {
          return true;
        }
      }
      return false;
    }

    public boolean addMessage(Message message) {
      if (message == null)
        return false;
      Set<Message> messages =messagesMap.get(message.getType());
      if (messages == null) {
        messages = new HashSet<Message>();
        messagesMap.put(message.getType(), messages);
      }
      return messages.add(message);
    }
  }
```

Code listing 19: Implementation of the ValidationReport interface

Please note that this code listing doesn't show the implementation of the equals, hashCode, and toString methods. All of them operate only on the message map.

Next, we'll look at the implementation of the ReportFactory interface. It simply creates a new instance of a DefaultMessage or a DefaultValidationReport object.

```
  public class DefaultReportFactory implements ReportFactory {
    public Message createMessage(Message.Type type,
        String messageKey, Object... context) {
      return new DefaultMessage(type, messageKey, Arrays
          .asList(context));
    }

    public ValidationReport createValidationReport() {
      return new DefaultValidationReport();
    }
  }
```

Code listing 20: Implementation of ReportFactory

Validation service

All rules are implemented the unit tests, and we can write a validation service that our clients can access. It will define one method for validating a customer. This is the `BankingValidationService` interface:

```
/**
 * service for validating the banking domain
 */
public interface BankingValidationService {
  /**
   * validates given customer and returns validation report
   */
  ValidationReport validate(Customer customer);
}
```

Code listing 21: Banking validation service interface

The interface defines one method that validates a `Customer` object and returns the `ValidationReport` interface. Since, in our domain model, all objects are accessible (traversable) from the `Customer` object, it is sufficient to just pass this class as the method parameter. The implementation is more interesting:

```
public class BankingValidationServiceImpl implements
    BankingValidationService {

  private KnowledgeBase knowledgeBase;
  private ReportFactory reportFactory;
  private BankingInquiryService bankingInquiryService;

  /**
   * validates provided customer and returns validation report
   */
  public ValidationReport validate(Customer customer) {
    ValidationReport report = reportFactory
        .createValidationReport();
    StatelessKnowledgeSession session = knowledgeBase
        .newStatelessKnowledgeSession();
    session.setGlobal("validationReport", report);
    session.setGlobal("reportFactory", reportFactory);
    session
        .setGlobal("inquiryService", bankingInquiryService);
    session.execute(getFacts(customer));
    return report;
  }
```

```
/**
 * @return facts that the rules will reason upon
 */
private Collection<Object> getFacts(Customer customer) {
  ArrayList<Object> facts = new ArrayList<Object>();
  facts.add(customer);
  facts.add(customer.getAddress());
  facts.addAll(customer.getAccounts());
  return facts;
}
```

Code listing 22: Section of banking validation service implementation

The implementation has the following dependencies: knowledgeBase, reportFactory, and bankingInquiryService. The setters for these properties are not shown; they are straightforward. The validation method creates a report that will be returned, creates a stateless rule session, sets three global objects, and finally calls the execute method with all facts grouped in one collection. Because a stateless session is used, all facts need to be passed in one go.

Note the different style of using a stateless session. In this case we set all three globals through the setGlobal method. By setting them this way, the global objects are scoped to the session, so we cannot reuse this session across multiple validate method invocations (across multiple threads). This is why the session variable is scoped to the validate method and not the class, as was the case with our unit tests. This is just to show you a different way of working with the session without using commands.

Summary

Let's look at what we've achieved in this chapter. By separating the validation rules from the rest of the application, we've made it easier for others to identify and understand them. Because of the declarative nature of rules, they can be maintained and refactored more easily. We can easily change rules or add new ones without increasing the overall complexity.

A simple extensible reporting model was defined and later used in the customer validation rules. Throughout this chapter a stateless session has been used, which is ideal for this type of decision rules. Remember that it is stateless only because it doesn't hold state between invocations. A special feature of a stateless session is that it can be executed in sequential mode, which has performance benefits for very simple rules. We've learned about the KnowledgeHelper object, which is present in every rule consequence as a convenient helper class. We've discussed the use of a validation report as a global variable versus being inserted into the session as an ordinary fact. We've also discussed the use of BigDecimal as a type for floating point numbers and Joda-Time as the date-time manipulation library.

4
Transforming Data

Almost any rewrite of an existing legacy system needs to do some kind of data transformation with the old legacy data before it can be used in the new system. It needs to load the data and transform them so that they meet the requirements of the new system and finally store them. This is just one example of where data transformation is needed.

Drools can help us with this data transformation task as well. Depending on our requirements it might be a good idea to isolate this transformation process in the form of rules. The rules can be reused later, maybe when our business will expand and we'll be converting data from a different third-party system. Of course, other advantages of using rules apply.

If performance is the most important requirement (for example, all data has to be converted within a specified time frame), rules may not be the ideal approach. Probably, the biggest disadvantage of using rules is that they need the legacy data in memory, so they are best suited to more complex data transformation tasks. However, consider carefully if your data transformation will grow in complexity as more requirements are added.

When writing these transformation rules, care should be taken not to confuse them with validation rules. In a nutshell, if a rule can be written working just with the domain model, it is most likely a validation rule. If it uses concepts that cannot be represented with our domain model, it is probably a transformation rule.

Process overview

Let's demonstrate this data transformation on an example. Imagine that we need to convert some legacy customer data into our new system.

Since not all legacy data is perfect, we'll need a way to report data that, for some reason, we've failed to transfer. For example, our system allows only one address per customer. Legacy customers with more than one address will be reported. We'll reuse the reporting component from *Chapter 3, Validating*.

In this chapter we'll:

- Load customer data from the legacy system. The data will include address and account information.
- Run transformation rules over this data and build an execution report.
- Populate the domain model with transformed data, running validation rules (from the previous section) and saving it into our system.

Getting the data

As a good practice, we'll define an interface for interacting with the other system. We'll introduce a `LegacyBankService` interface for this purpose. It will make it easier to change the way we communicate with the legacy system, and also the tests will be easier to write.

```
package droolsbook.transform.service;

import java.util.List;
import java.util.Map;

public interface LegacyBankService {

    /**
     * @return all customers
     */
    List<Map<String, Object>> findAllCustomers();

    /**
     * @return addresses for specified customer id
     */
    List<Map<String, Object>> findAddressByCustomerId(
        Long customerId);

    /**
     * @return accounts for specified customer id
     */
    List<Map<String, Object>> findAccountByCustomerId(
        Long customerId);

}
```

Code listing 1: Interface that abstracts the legacy system interactions

The interface defines three methods. The first one can retrieve a list of all customers, and the second and third ones retrieve a list of addresses and accounts for a specific customer. Each list contains zero or many maps. One map represents one object in the legacy system. The keys of this map are object property names (for example, addressLine1), and the values are the actual properties.

We've chosen a map because it is a generic data type that can store almost any data, which is ideal for a data transformation task. However, it has a slight disadvantage in that the rules will be a bit harder to write.

The implementation of this interface will be defined at the end of this chapter.

Loading facts into the rule session

Before writing some transformation rules, the data needs to be loaded into the rule session. This can be done by writing a specialized rule just for this purpose, as follows:

```
package droolsbook.transform;

import java.util.*;

import droolsbook.transform.service.LegacyBankService;
import droolsbook.bank.model.Address;
import droolsbook.bank.model.Address.Country;

global LegacyBankService legacyService;

rule findAllCustomers
  when
    $customerMap : Map( )
      fromlegacyService.findAllCustomers()
  then
    $customerMap.put("_type_", "Customer");
    insert( $customerMap );
end
```

Code listing 2: Rule that loads all Customers into the rule session (the dataTransformation.drl file).

The preceding `findAllCustomers` rule matches on a `Map` instance that is obtained from our `legacyService`. In the consequence part, it adds the type (so that we can recognize that this map represents a customer) and inserts this map into the session. There are a few things to be noted here, as follows:

- A rule is being used to insert objects into the rule session; this just shows a different way of loading objects into the rule session.

- Every customer returned from the `findAllCustomers` method is being inserted into the session. This is reasonable only if there is a small number of customers. If it is not the case, we can paginate, that is, process only *N* customers at once, then start over with the next *N* customers, and so on. Alternatively, the `findAllCustomers` rule can be removed and customers could be inserted into the rule session at session-creation time. We'll now focus on this latter approach (for example, only one `Customer` instance is in the rule session at any given time); it will make the reporting easier.

- A type of the map is being added to the map. This is a disadvantage of using a `Map` object for every type (`Customer`, `Address`, and so on): the type information is lost. It can be seen in the following rule that finds addresses for a customer:

```
rule findAddress
dialect "mvel"
  when
    $customerMap : Map( this["_type_"] == "Customer" )
    $addressMap : Map( )
      fromlegacyService.findAddressByCustomerId(
        (Long) $customerMap["customer_id"] )
  then
    $addressMap.put("_type_", "Address");
    insert( $addressMap )
end
```

Code listing 3: Rule that loads all Addresses for a Customer into the rule session (the dataTransformation.drl file)

Let's focus on the first condition line. It matches on `customerMap`. It has to test if this `Map` object contains a customer's data by executing `["_type_"] == "Customer"`. To avoid doing these type checks in every condition, a new map can be extended from `HashMap`, for example `LegacyCustomerHashMap`. The rule might look like the following line of code:

```
$customerMap :LegacyCustomerHashMap( )
```

The preceding line of code performs matching on the customer map without doing the type check.

We'll continue with the second part of the condition. It matches on addressMap that comes from our legacyService as well. The from keyword supports parameterized service calls. customer_id is passed to the findAddressByCustomerId method. Another nice thing about this is that we don't have to cast the parameter to java. lang.Long; it is done automatically.

The consequence part of this rule just sets the type and inserts addressMap into the knowledge session. Please note that only addresses for loaded customers are loaded into the session. This saves memory but it could also cause a lot of "chattiness" with the LegacyBankService interface if there are many child objects. It can be fixed by pre-loading those objects. The implementation of this interface is the right place for this.

Similar data-loading rules can be written for other types, for example Account.

Writing transformation rules

Now that all objects are in the knowledge session, we can start writing some transformation rules. Let's imagine that in the legacy system there are many duplicate addresses. We can write a rule that removes such duplication:

```
rule twoEqualAddressesDifferentInstance
  when
    $addressMap1 : Map( this["_type_"] == "Address" )
    $addressMap2 : Map( this["_type_"] == "Address",
      eval( $addressMap1 != $addressMap2 ),
      this == $addressMap1 )
  then
    retract( $addressMap2 );
    validationReport.addMessage(
      reportFactory.createMessage(Message.Type.WARNING,
      kcontext.getRule().getName(), $addressMap2));
end
```

Code listing 4: Rule that loads all Addresses for a Customer into the rule session (file dataTransformation.drl)

The rule matches two addresses. It checks that they don't have the same object identities by doing `eval( $addressMap1 != $addressMap2 )`. Otherwise, the rule could match on a single address instance. The next part, `this == $addressMap1`, translates behind the scenes to `$addressMap1.equal($addressMap2)`. If this equal check is true that means one of the addresses is redundant and can be removed from the session. The address map that is removed is added to the report as a warning message.

Testing

Before we'll continue with the rest of the rules, we'll set up unit tests. The test initialization method is similar to the one from *Chapter 3, Validating*. We'll still use a stateless session:

```
session = knowledgeBase.newStatelessKnowledgeSession();
session.setGlobal("legacyService",
newMockLegacyBankService());
```

Code listing 5: Section of the test setUpClass method (the DataTransformationTest file)

The `legacyService` global is set to a new instance of `MockLegacyBankService`. It is a dummy implementation that simply returns `null` from all methods. In most tests we'll insert objects directly into the knowledge session (and not through `legacyService`).

We'll now write a helper method for inserting objects into the knowledge session and running the rules. The helper method will create a list of commands, execute them, and the returned object, `BatchExecutionResults`, will be returned back from the helper method. The following command instances will be created:

- One for setting the global variable – `validationReport`; a new validation report will be created.
- One for inserting all objects into the session.
- One for firing only rules with a specified name. This will be done through an `AgendaFilter`. It will help us isolate a rule that we'll be testing.

org.drools.runtime.rule.AgendaFilter

When a rule is activated the `AgendaFilter` determines if this rule can be fired or not. The `AgendaFilter` interface has one `accept` method that returns `true`/`false`. We'll create our own `RuleNameEqualsAgendaFilter` that fires only rules with a specific name.

- One command for getting back all objects in a knowledge session that are of a certain type – `filterType` method parameter. These objects will be returned from the helper method as part of the `results` object under a given key – `filterOut` method parameter.

The following is the helper method:

```
/**
 * creates multiple commands, calls session.execute and
 * returns results back
 */
protected ExecutionResults execute(Collection<?> objects,
    String ruleName, final String filterType,
    String filterOut) {
  ValidationReport validationReport = reportFactory
      .createValidationReport();
  List<Command<?>> commands = new ArrayList<Command<?>>();
  commands.add(CommandFactory.newSetGlobal(
      "validationReport", validationReport, true));
  commands.add(CommandFactory.newInsertElements(objects));
  commands.add(new FireAllRulesCommand(
      new RuleNameEqualsAgendaFilter(ruleName)));
  if (filterType != null && filterOut != null) {
    GetObjectsCommand getObjectsCommand =
        new GetObjectsCommand( new ObjectFilter() {
          public boolean accept(Object object) {
            return object instanceof Map
                && ((Map) object).get("_type_").equals(
                    filterType);
          }
        });
    getObjectsCommand.setOutIdentifier(filterOut);
    commands.add(getObjectsCommand);
  }
  ExecutionResults results = session
      .execute(CommandFactory.newBatchExecution(commands));
  return results;
}
```

Code listing 6: Test helper method for executing the transformation rules (the DataTransformationTest file).

To write a test for the redundant address rule, two address maps will be created. Both will have their street set to `"Barrack Street"`. After we execute rules, only one address map should be in the rule session. The test looks as follows:

```
@Test
public void twoEqualAddressesDifferentInstance()
    throws Exception {
  Map addressMap1 = new HashMap();
  addressMap1.put("_type_", "Address");
  addressMap1.put("street", "Barrack Street");

  Map addressMap2 = new HashMap();
  addressMap2.put("_type_", "Address");
  addressMap2.put("street", "Barrack Street");
  assertEquals(addressMap1, addressMap2);

  ExecutionResults results = execute(Arrays.asList(
      addressMap1, addressMap2),
      "twoEqualAddressesDifferentInstance", "Address",
      "addresses");

  Iterator<?> addressIterator = ((List<?>) results
      .getValue("addresses")).iterator();
  Map addressMapWinner = (Map) addressIterator.next();
  assertEquals(addressMap1, addressMapWinner);
  assertFalse(addressIterator.hasNext());
  reportContextContains(results,
      "twoEqualAddressesDifferentInstance",
      addressMapWinner == addressMap1 ? addressMap2
          : addressMap1);
}
```

Code listing 7: Test for the redundant address rule

The `execute` method is called with the two address maps, the agenda filter rule name is set to `twoEqualAddressesDifferentInstance` (only this rule will be allowed to fire), and after the rules are executed all maps of the `Address` type are returned as part of the result. We can access them by `results.getValue("addresses")`. The test verifies that there is only one such map.

Another test helper method – reportContextContains verifies that the validationReport contains expected data. The implementation method, reportContextContains, is shown as follows:

```
/**
 * asserts that the report contains one message with
 * expected context (input parameter)
 */
void reportContextContains(ExecutionResults results,
    String messgeKey, Object object) {
  ValidationReport validationReport = (ValidationReport)
      results.getValue("validationReport");
  assertEquals(1, validationReport.getMessages().size());
  Message message = validationReport.getMessages()
      .iterator().next();
  List<Object> messageContext = message.getContextOrdered();
  assertEquals(1, messageContext.size());
  assertSame(object, messageContext.iterator().next());
}
```

Code listing 8: Helper method, which verifies that report the contains a supplied object

Address normalization

Our next rule will be a type conversion rule. It will take a String representation of country and it will convert it into Address.Countryenum. We'll start with a test:

```
@Test
public void addressNormalizationUSA() throws Exception {
  Map addressMap = new HashMap();
  addressMap.put("_type_", "Address");
  addressMap.put("country", "U.S.A");

  execute(Arrays.asList(addressMap),
      "addressNormalizationUSA", null, null);

  assertEquals(Address.Country.USA, addressMap
      .get("country"));
}
```

Code listing 9: Test for the country type conversion rule

The test creates an address map with `country` set to `"U.S.A"`. It then calls the execute method, passing in the `addressMap` and allowing only the `addressNormalizationUSA` rule to fire (no filter is used in this case). Finally, the test verifies that the address map has the correct country value. Next, we'll write the rule:

```
rule addressNormalizationUSA
dialect "mvel"
  when
    $addressMap : Map( this["_type_"] == "Address",
      this["country"] in ("US", "U.S.", "USA", "U.S.A"))
  then
    modify( $addressMap ) {
      put("country", Country.USA)
    }
end
```

Code listing 10: Rule that converts String representation of country into enum representation
(the dataTransformation.drl file)

The rule matches an address map. The `in` operator is used to capture various country representations. The rule's consequence is interesting in this case. Instead of doing simply `update( $addressMap )`, the modify construct is being used. Modify takes an argument and a block of code. Before executing the block of code it retracts the argument from the rule session, then it executes the block of code, and finally the argument is inserted back into the session. This has to be done because the argument's identity is modified. If we look at the implementation of `HashMap` `equals` or the `hashCode` method, they take into account every element in the map. By doing `$addressMap.put("country", Country.USA)`, we change the address map identity.

Fact's identity

As a general rule, do not change the object identity while it is in the knowledge session, otherwise the rule engine behavior will be undefined (same as changing an object while it is in `java.util.HashMap`).

Testing the findAddress rule

Before continuing, let's write a test for the `findAddress` rule from the third rule in the *Loading facts into the rule session* section. The test will use a special `LegacyBankService` mock implementation that will return the provided `addressMap`.

```
public class StaticMockLegacyBankService extends
    MockLegacyBankService {
  private Map addressMap;
```

```
    public StaticMockLegacyBankService(Map addressMap) {
      this.addressMap = addressMap;
    }
    public List findAddressByCustomerId(Long customerId) {
      return Arrays.asList(addressMap);
    }
  }
```

Code listing 11: StaticMockLegacyBankService which returns provided addressMap

StaticMockLegacyBankService extends MockLegacyBankService and overrides
the findAddressByCustomerId method. The findAddress test looks as follows:

```
  @Test
  public void findAddress() throws Exception {
    final Map customerMap = new HashMap();
    customerMap.put("_type_", "Customer");
    customerMap.put("customer_id", new Long(111));

    final Map addressMap = new HashMap();
    LegacyBankService service =
      new StaticMockLegacyBankService(addressMap);
    session.setGlobal("legacyService", service);

    ExecutionResults results = execute(Arrays
        .asList(customerMap), "findAddress", "Address",
        "objects");

    assertEquals("Address", addressMap.get("_type_"));
    Iterator<?> addressIterator = ((List<?>) results
        .getValue("objects")).iterator();
    assertEquals(addressMap, addressIterator.next());
    assertFalse(addressIterator.hasNext());

    // clean-up
    session.setGlobal("legacyService",
        new MockLegacyBankService());
  }
```

Code listing12: Test for the findAddress rule

The test then verifies that the address map is really in the knowledge session. It also
verifies that it has the "_type_" key set and that there is no other address map.

Unknown country

The next rule will create an error message if the country isn't recognizable by our domain model. The test creates an address map with some unknown country, executes rules, and verifies that the report contains an error.

```
@Test
public void unknownCountry() throws Exception {
    Map addressMap = new HashMap();
    addressMap.put("_type_", "Address");
    addressMap.put("country", "no country");

    ExecutionResults results = execute(Arrays
        .asList(addressMap), "unknownCountry", null, null);

    ValidationReport report = (ValidationReport) results
        .getValue("validationReport");
    reportContextContains(results, "unknownCountry",
        addressMap);
}
```

Code listing 13: Test for the unknownCountry rule

The rule implementation will test if the country value from the `addressMap` is of the `Address.Country` type. If it isn't, an error is added to the report.

```
rule unknownCountry
salience -10 //should fire after address normalizations
  when
   $addressMap : Map( this["_type_"] == "Address",
       !($addressMap.get("country") instanceof
       Address.Country))
  then
   validationReport.addMessage(
     reportFactory.createMessage(Message.Type.ERROR,
     kcontext.getRule().getName(), $addressMap));
end
```

Code listing 14: Rule that reports unknown countries (the dataTransformation.drl file)

The type checking is done with MVEL's `instanceof` operator. Note that this rule needs to be executed after all address normalization rules, otherwise we could get an incorrect error message.

Currency conversion

As a given requirement, the data transformation process should convert all accounts to EUR currency. The test for this rule might look like the following code snippet:

```
@Test
public void currencyConversionToEUR() throws Exception {
  Map accountMap = new HashMap();
  accountMap.put("_type_", "Account");
  accountMap.put("currency", "USD");
  accountMap.put("balance", "1000");

  execute(Arrays.asList(accountMap),
      "currencyConversionToEUR", null, null);

  assertEquals("EUR", accountMap.get("currency"));
  assertEquals(new BigDecimal("780.000"), accountMap
      .get("balance"));
}
```

Code listing 15: Test for the EUR conversion rule

At the end of the code snippet the test verified that currency and balance were correct. The exchange rate of 0.780 was used. The rule implementation is as follows:

```
rule currencyConversionToEUR
  when
    $accountMap : Map( this["_type_"] == "Account",
      this["currency"] != null && != "EUR" )
    $conversionAmount : String() from
      getConversionToEurFrom(
        (String)$accountMap["currency"])
  then
    modify($accountMap) {
      put("currency", "EUR"),
      put("balance", new BigDecimal(
        $conversionAmount).multiply(new BigDecimal(
        (String)$accountMap.get("balance"))))
    }
end
```

Code listing 16: Rule that converts account balance and currency to EUR (the dataTransformation.drl file).

The rule uses the default `'java'` dialect. It matches on an account map and retrieves the conversion amount using the `from` conditional element. In this case it is a simple function that returns hardcoded values. However, it can be easily replaced with a service method that could, for example, call some web service in a real bank.

```
function String getConversionToEurFrom(String currencyFrom) {
  String conversion = null;
  if ("USD".equals(currencyFrom)) {
    conversion = "0.780";
  } else if ("SKK".equals(currencyFrom)) {
    conversion = "0.033";
  }
  return conversion;
}
```

Code listing 17: Dummy function for calculating the exchange rate (the dataTransformation.drl file)

Notice how we're calling the function. Instead of calling it directly in the consequence, it is called from a condition. This way our rule will fire only if the function returns some non-null result.

The rule then sets the currency to EUR and multiplies the balance with the exchange rate. This rule doesn't cover currencies for which the `getConversionToEurFrom` function returns `null`. We have to write another rule that will report unknown currencies.

```
rule unknownCurrency
  when
    $accountMap : Map( this["_type_"] == "Account",
      this["currency"] != null && != "EUR" )
    not( String() from
      getConversionToEurFrom(
        (String)$accountMap["currency"]) )
  then
    validationReport.addMessage(
      reportFactory.createMessage(Message.Type.ERROR,
      kcontext.getRule().getName(), $accountMap));
end
```

Code listing 18: Rule that adds an error message to the report if there is no conversion for a currency (the dataTransformation.drl file)

Note that in this case the `getConversionToEurFrom` function is called from within the `not` construct.

One account allowed

Imagine that we have a business requirement that only one account from the legacy system can be imported into the new system. Our next rule will remove redundant accounts while aggregating their balances.

The test inserts two accounts of the same customer into the rule session and verifies that one of them was removed and the balance has been transferred.

```
@Test
public void reduceLegacyAccounts() throws Exception {
    Map accountMap1 = new HashMap();
    accountMap1.put("_type_", "Account");
    accountMap1.put("customer_id", "00123");
    accountMap1.put("balance", new BigDecimal("100.00"));

    Map accountMap2 = new HashMap();
    accountMap2.put("_type_", "Account");
    accountMap2.put("customer_id", "00123");
    accountMap2.put("balance", new BigDecimal("300.00"));

    ExecutionResults results = execute(Arrays.asList(
        accountMap1, accountMap2), "reduceLegacyAccounts",
        "Account", "accounts");

    Iterator<?> accountIterator = ((List<?>) results
        .getValue("accounts")).iterator();
    Map accountMap = (Map) accountIterator.next();
    assertEquals(new BigDecimal("400.00"), accountMap
        .get("balance"));
    assertFalse(accountIterator.hasNext());
}
```

Code listing 19: Test for the reduceLegacyAccounts rule

Before we can write this rule we have to ensure that the `Account` instance's `balance` is of the `BigDecimal` type. This is partially (non-EUR accounts) done by the currency conversion rules. For the EUR accounts a new rule can be written that simply converts the type to `BigDecimal` (we can even update the `unknownCurrency` rule to handle this situation).

```
rule reduceLegacyAccounts
  when
    $accountMap1 : Map( this["_type_"] == "Account" )
    $accountMap2 : Map( this["_type_"] == "Account",
      eval( $accountMap1 != $accountMap2 ),
```

```
            this["customer_id"] ==$accountMap1["customer_id"],
            this["currency"] == $accountMap1["currency"])
    then
        modify($accountMap1) {
            put("balance", (
                (BigDecimal)$accountMap1.get("balance")).add(
                (BigDecimal)$accountMap2.get("balance")))
        }
        retract( $accountMap2 );
    end
```

Code listing 20: Rule that removes redundant accounts and accumulates their balances (the dataTransformation.drl file)

The rule matches on two `accountMap` instances; it ensures that they represent two different instances (`eval( $accountMap1 != $accountMap2)` – note that `eval` is important here), which both belong to the same customer (`this["customer_id"] ==$accountMap1["customer_id"]`) and have the same currency (`this["currency"] == $accountMap1["currency"]`). The consequence sums up the two balances and retracts the second `accountMap`.

Note that the rule should fire after all currency conversion rules. This is creating dependencies between rules. In this case it is tolerable, as only a few rules are involved. However, with more complex dependencies we'll have to introduce a ruleflow.

Transformation results

Now that we've written all transformation rules, data from the legacy system is in a good shape for our model, and we can start with populating it. To extract data from the knowledge session we'll use Drools queries.

Query

Drools query looks like a normal rule without the `'then'` part. It can be executed directly from a stateful knowledge session, for example `session.getQueryResults("getAllCustomers")` or by using a `QueryCommand`. It returns a `QueryResults` object that can contain multiple `QueryResultsRow` objects. Every `QueryResultsRow` instance represents one match of the query. Individual objects/facts can be retrieved from `QueryResultsRow`. Drools queries are a convenient way of retrieving objects/facts from the knowledge session that match conditions specified by the query. Queries can be parameterized. In `KnowledgeBase`, all queries share the same namespace.

Let's implement queries for retrieving transformed data:

```
query getCustomer
  $customerMap : Map( this["_type_"] == "Customer" )
end

query getAccountByCustomerId(Map customerMap)
  $accountMap : Map( this["_type_"] == "Account",
    this["customer_id"] == customerMap["customer_id"] )
end
```

Code listing 21: Queries for retrieving customer and accounts (the dataTransformation.drl file)

The getCustomer query matches on any customer map. The second query, getAccountByCustomerId, takes one parameter, customerMap. The customerMap parameter is then used to match only the accounts that belong to this customer.

We have the ability to extract data from the knowledge session. Let's write the transformation service. It will have only one method for starting the transformation process. This method calls a processCustomer method for every customer map that comes from legacyService.findAllCustomers. The following is the body of the processCustomer method:

```
/**
 * transforms customerMap, creates and stores new customer
 */
protected void processCustomer(Map customerMap) {
  ValidationReport validationReport = reportFactory
      .createValidationReport();

  List<Command<?>> commands = new ArrayList<Command<?>>();
  commands.add(CommandFactory.newSetGlobal(
      "validationReport", validationReport));
  commands.add(CommandFactory.newInsert(customerMap));
  commands.add(new FireAllRulesCommand());
  commands.add(CommandFactory.newQuery(
      "address", "getAddressByCustomerId",
      new Object[] { customerMap }));
  commands.add(CommandFactory.newQuery(
      "accounts", "getAccountByCustomerId",
      new Object[] { customerMap }));
  ExecutionResults results = session.execute(
      CommandFactory.newBatchExecution(commands));
  if (!validationReport.getMessagesByType(Type.ERROR)
      .isEmpty()) {
    logError(validationReport
```

```
        .getMessagesByType(Type.ERROR));
    logWarning(validationReport
        .getMessagesByType(Type.WARNING));
} else {
    logWarning(validationReport
        .getMessagesByType(Type.WARNING));
    Customer customer = buildCustomer(customerMap,
        results);
    bankingService.add(customer); // runs validation
    }
}
```

Code listing 22: Executing the transformation rules and retrieving transformed customer data
(the DataTransformationServiceImpl file)

A new `validationReport` is created; rules are executed in a stateless session and the customer map is passed in. If the validation report contains any errors, all messages are logged and this method finishes. In case there is no error, only warnings are logged, and the customer is built and added to the system. The `buildCustomer` method takes `BatchExecutionResults`, which contains the results of our queries, as an argument. The `add` service call validates the customer (in this case represented in our domain model) before saving.

An excerpt from the `buildCustomer` method can be seen in the following code snippet. It creates all accounts for the customer. The accounts are retrieved from the knowledge session with the `getAccountByCustomerId` query.

```
QueryResults accountQueryResults = (QueryResults)
    results.getValue("accounts");
for (QueryResultsRow accountQueryResult :
    accountQueryResults) {
    Map accountMap = (Map) accountQueryResult
        .get("$accountMap");

    Account account = new Account();
    account.setNumber((Long) accountMap.get("number"));
    account.setBalance((BigDecimal) accountMap
        .get("balance"));
    //..
    customer.addAccount(account);
```

Code listing 23: Execution of the parameterized query (the DataTransformationServiceImpl file)

Note that the query command bounds all `accountMap` instances under the name `"accounts"` (from the code snippet listing the body of the `processCustomer` method – `CommandFactory.newQuery("accounts", "getAccountByCustomerId", new Object[] { customerMap })`).

The method retrieves the collection of `accountMap` instances (`results.getValue("accounts")`) and for each `accountMap` creates a new `Account` object. These accounts are then added to the `Customer` object (`customer.addAccount(account)`).

Implementation of the data loading

In this section we'll look closer at getting the data from the legacy system. If you're not interested in actually trying out this example, you can skip this section.

Database setup

The data can come from various sources – database, XML, CSV, and so on. Our application will pull data from a database; however, it shouldn't be a problem to work with any other data source. The table structure looks as follows:

```
CREATE TABLE  `droolsBook`.`customer` (
  `customer_id` bigint(20) NOT NULL,
  `first_name` varchar(255) NOT NULL,
  `last_name` varchar(255) NOT NULL,
  `email` varchar(255) NOT NULL,
  PRIMARY KEY  (`customer_id`)
)
```

Code listing 24: Table structure for legacy customers in a MySQL Database

```
CREATE TABLE  `droolsBook`.`address` (
  `address_id` bigint(20) NOT NULL default '0',
  `parent_id` bigint(20) NOT NULL,
  `street` varchar(255) NOT NULL,
  `area` varchar(255) NOT NULL,
  `town` varchar(255) NOT NULL,
  `country` varchar(255) NOT NULL,
  PRIMARY KEY  (`address_id`)
)
```

Code listing 24: Table structure for legacy addresses in a MySQL Database

The `'parent_id'` column from the preceding code snippet represents a foreign key to the customer's primary key. The same applies for the `'customer_id'` column, as shown next:

```
CREATE TABLE `droolsBook`.`account` (
  `account_id` bigint(20) NOT NULL,
  `name` varchar(255) NOT NULL,
  `currency` varchar(100) NOT NULL,
  `balance` varchar(255) NOT NULL,
  `customer_id` bigint(20) NOT NULL,
  PRIMARY KEY  (`account_id`)
)
```

Code listing 25: Table structure for legacy account in a MySQL Database

As can be seen from the table structures, there is a one-to-many relationship between a customer and addresses/accounts. Note that the table column names are different to the property names used in our domain model.

You need to set up a database, create the tables using the previous code snippets, and populate them with some sample data.

Project setup

For loading data from a database we'll use iBatis (more information about project iBatis can be found at `http://ibatis.apache.org/`). It is an easy-to-use data mapper framework. iBatis has a rich set of functionality; we'll use it only for a simple task – to load data from the database as `java.util.Map` objects. Our rules will then reason over these objects.

We'll need the following additional libraries on the classpath:

- `ibatis-2.3.3.720.jar` – binary distribution of iBatis
- JDBC driver for your database; in the case of MySQL it is `mysql-connector-java-5.1.6-bin.jar` (the MySQL database driver for Java can be downloaded from `http://dev.mysql.com/downloads/connector/j/`)

iBatis configuration

Before any data can be loaded, iBatis needs to be configured. It needs to know about the database and its structure. This is configured in the SqlMapConfig.xml file:

```
<?xml version="1.0" encoding="UTF-8" ?>
<!DOCTYPEsqlMapConfig
    PUBLIC "-//ibatis.apache.org//DTD SQL Map Config 2.0//EN"
    "http://ibatis.apache.org/dtd/sql-map-config-2.dtd">
<sqlMapConfig>
  <transactionManager type="JDBC" commitRequired="false">
    <dataSource type="SIMPLE">
      <property name="JDBC.Driver"
        value="com.mysql.jdbc.Driver" />
      <property name="JDBC.ConnectionURL"
        value="jdbc:mysql://localhost/droolsBook?createDatabaseIfNotEx
ist=true&amp;useUnicode=true&amp;characterEncoding=utf-8" />
      <property name="JDBC.Username" value="root" />
      <property name="JDBC.Password" value="" />
    </dataSource>
  </transactionManager>
  <sqlMap resource="Banking.xml" />
</sqlMapConfig>
```

Code listing 26: Table structure for legacy account in a MySQL Database

The configuration is straightforward. The JDBC driver, connection URL, username, and password are given. Further down the configuration, the sqlMap element refers to an external file (Banking.xml) that specifies the table structure.

```
<?xml version="1.0" encoding="UTF-8" ?>
<!DOCTYPEsqlMap
    PUBLIC "-//ibatis.apache.org//DTD SQL Map 2.0//EN"
    "http://ibatis.apache.org/dtd/sql-map-2.dtd">
<sqlMap namespace="Banking">
<select id="findAllCustomers"
  resultClass="java.util.HashMap">
select * from customer
</select>
<select id="findAddressByCustomerId" parameterClass="long"
  resultClass="java.util.HashMap" >
select * from address where parent_id = #id#
</select>
```

```
<select id="findAccountByCustomerId" parameterClass="long"
  resultClass="java.util.HashMap" >
select * from account where customer_id = #id#
</select>
</sqlMap>
```

Code listing 27: iBatis configuration file – Banking.xml

The `sqlMap` element defines three `select` statements: one for loading all customers, one for loading customer' addresses, and one for customers' accounts. All `select` statements specify `java.util.HashMap` as the result class. When the `select` statement executes, it creates and populates this map. Each row in a table will be represented by one `HashMap` instance. Table column names are mapped to the map's keys and values to the map's values. The two other `select` elements – `findAddressByCustomerId` and `findAccountByCustomerId` – take one parameter of the `long` type. This parameter is used in the `select` statement's where clause. It represents the foreign key to the customer table.

Running iBatis

The main interface that will be used to interact with iBatis is `com.ibatis.sqlmap.client.SqlMapClient`. An instance of this class can be obtained as follows:

```
Reader reader = Resources
    .getResourceAsReader("SqlMapConfig.xml");
SqlMapClientsqlMapClient = SqlMapClientBuilder
    .buildSqlMapClient(reader);
reader.close();
```

Code listing 28: iBatis set up – building the SqlMapClient instance

After we have the `SqlMapClient` instance it can be used to load data from the database:

```
List customers = sqlMapClient
    .queryForList("findAllCustomers");

List addresses = sqlMapClient.queryForList(
    "findAddressByCustomerId", new Long(654258));
```

Code listing 29: Running iBatis queries

The second query shows how we can pass parameters to iBatis. The `returned` object in both cases is of the `java.util.List` type. The list contains zero or many `HashMap` instances. Remember? Each map represents one database record.

We can now write the implementation of the `LegacyBankService` interface from the first code snippet in this chapter. The implementation is straightforward. It simply delegates to `sqlMapClient`, as we've seen, for example, in the previous two code snippets.

Alternative data loading

Drools supports various data loaders – Smooks (`http://milyn.codehaus.org/Smooks`), JAXB (`https://jaxb.dev.java.net/`), and so on. They can be used as an alternative to iBatis. For example, Smooks can load data from various sources such as XML, CSV, Java, and others. It is itself a powerful **Extract, Transform, Load** (ETL) tool. However, we can use it to do just the data-loading part, probably with some minor transformations.

Summary

In this chapter we've seen how to use rules to perform more complex data transformation tasks. These rules are easy to read and can be expanded without increasing the overall complexity. However, it should be noted that Drools is probably not the best option if we want to do high-throughput/high-performance data transformations.

We've seen how to write rules over a generic data type such as `java.util.Map`. You should try to avoid using this kind of generic data type. However, it is not always possible, especially when doing data transformation and if you don't know much about the data.

Some testing approaches were shown; the use of `AgendaFilter` as a way to isolate the individual rule tests. Please note that upon execution, all rules are matched and placed onto the agenda; however, only those that pass this filter are executed. `ObjectFilter` was used to filter facts from the knowledge session, when we were verifying test assertions.

Finally, some examples were given on how to use Drools queries. They represent a very convenient way of accessing facts in the knowledge session.

5
Creating Human-readable Rules

The business rules implementations presented so far were aimed mostly at developers. However, it is sometimes needed that these rules are readable and understandable by business analysts. Ideally, they should be able to change the rules or even write new ones. An important aspect of business rules is their readability and user friendliness. A quick glance at a rule should give you an idea of what is it about. In this chapter we'll look at **domain-specific language** (DSL), decision tables, and rule flows to create human-readable rules.

Domain-specific language

The domain in this sense represents the business area (for example, life insurance or billing). Rules are expressed with the terminology of the problem domain. This means that domain experts can understand, validate, and modify these rules more easily.

You can think of the DSL as a translator. It defines how to translate sentences from the problem-specific terminology into rules. The translation process is defined in a .dsl file. The sentences themselves are stored in a .dslr file. The result of this process must be a valid .drl file.

Building a simple DSL might look like this:

```
[condition][]There is a Customer with firstName {name}=$customer :
Customer(firstName == {name})
[consequence][]Greet Customer=System.out.println("Hello " +
$customer.getFirstName());
```

Code listing 1: Simple DSL file simple.dsl

Note that the code listing contains only two lines (each begins with []; however, because the lines are too long, they are wrapped and effectively create four lines. This will be the case in most code listings. When using the Drools Eclipse plugin to write this DSL, enter the text before the first equal sign into the field called **Language Expression**, the text after the equal sign into **Rule Language Mapping**, leave the **Object** field blank, and select the correct scope.

The DSL just shown defines two DSL mappings. They map a DSLR sentence to a DRL rule. The first one translates to a condition that matches on a `Customer` object with a specified first name. The first name is captured into a variable called `name`. This variable is then used in the rule condition. The second line translates to a greeting message that is printed on the console. The following `.dslr` file can be written based on the DSL:

```
package droolsbook.dsl;
import droolsbook.bank.model.*;
expander simple.dsl
rule "hello rule"
  when
    There is a Customer with firstName "David"
  then
    Greet Customer
end
```

Code listing 2: The simple .dslr file (simple.dslr) with rule that greets a customer with name David

As can be seen, the structure of a `.dslr` file is same as the structure of a `.drl` file. Only the rule conditions and consequences are different. Another thing to note is the line containing `expander simple.dsl`. It informs Drools how to translate sentences in this file into valid rules. Drools reads the `simple.dslr` file and tries to translate/expand each line by applying all mappings from the `simple.dsl` file (it does it in a single pass process, line-by-line from top to bottom). The order of lines is important in a `.dsl` file. Please note that one condition/consequence doesn't have to be written on one line. If a condition/consequence is spread on multiple lines, it will be merged into one line in the resulting `.drl` file. You can use `\n` to force a newline character in the resulting `.drl` file.

When writing the `.dslr` files, consider using the Drools Eclipse plugin. It provides a special editor for the `.dslr` files that has an editing mode and a read-only mode for viewing the resulting `.drl` file. A simple DSL editor is provided as well.

The result of the translation process will look like the following screenshot:

```
simple.dslr ⊠

    package droolsbook.dsl;
    import droolsbook.bank.model.*;

    rule| "hello rule"
      when
        $customer : Customer(firstName == "David")
      then
        System.out.println("Hello " + $customer.getFirstName());
    end

Text Editor | DRL Viewer
```

Figure 1: The result of a DSL translation is a .drl file (open with the .dslr file editor)

This translation process happens in memory and no `.drl` file is physically stored. We can now run this example. First of all, a knowledge base must be created from the `simple.dsl` and `simple.dslr` files. The process is as follows (only the package creation is shown, the rest is the same as we've seen in the *Executing rules* section of *Chapter 2, Writing Basic Rules*):

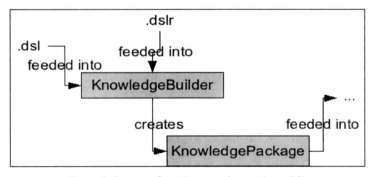

Figure 2: Process of creating a package using a DSL

The `KnowledgeBuilder` object acts as the translator. It takes the `.dslr` file, and based on the `.dsl` file, it creates the DRL. This DRL is then used as normal (we don't see it, it is internal to the `KnowledgeBuilder` object). The implementation is as follows:

```
private KnowledgeBase createKnowledgeBaseFromDSL()
    throws Exception {
```

```
KnowledgeBuilder builder =
    KnowledgeBuilderFactory.newKnowledgeBuilder();
builder.add(ResourceFactory.newClassPathResource(
    "simple.dsl"), ResourceType.DSL);
builder.add(ResourceFactory.newClassPathResource(
    "simple.dslr"), ResourceType.DSLR);
if (builder.hasErrors()) {
  throw new RuntimeException(builder.getErrors()
      .toString());
}

KnowledgeBase knowledgeBase = KnowledgeBaseFactory
    .newKnowledgeBase();
knowledgeBase.addKnowledgePackages()
    builder.getKnowledgePackages());
return knowledgeBase;
}
```

Code listing 3: Creating a knowledge base from the .dsl and .dslr files

The `.dsl` and subsequently the `.dslr` files are passed into the `KnowledgeBuilder` object. The rest is similar to what we've seen before.

DSL as an interface

DSLs can also be looked at as another level of indirection between your `.drl` files and business requirements. It works like this:

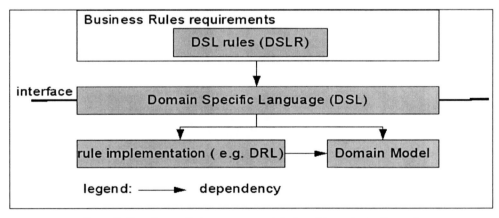

Figure 3: Domain-specific language as an interface (dependency diagram)

At the top are the business requirements as defined by the business analyst. These requirements are represented as DSL sentences (the `.dslr` file). The DSL then represents the interface between DSL sentences and rule implementation (the `.drl` file) and the domain model. For example, we can change the transformation to make the resulting rules more efficient without changing the language. Furthermore, we can change the language, for example, to make it more user friendly without changing the rules. All this can be done just by changing the `.dsl` file.

DSL for validation rules

The first three implemented object/field required rules from *Chapter 3, Validating,* can be rewritten as:

- If the `Customer` object does not have an address, then display a warning message

- If the `Customer` object does not have a phone number or it is blank, then display an error message

- If the `Account` object does not have an owner, then display an error message for the `Account` object

We can clearly see that all of them operate on some object (`Customer`/`Account`), testing its property (address/phone/owner), and displaying a message (warning/ error) possibly with some context (account). Our `validation.dslr` file might look as follows:

```
expander validation.dsl

rule "address is required"
  when
    The Customer does not have address
  then
    Display warning
end

rule "phone number is required"
  when
    The Customer does not have phone number or it is blank
  then
    Display error
end

rule "account owner is required"
  when
```

```
      The Account does not have owner
   then
      Display error for Account
 end
```

Code listing 4: First DSL approach at defining the required object/field rules (the validation.dslr file)

The conditions could be mapped like this:

```
[condition][]The {object} does not have {field}=${object} : {object}(
{field} == null )
```

Code listing 5: validation.dsl

This covers the address and account conditions completely. For the phone number rule, we have to add the following mapping at the beginning of the `validation.dsl` file:

```
[condition][] or it is blank =  == "" ||
```

Code listing 6: Mapping that checks for a blank phone number

As it stands, the phone number condition will be expanded to:

```
$Customer : Customer( phone number  == "" || == null )
```

Code listing 7: Unfinished phone number condition

To correct it, the phone number has to be mapped to `phoneNumber`. This can be done by adding the following at the end of the `validation.dsl` file:

```
[condition][]phone number=phoneNumber
```

Code listing 8: Phone number mapping

The conditions are working; let's now focus on the consequences. This mapping will do the job:

```
[consequence][]Display {message_type} for {object}={message_type}(
drools, ${object} );
[consequence][]Display {message_type}={message_type}( drools );
```

Code listing 9: Consequence mappings

The three validation rules are now being expanded to the same `.drl` representation as we've seen in the *Object required type rules* section of *Chapter 3, Validating*.

File formats

Before we go further, we'll examine each file format in more detail.

The DSL file format

A line in a `.dsl` file has the following format:

```
[<scope>][<Type>]<language expression>=<rule mapping>
```

Code listing 10: The format of one line in a .dsl file

An example of a line in a DSL file might look like this:

```
[condition][droolsbook.bank.model.Customer]The Customer does not have
address=Customer(address == null)
```

Code listing 11: Sample line from a DSL file (note that it is just one line that has been wrapped)

The scope can have the following values:

- `condition`: This specifies that this mapping can be used in the condition part of a rule.
- `consequence`: This specifies that this mapping can be used in the consequence part of a rule.
- `*`: This specifies that this mapping can be used in both the condition and consequence parts of a rule.
- `keyword`: This mapping is applied to the whole rule (not just a condition or consequence part). It is used mainly when writing DSLs in other languages than English or if we want to customize the basic `rule-when-then-end` structure.

`Type` can be used to further limit the scope of the mapping. `Scope` and `Type` are used by the Drools Eclipse plugin to provide auto-completion when writing the `.dslr` files (when pressing *Ctrl* + Space bar, only relevant choices are offered). This is especially useful with the multiple constraints feature.

DSL supports comments by starting the line with the hash character (#). For example:

```
#this is a comment in a .dsl file
```

The DRL file format

As a side note, in a `.drl` file, it is valid to write the whole rule on a single line. This allows us to write more complex DSLs, since one sentence in the `.dslr` file can be translated into multiple conditions and even a whole rule. For example, these are valid rules on a single line:

```
rule "addressRequired" when Customer( address == null ) then
warning(drools); end
```

Code listing 12: The addressRequired rule on one line

Be sure you add spaces between the Drools keywords. Another complex example of a rule on one line:

```
rule "studentAccountCustomerAgeLessThan" when Customer(
yearsPassedSince(dateOfBirth) >= 27 ) and $account : Account( type
== Account.Type.STUDENT ) then error(drools, $account); System.out.
println("another statement"); end
```

Code listing 13: The studentAccountCustomerAgeLessThan rule on one line

This rule contains two conditions and two Java statements in the consequence block. Also, there is an optional `and` keyword between the conditions to make it more readable.

The DSLR file format

A `.dslr` file contains the sentences written using DSL. The `.dslr` file is very similar to the `.drl` file. One thing to note is that by prepending a line with the > symbol, we can turn off the expander for the line. This allows us to write a hybrid `.dslr` file that contains traditional DRL rules and DSL rules. For example, if we are not yet sure how to map some complex rule, we can leave it in its original `.drl` file format.

DSL for multiple constraints in a condition

We'll go through more complex DSLs. Let's look at a standard condition.
For example:

```
Account( owner != null, balance > 100, currency == "EUR" )
```

Code listing 14: Condition that matches on some account

It is very easy to write DSL that will allow us to create conditions with any subset of constraints from this code listing using the - feature:

```
[condition][]There is an Account that=$account : Account( )
[condition][]-has owner=owner != null
[condition][]-has balance greater than {amount}=balance > {amount}
[condition][]-has currency equal to {currency}=currency == {currency}
```

Code listing 15: DSL using the - feature, which can create seven combinations of constraints

When the DSL condition starts with -, the DSL parser knows that this constraint should be added to the last condition (in a .dslr file). With the DSL just shown, the following condition can be created:

```
There is an Account that
    has currency equal to "USD"
    has balance greater than 2000
```

Code listing 16: Condition using the - feature (in a .dslr file)

The - feature increases the flexibility of the resulting language. It works just fine for simple cases involving only one pair of brackets. In the case of multiple brackets in the condition, Drools always adds the constraint to the last pair of brackets. This may not be always what we want. We have to find different way of specifying multiple constraints in a condition. We can write our DSL, which looks like this:

```
[condition][]There is an Account that {constraints} = Account(
{constraints} )
[condition][]has {field} equal to {value}={field} == {value}
[condition][]and has {field} equal to {value}=, {field} == {value}
```

Code listing 17: Flexible DSL that can be expanded to a condition with two field constraints

With this DSL, the following DSLR can be written:

```
There is an Account that has owner equal to null and has balance equal
to 100
```

Code listing 18: DSLR that describes an Account object with two constraints

If we want to have more conditions, we can simply duplicate the last line in the DSL. Keep in mind that translation is a single pass process.

Named capture groups

Sometimes, when a more complex DSL is needed, we need to be more precise at specifying what is a valid match. We can use named capture groups with regular expressions to give us the needed precision. For example:

```
{name:[a-zA-Z]+}
```

Code listing 19: Name that matches only on characters

Regular expressions (`java.util.regex.Pattern`) can be used not only for capturing variables but also within the DSL itself. For example, the DSL from 18 isn't very flexible in terms of whitespace characters. If we had the `There    is an Account that ...` line in the `.dslr` file, the expander would not have expanded this line. The DSL can be made more whitespace friendly by performing `[condition][]` `There\s+is\s+an\s+Account\s+that ....`

Each `\s+` matches one or more spaces and adds the flexibility that we need. Another useful example is to do case-insensitive matching, that is, the users should be allowed to type `Account`, `account`, `ACCOUNT`, or even `aCcount`. This can be done by enabling the embedded case-insensitive flag expression (`?i`). For example, `[condition][]There\s+is\s+an\s+(?i:account)\s+that ....`

The transformation functions

With transformation functions we can modify the captured text that is written out. For example, let's say we have the following DSL:

```
[when][]There is an? {fact}=${fact!lc} : {fact!ucfirst}( )
```

Code listing 20: DSL with transformation functions

The `There is a License` (*Code listing 21: DSLR sentence*) sentence will be translated into `$license : License( )` (*Code listing 22: Resulting DRL*):

Some of the functions that are supported are:

- `uc`: This converts all letters to uppercase
- `lc`: This converts all letters to lowercase
- `ucfirst`: This converts the first letter to uppercase and all remaining letters to lowercase

DSL for data transformation rules

We'll now implement DSL for the data transformation rules from the *Writing transformation rules* section of *Chapter 4, Transforming Data*. We'll reuse our unit test rule to verify that we don't change the functionality of the rules but only their representation. The unit test class will be extended and the method for creating the `KnowledgeBase` object will be overridden to use the `.dsl` and `.dslr` files as inputs. Rule names will stay the same. Let's start with the `twoEqualAddressesDifferentInstance` rule:

```
rule twoEqualAddressesDifferentInstance
  when
    There is legacy Address-1
    There is legacy Address-2
    - same as legacy Address-1
  then
    remove legacy Address-2
    Display WARNING for legacy Address-2
end
```

Code listing 23: Rule for removing redundant addresses (dataTransformation.dslr)

The conditions can be implemented with the following DSL:

```
[condition][] legacy {object}-{id} = {object}-{id}
[condition][] There is {object}-{id} = ${object}{id} : Map( this["_
type_"] == "{object}" )
[condition][]- {object}-{id1} same as {object}-{id2} = this ==
${object}{id2}, eval( ${object}{id1} != ${object}{id2} )
```

Code listing 24: DSL for conditions (dataTransformation.dsl)

The first mapping is a simple translation rule, where we remove the word `legacy`. The next mapping captures a map with its type. The last mapping includes the equality test with an object identity test. The mapping for consequences is as follows:

```
[consequence][] legacy {object}-{id} = ${object}{id}
[consequence][]Display {message_type_enum} for
{object}=validationReport.addMessage(reportFactory.
createMessage(Message.Type.{message_type_enum}, drools.getRule().
getName(), {object}));
[consequence][]remove {object} = retract( {object} );
```

Code listing 25: DSL for consequences

The first mapping just removes the word legacy. The second mapping adds a message to the validationReport object. And the last mapping removes an object from the knowledge session. This is all we need for the twoEqualAddressesDifferentInstance rule.

As you can see, we started with the sentence in the DSL (23) and then we've written the transformation to reflect the rules (from *Chapter 4, Transforming Data*). In reality this is an iterative process. You'll modify the .dslr and .dsl files until you are happy with the results. Also, it is a good idea to first write your rules in standard .drl and only then try to write a DSL for them.

We'll move to the next rule, addressNormalizationUSA:

```
rule addressNormalizationUSA
  when
    There is legacy Address-1
    - country is one of "US", "U.S.", "USA", "U.S.A"
  then
    for legacy Address-1 set country to USA
end
```

Code listing 26: DSLR rule for normalizing address country field

The rule just needs another constraint type:

```
[condition][]- country is one of {country_list} = this["country"] in
({country_list})
```

Code listing 27: Another condition mapping

The consequence is defined with two mappings. The first one will translate the country object to enum, and the second will then perform the assignment.

```
[consequence][]set country to {country}=set country to Address.
Country.{country}
[consequence][]for {object}set {field} to {value} = modify( {object} )
\{ put("{field}", {value} ) \}
```

Code listing 28: Consequence mapping for the country normalization rule

Please note that the curly brackets are escaped. Also, the original rule used the mvel dialect. It is a good idea to write your rules using the same dialect. It makes the DSL easier. Otherwise, the DSL will have to be dialect aware.

The other country normalization rule can be written without modifying the DSL. We'll now continue with the `unknownCountry` rule:

```
rule unknownCountry
Apply after address normalizations
  when
    There is legacy Address-1
    - country is not normalized
  then
    Display ERROR for legacy Address-1
end
```

Code listing 29: DSLR representation of the unknownCountry rule

The whole sentence, `Apply after address normalizations`, is mapped as a keyword mapping:

```
[keyword][] Apply after address normalizations = salience -10
```

Code listing 30: Salience keyword mapping

Now, we can use other rule attributes to achieve the same goal just by changing the DSL.

Additional mapping that is needed:

```
[condition][]- country is not normalized = !($Address1.get("country")
instanceof Address.Country)
```

Code listing 31: Another condition mapping

In the condition mapping the `$Address1` object is hardcoded. This is fine for the rules that we have.

As you can imagine, the rest of the rules follow similar principles.

What we have achieved by writing this DSL is better readability. A business analyst can more easily verify the correctness of these rules. We could push this further by defining a complete DSL that can represent any concept from the problem domain. The business analyst will then be able to express any business requirement just by editing the `.dslr` file.

The decision tables

The decision tables are another form of human-readable rules that is useful when there are lots of similar rules with different values. Rules that share the same conditions with different parameters can be captured in a decision table. Decision tables can be represented in an Excel spreadsheet (the `.xls` file) or a comma-separated value (the `.csv` file) format. Starting from Version 5.0, Drools supports web-based decision tables as well. They won't be discussed in this book; however, they are very similar. Let's look at a simple decision table in the `.xls` format.

1 2		A	B	C	D
	1	**RuleSet**	droolsbook.decisiontables.validation		
	2	**Import**	droolsbook.bank.model.*, droolsbook.bank.service.*, function droolsbook.bank.service.ValidationHelper.error, function droolsbook.bank.service.ValidationHelper.warning,		
	3	**Variables**	ValidationReport validationReport, ReportFactory reportFactory, BankingInquiryService inquiryService		
	4	**Notes**	Decision tables for customer validation		
	5				
	6	**RuleTable Customer validation**			
	7	NAME	CONDITION	CONDITION	ACTION
	8		$customer : Customer		
	9		$param == null	$param == null || == ""	$param == null || $param(drools);
	10	**name**	**has no**	**has blank or no**	**report**
	11	addressRequired	address		warning
	12	phoneNumberRequired		phoneNumber	error
	13		dateOfBirth		error
	14				

Figure 4: Example decision table in validation.xls opened with the OpenOffice Calc editor

The screenshot shows one decision table for validating a customer. Line number **10** shows four columns. The first one defines the rule name, the next two define conditions, and the last one is for defining actions/consequences. Lines from **11** to **13** represent the individual rules; one line per rule. Each cell defines the parameters for conditions/consequences. If a cell doesn't have a value, that condition/action is ignored and some rows in the spreadsheet are grouped and hidden (see the two plus signs in the left-hand side). This makes the decision tables more user friendly, especially for business users. Please note that tables don't have to start on the first column.

The full `validation.xls` file follows:

RuleSet	droolsbook.decisiontables.validation
Import	droolsbook.bank.model.*, droolsbook.bank. service.*, function droolsbook.bank.service. ValidationHelper.error, function droolsbook. bank.service.ValidationHelper.warning
Variables	ValidationReport validationReport, ReportFactory reportFactory, BankingInquiryService inquiryService
Notes	Decision tables for customer validation

RuleTable Customer validation			
NAME	**CONDITION**	**CONDITION**	**ACTION**
	$customer : Customer		
	$param == null	**$param == null || == ""**	**$param(drools);**
name	has no	has blank or no	report
addressRequired	address		warning
phoneNumberRequired		phoneNumber	error
	dateOfBirth		error

Table 1: Decision table for customer validation – complete source

Every file for defining decision tables starts with a global configuration section. The configuration consists of the name-value pairs. As can be seen:

- `RuleSet` defines the package
- `Import` specifies the used classes, including static imported functions
- `Variables` are used for globals
- `Notes` can be any text
- `Functions` can be used to write local functions (as in the `.drl` format)
- `Worksheet` specifies the sheet to be used; by default only the first sheet is checked for rules

The `RuleTable` validation then denotes the start of the decision table. It has no specific purpose, only to group rules that operate on the same objects and share conditions. The next line defines column types. The following column types are available:

- `CONDITION`: This defines a single rule condition or constraint and checks whether the following row can contain a type for this condition, and if it doesn't, then the next row must define a full condition (with a type, not just a constraint as is the case we just saw).

- ACTION: This is a rule action. Similar to condition, in this, the next line contains any global or bound variable. Drools will then assume that the next line is a method that should be called on this global/variable.

- PRIORITY: This is used for defining rule salience.

- NAME: By default, rule names are autogenerated, and NAME can be used to explicitly specify the name.

- No-loop or Unloop: This specifies the rule No-loop attribute.

- XOR-GROUP: This specifies the rule agenda-group (this will be discussed in the next section about jBPM).

For full configuration options please consult the Drools manual (http://www.jboss.org/drools/documentation.html).

The next line from *Table 1* ($customer : Customer) looks similar to what we see in a .drl file. It is a simple condition that matches on any Customer object and exposes this object as a $customer variable. The only difference is that there are no brackets. They will be added automatically by Drools at parsing time. Please note that this line contains only two columns. The first two columns are merged into one column. This is because they operate on the same type (Customer). If we didn't merge the two columns, they'll be matching on two separate objects (which may or may not be the same instance).

The next line (starting with: $param == null) then defines individual constraints (in case of conditions) or code blocks (in case of actions). Special parameters can be used as $param or $1, $2, $3, and so on. The first one is used if our constraint needs only one parameter, otherwise the $n format should be used.

The following line (starting with Name, has no, corresponds to line 10 from *Table 1*) is for pure informational purposes. It should contain some meaningful description of the column/action so that we don't have to always look how it is implemented (by expanding/collapsing rows).

Finally, the actual values follow in subsequent rows. Each line represents one rule. For example, the first line gets translated behind the scenes to the following .drl rule:

```
#From row number: 11
rule "addressRequired"
  when
    $customer : Customer(address == null)
  then
    warning(drools);
end
```

Code listing 32: Generated rule from a decision table

The `.drl` rule is exactly the same as we've implemented in *Chapter 3, Validation*. We can even reuse the same unit test to test this rule.

Advantages of a decision table

Here are the advantages of a decision table:

- They are easy to read and understand.
- They are a very common tool used by analysts, which makes importing existing business rules into Drools an easy task rather than having to rewrite them in the `.drl` format.
- Refactoring can be quicker because we just have to change the column header to related rules (that is, it is easy to change conditions across the group of rules).
- They feature isolation; similar to DSL, decision tables can hide the rule implementation details.
- They provide some separation between the rules and data (they are still in one file but separated).
- Any formatting available in a spreadsheet editor can be applied to present these data in a more readable manner (for example, using a drop-down list of values). It can reduce errors from mistyping a value into a cell by allowing only valid values.
- The Eclipse Drools plugin can also be used to validate a spreadsheet. This is very useful when writing rules. The problems view in Eclipse shows what exactly is wrong with the generated `.drl` file.

Disadvantages of a decision table

On the other hand, these are the disadvantages of a decision table:

- They can be awkward to debug/write these rules. Sometimes it helps to convert the spreadsheet to a `.drl` file; then save this file and fix it as we're used to.
- Decision tables shouldn't be used if the rules don't share many conditions. Furthermore, the order of conditions is important. In a decision table the order of a condition is given by the order of a column. Care should be taken if you want to convert existing DRL rules into decision tables, as the order of conditions may change (to take advantage of the reuse). Note that the rule templates don't have this disadvantage.
- XLS is a binary format, which makes version management more difficult.

Calculating the interest rate

As an example we'll calculate the interest rate based on the account's balance, currency, duration, and type. This calculation is ideal for a decision table, because we have a lot of constraints that are reused across rules with different data. The decision table looks as follows:

RuleSet	droolsbook.decisiontables
Import	droolsbook.decisiontables.bank.model.*, droolsbook. bank.model.Customer, droolsbook.bank.model. Account.Type, java.math.*,
Notes	Decision tables for calculating interest rates

RuleTable Interest Calculation

CONDITION	CONDITION	CONDITION	CONDITION	ACTION
$a:Account				
type == Account. Type.$param	currency	balance >= $1 && < $2	monthsBetween StartAnd EndDate >= $1 && < $2	$a.set Interest Rate(new BigDecimal ($param)); set interest
type	currency	balance <min, max)	months	rate
TRANSACTIONAL	EUR			"0.01"
STUDENT	EUR	0, 2000		"1.00"
SAVINGS	EUR	0, 100	0, 1	"0.00"
SAVINGS	EUR	0, 100	1, 3	"0.10"
SAVINGS	EUR	0, 100	3, 12	"2.00"
SAVINGS	EUR	100, 1000	0, 1	"0.10"
SAVINGS	EUR	100, 1000	1, 3	"3.00"
SAVINGS	EUR	100, 1000	3, 12	"3.25"
SAVINGS	EUR	1000, 5000	0, 1	"0.10"
SAVINGS	EUR	1000, 5000	1, 3	"3.25"
SAVINGS	EUR	1000, 5000	3, 12	"3.50"
SAVINGS	EUR	5000, 10000	0, 1	"0.10"
SAVINGS	EUR	5000, 10000	1, 3	"3.50"
SAVINGS	EUR	5000, 10000	3, 12	"3.75"
SAVINGS	USD	0, 100	0, 1	"0.00"

Table 2: Decision table for calculating the interest rates

Please note that the `Account` object is used in every condition, so the `CONDITION` columns are merged. We can see the use of parameters `$1` and `$2`. The first line can be read as: `For every transactional account with currency EUR set its interest rate to 0.01 percent (regardless of the balance)`. Another line can be read as: `For every savings account whose balance is between 100 EUR and 1000 EUR that is opened for one to three months, set its interest rate to 3 percent`. The following rule will be generated:

```
#From row number: 16
rule "Interest Calculation_16"
  when
    $a:Account(type == Account.Type.SAVINGS,
      currency == "EUR", balance >= 100 && < 1000,
      monthsBetweenStartAndEndDate >= 1 && < 3)
  then
    $a.setInterestRate(new BigDecimal("3.00"));
end
```

Code listing 33: Generated rule for calculating the interest rate

If we didn't use a decision table, we'll have to write such rules by hand. Please note that the second condition column in the decision table shown doesn't have any operator or operand. It simply says currency. It is a special feature and this is automatically translated to currency `== $param`.

The last condition column uses the `getMonthsBetweenStartAndEndDate` method on the `Account` class:

```
private DateMidnight startDate;
private DateMidnight endDate;

/**
 * @return number of months between start and end date
 */
public int getMonthsBetweenStartAndEndDate() {
  if (startDate == null || endDate == null) {
    return 0;
  }
  return Months.monthsBetween(startDate, endDate)
      .getMonths();
}
```

Code listing 34: Implementation of the getMonthsBetweenStartAndEndDate method of Account

The implementation uses the Joda-Time library to do the calculation.

Project setup

The following libraries are needed on the classpath:

- `drools-decisiontables-5.5.0.Final.jar`: This is used for compiling spreadsheets into the `.drl` file format. It knows how to handle the `.xls` and `.csv` formats.

- `jxl-2.6.10.jar` - XLS API: This is used for parsing the `.xls` spreadsheets.

Testing

For testing the interest calculation rules, we'll use a stateless knowledge session, an account, and a date object. All tests will reuse the stateless session. The test can be set up as follows:

```
static StatelessKnowledgeSession session;
Account account;
static DateMidnight DATE;

@BeforeClass
public static void setUpClass() throws Exception {
  KnowledgeBase knowledgeBase =
    createKnowledgeBaseFromSpreadsheet();
  session = knowledgeBase.newStatelessKnowledgeSession();
  DATE = new DateMidnight(2008, 1, 1);
}

@Before
public void setUp() throws Exception {
  account = new Account();
}
```

Code listing 35: Setup of the decision table test

The date will be used to set deposit durations. An account is created for every test method. The `createKnowledgeBaseFromSpreadsheet` method is implemented as shown:

```
private static KnowledgeBase createKnowledgeBaseFromSpreadsheet()
    throws Exception {
  DecisionTableConfiguration dtconf =KnowledgeBuilderFactory
    .newDecisionTableConfiguration();
  dtconf.setInputType( DecisionTableInputType.XLS );
```

```
KnowledgeBuilder knowledgeBuilder =
  KnowledgeBuilderFactory.newKnowledgeBuilder();
knowledgeBuilder.add(ResourceFactory.newClassPathResource(
    "interest calculation.xls"), ResourceType.DTABLE,
    dtconf);

if (knowledgeBuilder.hasErrors()) {
  throw new RuntimeException(knowledgeBuilder.getErrors()
      .toString());
}

KnowledgeBase knowledgeBase = KnowledgeBaseFactory
  .newKnowledgeBase();
knowledgeBase.addKnowledgePackages(
    knowledgeBuilder.getKnowledgePackages());
return knowledgeBase;
}
```

Code listing 36: Creating a knowledgeBase object from a spreadsheet

As opposed to other knowledge definitions, the decision table needs a special configuration that is encapsulated in the DecisionTableConfiguration class. This configuration specifies the type of decision table and it is then passed to the knowledge builder. The rest should be familiar. If we want to use a decision table in a .csv format, we'd have to use the DecisionTableInputType.CSV object as the input type.

Note that if you want to see the generated .drl source, you can get it like this:

```
String drlString = DecisionTableFactory
    .loadFromInputStream(ResourceFactory
        .newClassPathResource("interest calculation.xls")
        .getInputStream(), dtconf);
```

Code listing 37: Getting the .drl representation of the decision table

It is stored in a drlString string variable; it can be printed to the console and used for debugging purposes.

We'll now write a test for depositing 125 EUR for 40 days:

```
@Test
public void deposit125EURfor40Days() throws Exception {
  account.setType(Account.Type.SAVINGS);
  account.setBalance(new BigDecimal("125.00"));
  account.setCurrency("EUR");
  account.setStartDate(DATE.minusDays(40));
```

```
        account.setEndDate(DATE);

        session.execute(account);

        assertEquals(new BigDecimal("3.00"), account
            .getInterestRate());
    }
```

Code listing 38: Test for depositing 125 EUR for 40 days

The test verifies that the correct interest rate is set on the account. And one test for the default transactional account rate is:

```
    @Test
    public void defaultTransactionalRate() throws Exception {
        account.setType(Account.Type.TRANSACTIONAL);
        account.setCurrency("EUR");

        session.execute(account);

        assertEquals(new BigDecimal("0.01"), account
            .getInterestRate());
    }
```

Code listing 39: Test for the default transactional account rate

Again, the test verifies that the correct interest rate is set.

Comma separated values

The XLS spreadsheet can be easily converted into CSV format. Just select Save as CSV in your spreadsheet editor. However, there is one caveat. CSV format doesn't support merging of columns by default. However, Drools has the following workaround: if we add three dots at the end of type declarations, they will be merged into one. It can be seen on the last line of the following CSV excerpt:

```
    "RuleTable Interest Calculation",,,,
    "CONDITION","CONDITION","CONDITION","CONDITION","ACTION"
    "$a:Account...","$a:Account...","$a:Account...","$a:Account...",
```

Code listing 40: Excerpt from the interest calculation.csv file

It is the only change that needs to be done. Tests should pass for CSV format as well.

CSV is a text format as opposed to XLS, which is a binary format. The binary format makes version management harder. For example, it is very difficult to merge changes between two binary files. CSV doesn't have these problems. On the other hand, the presentation suffers.

Rule templates

If you like the concept of decision tables, you may want to look at "Drools Rule Templates". They are similar to decision tables but more powerful. With Drools Rule Templates the data is fully separated from the rule (for example, it can come from a database and have different templates over the same data). You have more power in defining the resulting rule. The data can define any part of a rule (for example, condition operator, class, or property name). For more information look into the Drools Experts User Guide section on Rule Templates.

jBPM

Processes can also help us toward more human-readable rules. It is not a substitute to rules as was the case with DSLs and decision tables. It is a way of defining the execution flow between complex rules. The rules are then easier to understand.

With jBPM we can externalize the execution order from the rules. The execution order can then be managed externally. Potentially, you may define more execution orders for one `KnowledgeBase` object.

jBPM is a process engine, a standalone product that is very closely integrated with Drools. It can execute arbitrary actions or user-defined work items at specific points within the process. It can even be persisted, as we'll see in *Chapter 8, Defining Processes with jBPM*, which shows a bigger example of using processes.

Drools agenda

Before we talk about how to manage rule execution order, we have to understand Drools Agenda. When a object is inserted into the knowledge session, Drools tries to match this object with all the possible rules. If a rule has all its conditions met, its consequence can be executed. We say that a rule is activated. Drools records this event by placing this rule onto its agenda (it is a collection of activated rules). As you may imagine, many rules can be activated and also deactivated depending on what objects are in the rule session. After the `fireAllRules` method call, Drools picks one rule from the agenda and executes its consequence, which may or may not cause further activations or deactivations. This continues until the Drools agenda is empty.

The purpose of the agenda is to manage the execution order of rules.

Methods for managing the rule execution order

The following are the methods for managing the rule execution order (from the user's perspective). They can be viewed as alternatives to processes. All of them are defined as rule attributes:

- `salience`: This is the most basic one. Every rule has a `salience` value. By default it is set to `0`. Rules with a higher salience value will fire first. The problem with this approach is that it is hard to maintain. If we want to add a new rule with some priority, we may have to shift the priorities of existing rules. It is often hard to figure out why a rule has a certain salience, so we have to comment every salience value. It creates an invisible dependency on other rules.

- `activation-group`: This used to be called `xor-group`. When two or more rules with the same activation group are on agenda, Drools will fire just one of them. Be careful when using `activation-group` if you are processing more sets of facts in one session (for example, more customers), and let's say there are two rules, `goldenCustomer` and `standardCustomer` that share the same `activation-group` attribute. If one of these rules fire for any customer, then the other rule won't fire for any customer, which is probably not what we want.

- `agenda-group`: Every rule has an agenda group. By default it is `MAIN`; however, it can be overridden. This allows us to partition Drools agenda into multiple groups that can be executed separately at different times.

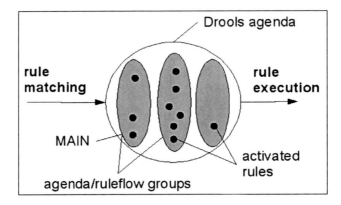

Figure 7: Partitioned Agenda with activated rules

This picture shows matched rules coming from the left-hand side, going into agenda. One rule is chosen from the agenda at a time and then executed/fired.

At runtime we can programmatically set the active agenda group (through the `setFocus` method of `KnowledgeHelper`: the `drools.setFocus(String agendaGroup)` method), or declaratively by setting the rule attribute's autofocus to `true`. When a rule is activated and has this attribute set to `true`, the active agenda group is automatically changed to the rule's agenda group. Drools maintains a stack of agenda groups. Whenever the focus is set to a different agenda group, Drools adds this group onto this stack. When there are no rules to fire in the current agenda group, Drools pops from the stack and sets the current agenda group to the next one.

Note that only one instance of each of these attributes is allowed per rule (for example, a rule can be only in one `ruleflow-group`; however, it can also define a `salience` value within that group).

The ruleflow-group attribute

As we've already said, processes can externalize the execution order from the rule definitions. Rules have to just define a `ruleflow-group` attribute, which is similar to the `agenda-group` attribute. It is then used to define the execution order. A simple process is shown in the following screenshot:

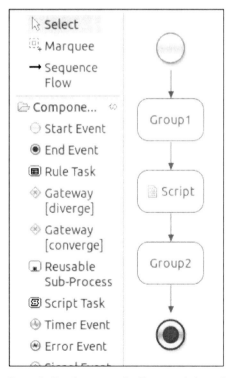

Figure 8: Simple process (in file example.bpmn)

This is a process opened with the Drools Eclipse plugin. On the left-hand side are components that can be used when building a process. On the right-hand side is the process itself. It has a start node, which goes to `rule-flow group` called `Group1`. After it finishes execution a script is executed, then the flow continues to another ruleflow group called `Group2`, and finally it finishes in an end node.

Process definitions are stored in a file with the `.bpmn` extension. This file has an XML format and defines the structure and layout for presentational purposes.

> Another useful rule attribute for managing whose rules can be activated is `lock-on-active`. It is a special form of the `no-loop` attribute. It can be used in combination with `ruleflow-group` or `agenda-group`. If it is set to `true` and an `agenda-group` or `ruleflow-group` attribute becomes active/focused, it discards any further activations for a rule until a different group becomes active. Please note that activations that are already on the agenda are allowed to fire.

A process consists of various nodes. Each node has a name, type, and other specific attributes. You can see and change these attributes by opening the standard **Properties view** in Eclipse while editing the process file. Now let's take a look at the basic node types.

Start event

This is an initial node. The process begins here. Each process needs one start node. This node has no incoming connection, just one outgoing connection.

End event

It is a terminal node. When an execution reaches this node, the whole process is terminated (all active nodes are canceled). This node has one incoming connection and no outgoing connections.

Script task

This is used to execute some arbitrary block of code. It is similar to a rule consequence; it can reference global variables and can specify dialect.

Rule task

This node will activate a `ruleflow-group` attribute, as specified by its `RuleFlowGroup` attribute. It should match the value in `ruleflow-group` attribute.

Gateway — diverging

This node splits the execution flow into one or many branches. It has two properties: `name` and `type`. The `name` property is just for display purposes. The `type` property can have three values: `AND`, `OR`, and `XOR`:

- `AND`: With this, the execution continues through all branches.

- `OR`: With this, each branch has a condition. The condition is basically the same as a rule condition. If the condition is `true`, the flow continues through this branch. There must be at least one condition that is `true`; otherwise, an exception will be thrown.

- `XOR`: Similar to the `OR` type, each branch has a condition, but in this case with a priority. The flow continues through just one branch, whose condition is `true` and has the lowest value in the priority field. There must be at least one condition that is `true`; otherwise, an exception will be thrown. Please note that this concept (lowest value means highest priority) is different from the concept used with the `salience` value (lowest value means lowest priority).

The dialog for defining `OR` and `XOR` split types looks as follows:

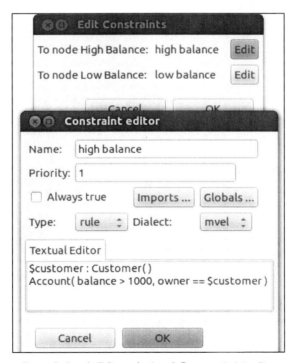

Figure 9: Drools Eclipse plugin ruleflow constraint editor

It is accessible from the standard Eclipse **Properties view**.

Gateway – converge

This joins multiple branches into one. It has two properties: name and type. The name property is for display purposes. The type property decides when the execution will continue. It can have the following values:

- AND: With this, join waits for all incoming branches; the execution then continues
- XOR: With this, the join node waits for one incoming branch

Please consult the Drools manual for additional node types.

Example – defining an execution order

If you look at the data transformation rule in *Chapter 4, Transforming Data*, you'll see that in some rules we've used the salience value to define a rule execution order. For example, all addresses needed to be normalized (that is, converted to enums) before we could report the unknown countries. The unknown country rule used salience value of -10, which meant that it would fire only after all address normalization rules. We'll now extract this execution order logic into a process to demonstrate how it works. The process might look as follows:

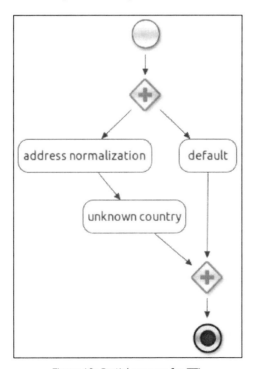

Figure 10: Partial process for ETL

When the execution starts, it goes through the start node straight into the diverging gateway. In this case it is an and type gateway. It basically creates two parallel branches that will be executed concurrently (note that this doesn't mean multiple threads). We can see that the flow is explicitly specified. Address normalization happens before the unknown country reporting. Parallel to this branch is a default rule task. It contains the other rules. Finally, a converging gateway of type and is used to block until all branches complete and then the flow continues to the end node. We had to use the converging gateway (instead of going straight to the end node), because as soon as some branch in a process reaches the end node, it terminates the whole process (that is, our branches may be canceled before competition, which is not what we want).

The process ID is set to dataTransformation. It can be done by clicking on the canvas in the process editor and then in **Properties view** setting the ID to this value.

Rules

Next, we create a copy of the dataTransformation.drl file from *Chapter 4, Transforming Data*, and we'll name it dataTransformation-ruleflow.drl. We'll make the following changes:

- Each rule gets a new attribute: ruleflow-group "default".

- Except the address normalization rules. For example:

```
rule addressNormalizationUSA
ruleflow-group "address normalization"
```

Code listing 41: Top part of the USA address normalization rule

- Except unknown country rule that gets the unknown country ruleflow-group.

KnowledgeBase set up

We can now create a knowledge base out of the .bpmn and the .drl files:

```
static KnowledgeBase createKnowledgeBaseFromRuleFlow()
    throws Exception {
  KnowledgeBuilder builder = KnowledgeBuilderFactory
    .newKnowledgeBuilder();
  builder.add(ResourceFactory.newClassPathResource(
      "dataTransformation-ruleflow.drl"), ResourceType.DRL);
  builder.add(ResourceFactory.newClassPathResource(
      "dataTransformation.bpmn"), ResourceType.BPMN2);
  if (builder.hasErrors()) {
```

```
        throw new RuntimeException(builder.getErrors()
            .toString());
    }

    KnowledgeBase knowledgeBase = KnowledgeBaseFactory
        .newKnowledgeBase();
    knowledgeBase.addKnowledgePackages(builder
        .getKnowledgePackages());
    return knowledgeBase;
}
```

Code listing 42: Method that creates a KnoweldgeBase object with a ruleflow-group

Note that a knowledge base is created from both files, `.drl` and `.bpmn`. To achieve true isolation of unit tests, consider constructing the knowledge base only from the `.drl` file or `.bpmn` file. That way the unit tests can focus only on the relevant part.

Tests

The test setup needs to be changed as well. Processes are fully supported only for stateful sessions. Stateful sessions can't be shared across tests because they maintain state. We need to create a new stateful session for each test. We'll move the session initialization logic from the `setupClass` method that is called once per test class into the initialize method that will be called once per test method:

```
static KnowledgeBase knowledgeBase;
StatefulKnowledgeSession session;

@BeforeClass
public static void setUpClass() throws Exception {
    knowledgeBase = createKnowledgeBaseFromRuleFlow();
}

@Before
public void initialize() throws Exception {
    session = knowledgeBase.newStatefulKnowledgeSession();
```

Code listing 43: Excerpt from the unit test initialization

Once the stateful session is initialized, we can use it.

We'll write a test that will create a new address map with an unknown country. This address map will be inserted into the session; we'll start the process and execute all rules. The test will verify that the `unknownCountry` rule has been fired:

```
@Test
public void unknownCountryUnknown() throws Exception {
    Map addressMap = new HashMap();
    addressMap.put("_type_", "Address");
    addressMap.put("country", "no country");

    session.insert(addressMap);
    session.startProcess("dataTransformation");
    session.fireAllRules();

    assertTrue(validationReport.contains("unknownCountry"));
}
```

Code listing 44: Test for the unknown country rule with an unknown country

Note that the order of the session methods is important. All facts need to be in the session before the process can be started and rules can be executed.

Please note that in order to test this scenario, we didn't use any agenda filter. This test is more like an integration test where we need to test more rules cooperating together.

Another test that exercises case, where the country is known, is shown here. It proves that the process works:

```
@Test
public void unknownCountryKnown() throws Exception {
    Map addressMap = new HashMap();
    addressMap.put("_type_", "Address");
    addressMap.put("country", "Ireland");

    session.startProcess("dataTransformation");
    session.insert(addressMap);
    session.fireAllRules();

    assertFalse(validationReport.contains("unknownCountry"));
}
```

Code listing 45: Test for the unknown country rule with a known country

Since a stateful session is being used, every test should call the `dispose` method on the session after it finishes. It can be done like this:

```
@After
public void terminate() {
  session.dispose();
}
```

Code listing 46: Calling the session dispose method after every test

Summary

In this chapter we've learned about writing more user friendly rules using DSLs, decision tables, and processes. You can mix and match these various approaches. It makes sense to write some rules using DSL, some using decision tables, and more complex rules using the pure `.drl` file format. A `KnowledgeBase` object can be created from multiple sources.

DSLs are very useful if there is a need for the business analyst to read and understand existing rules and even write new rules. The resulting language uses business terminology, making it more natural for the business analyst. The DSL provides an abstraction layer that hides complicated rule implementations. The Eclipse editor brings autocompletion so that the rules are easier to write.

Decision tables on the other hand are shining when we have lot of similar rules that use different values. As was the case in the interest rate calculation example. It makes it easy to change such rules, because the rule implementation is decoupled from the values they use. The spreadsheet format is also more concise. We can fit more rules into one screen, which makes it easier to get the overall picture.

In the last section we've learned about jBPM, agenda, and various ways of managing the rule execution order. jBPM was one that manages the execution order in a nice human-readable graphical representation.

6

Working with Stateful Session

In this chapter we'll look at using stateful knowledge sessions for executing validation rules from *Chapter 3, Validating*. We'll discuss the advantages and disadvantages that this brings. Since a stateful session maintains state, we'll go through various serialization modes that are supported. We'll also cover logical assertions, fact handles, and a new rule conditional element called `collect`.

StatefulKnowledgeSession

Drools supports two kinds of knowledge sessions for executing rules: stateful and stateless. The names might be a bit misleading at first, because both sessions maintain state. The difference is that a stateful session also maintains its state between session invocations (calls to the `fireAllRules` method). This is useful when we need to call rules multiple times over a period of time while making iterative changes to its state.

Another use case is if we need to execute the same set of rules over the same facts that don't change very often over time. It would be a waste of computer resources to insert all facts over and over again. Instead, we should use a stateful session and tell it about the facts that have been changed since the last execution.

The disadvantages are that working with this session is more complex, because we have to take into account its state unlike in a stateless session, where a new state is formed with each session invocation. A stateful session needs to be destroyed when we finish working with it. Only then can the garbage collector reclaim the resources it holds.

Generally speaking, if a task can be done just with a stateless session, this should be preferred. It is in line with the **keep it short and simple (KISS)** principle.

org.drools.runtime.StatefulKnowledgeSession

StatefulKnowledgeSession is the interface for all Drools stateful sessions. A stateful knowledge session keeps state between session invocations. It can be created by calling the newStatefulKnowledgeSession method on a KnowledgeBase object. By default, the KnowledgeBase object keeps a reference to all stateful sessions. By keeping the references, the sessions can be updated when a new rule is added or an existing rule is removed. In case a new rule is added to the knowledge base, it notifies all existing sessions and all objects/facts are automatically matched with the rule's conditions as if the rule was always there. If an existing rule is removed from the knowledge base, it is removed from each knowledge session as well. If we've finished working with the session, the engine should be notified by calling the dispose() method on the StatefulKnowledgeSession object. The rule engine can then disassociate this session from the KnowledgeBase object, free all session's memories, and remove attached event listeners so that the session can be garbage collected. If a lot of stateful sessions are created and we forgot to call the dispose() method, the program may soon run out of memory.

StatefulKnowledgeSession, similar to the StatelessKnowledgeSession object, implements the CommandExecutor interface. It allows us to execute commands that implement the org.drools.command.Command interface. The only difference to StatelessKnowledgeSession is that a stateless session automatically executes FireAllRulesCommand if we haven't done it explicitly. Note that there is a special command implementation, BatchExecutionCommandImpl, that allows us to execute multiple commands at once.

It should be noted that from the rules perspective it makes no difference if we use a stateful or stateless session. We can switch from stateless to stateful and vice versa without changing rules.

Both stateful and stateless sessions are thread-safe. However, note that if we want to use Drools in a multithreaded environment, the facts that we create need to be thread-safe too.

Validation using stateful session

Our implementation of the validation service from *Chapter 3, Validating*, is working seamlessly, but it might be doing more work than it needs to. The state of the session isn't kept and so all rules have to be processed every time. Imagine a web application where a user logs in to his/her bank account and wants to do a couple of changes. Every change needs to leave the system in a consistent state. The validation must run as part of every request. However, with the validation implementation that we have, all objects will have to be inserted into a new stateless knowledge session over and over again, which is unnecessary. With a stateful session, we just need to insert all objects once and then simply update only those that changed. This can save us computing time, especially if we have lots of facts that need to be inserted. Of course, one needs to know which objects did change, but this shouldn't be a problem. If, for example, a customer is changing his/her demographic data, only the `Customer` and `Address` objects need to be updated. The client of this service API can make these decisions and update only the `Customer` and `Address` objects.

Design overview

If we think about the implementation, there are at least two approaches to stateful sessions. The first one is to have the stateful session in the domain model itself. The advantage is that you'll get a rich model that knows how to validate itself. Domain objects can even be intelligent enough to know if they've been changed, and only then call `session.update`, removing the burden from the user of this API. Every domain object will have `FactHandle`, which is a handle to its representation in the knowledge session. `FactHandles` are needed for external (that is, not from within a DRL file) interactions with the knowledge session. The disadvantage is that the model will depend on the Drools API or at least some abstraction of it. Also, each object will need to have access to the knowledge session probably through its parent. This is not ideal from the point of domain modeling.

The second option is to separate this logic completely from the domain model by having a separate stateful service. The disadvantage of this approach is that we'll get a more anemic domain model (where business logic is implemented outside of the domain model). The stateful service will have to maintain a map of fact to `FactHandle`. Alternatively, it could use such existing map that Drools maintains internally, namely delegate to the session's `getFactHandle` method for the retrieval of FactHandles. By default, it retrieves `FactHandles` by fact identity. It works fine as long as the identities don't change. If they do, then we have to repopulate the session.

Stateful Validation Service

We'll implement the second option (note that both options are valid and it shouldn't be that much different to perform the first option). Let's start with a stateful service interface. Firstly, the service needs to know about our domain objects probably through some register method. Then it needs to be notified when an object has been changed. Finally, it needs to generate a validation report. The interface is as follows:

```
public interface StatefulService {
  /**
```

```
   * registers new objects with this service or notifies this
   * service that an object has been modified
   */
  void insertOrUpdate(Object object);

  /**
   * same as insertOrUpdate(Object object); plus this method
   * calls insertOrUpdate on child objects
   */
  void insertOrUpdateRecursive(Customer customer);

  /**
   * executes validation rules and returns report
   */
  ValidationReport executeRules();

  /**
   * releases all resources held by this service
   */
  void terminate();
}
```

Code listing 1: Stateful validation service interface (the StatefulService.java file)

The stateful service works similar to a stateful session. New objects can be inserted into the stateful service, and existing objects can be updated. The first two methods of this service are exactly for this purpose. The second method is a convenient method that will traverse the tree of objects starting with the Customer (argument of the method) object. We can use this approach because all of our domain objects are traversable/reachable from the Customer object.

After all the needed objects have been inserted/updated, the executeRules method can be called. It will execute all rules and return back a validation report. If the validation has failed, this report can be displayed to the user. The user can make changes, which translates to inserting new or updating an existing object using the two methods mentioned earlier. Then the rules are executed again, and the process may continue until we're happy with the validation result (for example, the validation report has no errors). When we've finished working with the stateful service, we should call its terminate method to properly release all resources it holds. The following is a graphical representation of this whole process:

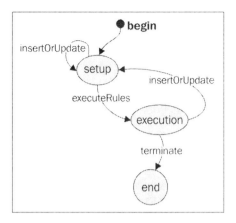

Figure 1: State diagram of the StatefulService interface

Let's now start implementing this service. It will use some classes that we should be familiar with from *Chapter 3, Validating*:

```
public class StatefulServiceImpl implements StatefulService,
    Serializable {
  private transient KnowledgeBase knowledgeBase;
  private transient StatefulKnowledgeSession statefulSession;
  private transient ReportFactory reportFactory;

  public StatefulServiceImpl(KnowledgeBase knowledgeBase,
      ReportFactory reportFactory,
      BankingInquiryService inquiryService) {
    this.reportFactory = reportFactory;
    this.knowledgeBase = knowledgeBase;
    statefulSession = createKnowledgeSession(inquiryService);
  }
```

Code listing 2: Service constructor and properties (the StatefulServiceImpl.java file)

The service implements the `StatefulService` interface and also the `java.io.Serializable` interface. It has three properties: `knowledgeBase`, the session itself, and the `reportFactory` object. They are all declared as transient, which means they won't be serialized by default. We'll talk about serialization later in this chapter. The constructor sets the properties and delegates the creation of the stateful knowledge session to the method `createKnowledgeSession`. This method is as follows:

```
private StatefulKnowledgeSession createKnowledgeSession(
    BankingInquiryService inquiryService) {
  StatefulKnowledgeSession session = knowledgeBase
    .newStatefulKnowledgeSession();
  session.setGlobal("reportFactory", reportFactory);
```

```
      session.setGlobal("inquiryService", inquiryService);
      return session;
  }
```

Code listing 3: Method for creating and setting up the stateful knowledge session (the StatefulServiceImpl.java file)

The `createKnowledgeSession` method also sets the global variables as required by the validation rules. The `knowledgeBase` object will be created from the same file, `validation.drl`.

The next code listing shows the implementation of the two setup methods:

```
public void insertOrUpdate(Object fact) {
  if (fact == null) {
    return;
  }

  FactHandle factHandle = statefulSession
      .getFactHandle(fact);

  if (factHandle == null) {
    statefulSession.insert(fact);
  } else {
    statefulSession.update(factHandle, fact);
  }
}

public void insertOrUpdateRecursive(Customer customer) {
  insertOrUpdate(customer);
  insertOrUpdate(customer.getAddress());
  if (customer.getAccounts() != null) {
    for (Account account : customer.getAccounts()) {
      insertOrUpdate(account);
    }
  }
}
```

Code listing 4: Two stateful service setup methods (the StatefulServiceImpl.java file)

The `insertOrUpdate` generic method takes a fact and checks if this fact already exists in the knowledge session. If it exists, it updates this fact ,and if it doesn't exist, it inserts this fact into the session. The `statefulSession.getFactHandle` method is used to check the fact existence. It takes the fact and returns `FactHandle`.

org.drools.FactHandle

As the name suggests, it is a handle to an already inserted fact in the knowledge session. When a fact is inserted, the `insert` method returns `FactHandle`. An object inside the knowledge session can be modified only through its `FactHandle`. The session's `update` method actually takes two parameters: `FactHandle` and the updated object. You may be wondering why the `update` method worked in the rule consequences that we've written so far. It is because behind the scenes, Drools provides the fact handle for us, since it is known in the rule consequence.

The rule engine needs `FactHandles` to correctly identify the fact we're referring to. Let's say that the insertion mode is set to identity and we want to change the value of some immutable object (for example, `java.math.BigDecimal`). The only way to change it is to create a new instance. Then, if the `session.update` method is called by passing in `FactHandle` together with the object, the engine can correctly update itself. Another example is if the insertion mode is set to equality and we're changing the object state that is part of the equals contract. Only through `FactHandle` will the engine recognize the object.

Drools supports two fact insertion modes: equality and identity. They can be set at `KnowledgeBase` creation time in the `org.drools.KnowledgeBaseConfiguration` object. Identity mode means that no two objects with the same JVM object reference can be inserted into the knowledge session. Equality mode works based on the `equals` method. The default mode is identity. Changing the insertion mode also changes the way the `session.getFactHandle` method behaves (if it is changed to equality mode it will retrieve facts based on the equals method).

Note that `FactHandles` are not serializable out of the box.

The `insertOrUpdateRecursive` method takes a `Customer` object and simply calls the `insertOrUpdate` method for the `Customer` object and all its descending objects.

The method that represents the second state of the stateful service (execution of validation rules) is shown:

```
public ValidationReport executeRules() {
  ValidationReport validationReport =
      reportFactory.createValidationReport();
  statefulSession.setGlobal("validationReport",
      validationReport);
  statefulSession.fireAllRules();
  return validationReport;
}
```

Code listing 5: Method for rule execution (the StatefulServiceImpl.java file)

It creates a validation report, sets it as a global variable, fires all rules, and returns this validation report. A new validation report is created for every rule execution.

Finally, the method that handles the termination of this service is shown here:

```
public void terminate() {
  statefulSession.dispose();
}
```

Code listing 6: Method for terminating the service (the StatefulServiceImpl.java file)

It calls the session `dispose` method, which releases all resources held by this session.

Integration testing

If we run the tests implemented in *Chapter 3, Validating*, they would run just fine. However, the purpose of this section is to test interactions that include multiple user requests. The following test will cover a scenario where the user logs in, performs multiple operations, and then logs out.

The setup of `StatefulServiceIntegrationTest` is similar to what we've done before:

```
public class StatefulServiceIntegrationTest {
  StatefulServiceImpl statefulService;
  static KnowledgeBase knowledgeBase;

  @BeforeClass
  public static void setUpClass() throws Exception {
    knowledgeBase = DroolsHelper.createKnowledgeBase(
        "validation-stateful.drl");
  }

  @Before
  public void initialize() throws Exception {
    ReportFactory reportFactory = new DefaultReportFactory();
    BankingInquiryService inquiryService =
        new BankingInquiryServiceImpl();

    statefulService = new StatefulServiceImpl(knowledgeBase,
        reportFactory, inquiryService);
  }

  @After
  public void terminate() {
    statefulService.terminate();
  }
```

Code listing 7: The StatefulServiceIntegrationTest setup

In the `setUpClass` method, the `knowledgeBase` object is created from the file `validation-stateful.drl`. This file is, for now, a pure copy of the file `validation.drl`. The `initialize` method will run before every `test` method and it will create the `statefulService` object that we'll test. After each `test` method, the `statefulService` object will be discarded by calling the `terminate` method.

Before writing the `test` method, a `helper` method for creating a valid customer will be needed:

```
private Customer createValidCustomer() {
    Customer customer = new Customer();
    customer.setPhoneNumber("123 456 789");
    customer.setAddress(new Address());

    statefulService.insertOrUpdateRecursive(customer);
    ValidationReport report = statefulService.executeRules();
    assertEquals(0, report.getMessages().size());
    return customer;
}
```

Code listing 8: Helper method for creating a valid customer (the StatefulServiceIntegrationTest.java file)

This method creates a new valid `Customer` object and sets the required fields. This customer is then passed into the `insertOrUpdateRecursive` method, which behind the scenes inserts the `Customer` and `Address` object into a stateful session. Since this is a valid customer, the method also verifies that the validation report has no messages.

Let's write a `test` method. It will use the previous method to create a valid Customer object. Since we'll be testing a full user session interaction, the `test` method will be split into three sections. The first part is shown in *Code listing 9*. It will blank the customer phone number, notify the service, and verify that it contains the correct report:

```
@Test
public void statefulValidation() throws Exception {
    Customer customer = createValidCustomer();

    customer.setPhoneNumber("");
    statefulService.insertOrUpdate(customer);
    ValidationReport report = statefulService.executeRules();
    assertEquals(1, report.getMessages().size());
    assertTrue(report.contains("phoneNumberRequired"));
```

Code listing 9: First part of statefulValidation test method (the StatefulServiceIntegrationTest.java file)

Since we've modified the Customer object, the statefulService object is notified about this by calling insertOrUpdateMethod and passing in the Customer object. After executing the rules, the test verifies that there is one message in the validation report.

Let's imagine that the user now creates a new account. The next part tests this scenario:

```
Account account = new Account();
account.setOwner(customer);
customer.addAccount(account);
statefulService.insertOrUpdate(customer);
statefulService.insertOrUpdate(account);
report = statefulService.executeRules();
assertEquals(3, report.getMessages().size());
assertTrue(report.contains("accountNumberUnique"));
assertTrue(report.contains("accountBalanceAtLeast"));
assertTrue(report.contains("phoneNumberRequired"));
```

Code listing 10: Second part of the statefulValidation test method (the StatefulServiceIntegrationTest.java file)

After creating the new Account object and setting its properties, the statefulService object is notified. Please note that the notification is done not only for the new Account object but also for the Customer object, because it has changed.

Our expectation is that there will be three messages in the report. The balance object hasn't been set, the customer's phone number is still missing, and the accountNumberUnique rule should fire, because our stub implementation of the bankingInquiryService.isAccountNumberUnique method simply always returns false.

If we run this test, everything will work as expected. Let's continue with the last part of this test method. It will set the account owner to null and expect one more message in the validation report (accountOwnerRequired):

```
account.setOwner(null);
statefulService.insertOrUpdate(account);
report = statefulService.executeRules();
assertEquals(4, report.getMessages().size());
assertTrue(report.contains("accountNumberUnique"));
assertTrue(report.contains("accountOwnerRequired"));
assertTrue(report.contains("accountBalanceAtLeast"));
assertTrue(report.contains("phoneNumberRequired"));
}
```

Code listing 11: Third and last part of the statefulValidation test method (the StatefulServiceIntegrationTest.java file)

Again, the `statefulService` object is notified that the account fact has been changed. Please note that only the `Account` object has changed this time. Our expectation is that there will be four messages in the report (four validation rules are violated). However, after running the test, only three account validation messages are in the report. The `phoneNumberRequired` message is missing. If we look at the rule, we'll see that it has only one condition: `Customer( phoneNumber == null || == "" )`. Since we haven't updated the `Customer` object, the rule didn't fire.

The problem is that a new report is created every time the `executeRules` method is called. It contains only messages from rules that fired during the last execution. You may ask: why do we create a new report with each rule execution? If we had a report for the whole duration of the `statefulService` object, we wouldn't know when an error had been corrected (for example, in this case, that the customer's phone number has been set). We'd need some way to remove invalid messages from the report. Logical assertions provide a nice solution to this problem.

Logical assertions

Similar to the standard assertions (we previously referred to them as inserts), a logical assertion adds facts into the knowledge session. If the same fact is logically inserted by more rules, only one equal instance will be physically present in the session. Furthermore, a logically inserted fact will be automatically retracted when the conditions of all rules that inserted it are no longer true. Enough theory; let's explain this with an example.

Imagine that we have couple of rules for checking fraudulent transactions. We'll create a special type, `SuspiciousTransaction`, to mark that the transaction is suspicious.

```
rule notification
  when
    $transaction : Transaction( )
    Notification( transaction == $transaction )
  then
    insertLogical(new SuspiciousTransaction($transaction))
end
```

Code listing 12: Rule that triggers on user notifications and adds the SuspiciousTransaction logical assertion (the fraudulent-transactions.drl file)

This `Notification` may, for example, represent a customer service department, receiving a notification of some sort. The rule consequence inserts the logical fact `SuspiciousTransaction`.

There can be many rules that insert `SuspiciousTransaction`. For example:

```
rule unusualLocation
  when
    $transaction : Transaction( )
    RiskFactor( unusualLocation > 10,
      transaction == $transaction )
  then
    insertLogical(new SuspiciousTransaction($transaction))
end
```

Code listing 13: Rule that adds the SuspiciousTransaction logical assertion based on an unusual location risk factor (the fraudulent-transactions.drl file)

This rule will fire if a risk factor is greater than a certain value (in this case, it is `10`). This `RiskFactor` fact can be calculated and updated by many other rules.

Each logically inserted fact has a counter, which is incremented every time an equal fact is inserted (our suspicious transaction facts are equal if they refer to the same transaction). If the conditions of this rule are no longer `true`, for example, the `unusualLocation` value of `RiskFactor` is changed to `5` and the `RiskFactor` fact is updated, the counter for this logically inserted fact will be decremented. If the value reaches zero, the fact will be automatically retracted. The transaction is no longer considered suspicious if the risk factor is small.

Next, we may have a different set of rules with very low priority firing at the end, which reacts to the presence of a `SuspiciousTransaction` fact. If there is a suspicious transaction, the account will be put on hold:

```
rule freezeAccount
salience -1000
  when
    $from : Account( )
    $transaction : Transaction( from == $from )
    SuspiciousTransaction( transaction == $transaction)
  then
    $from.setStatus(Account.Status.ON_HOLD);
end
```

Code listing 14: Rule that puts an account on hold if there is a suspicious transaction originating from it (the fraudulent-transactions.drl file)

The introduction of the `SuspiciousTransaction` fact provides a level of insulation between two set of rules: rules that identify a threat and rules that react to it.

If we logically insert a fact, we can override it with a standard insert. It then becomes an ordinary fact that was inserted using the standard `insert` method. For more information about logical assertions, please see the Drools documentation (Drools Expert – section "Truth Maintenance with Logical Objects").

Keeping the validation report up-to-date

Let's now move back to our validation example. Logical assertions can be used to keep the report up-to-date. Instead of adding messages to a global validation report, we can insert them into the session just as another fact. A logical insert will be used so that messages that are no longer valid will be automatically retracted. A query can be used to fetch all messages and create the validation report.

In *Chapter 3, Validating,* all messages were created and added to the validation report in the `ValidationHelper` utility class, by error and warning methods. We'll now create another version of `ValidationHelper` that will insert all messages into the knowledge session by calling the `insertLogical` method. The error method of the utility class is as follows:

```
public class ValidationHelper {
  /**
   * inserts new logical assertion - a message
   * @param kcontext RuleContext that is accessible from
   *  rule condition
   * @param context for the message
   */
  public static void error(RuleContext kcontext,
      Object... context) {
    KnowledgeRuntime knowledgeRuntime = kcontext
        .getKnowledgeRuntime();
    ReportFactory reportFactory = (ReportFactory)
        knowledgeRuntime.getGlobal("reportFactory");

    kcontext.insertLogical(reportFactory.createMessage(
        Message.Type.ERROR, kcontext.getRule().getName(),
        context));
  }
```

Code listing 15: The ValidationHelper utility class that uses logical assertions

Modify the `validation-stateful.drl` file to import these two helper functions instead of the old ones. Next, add the following query for message retrieval to the `.drl` file:

```
query getAllMessages
  $message : Message( )
end
```

Code listing 16: Query for retrieving all messages (the validation-stateful.drl file)

The global variable `validationReport` can be removed completely from this file. The validation report will be created inside the stateful service. Just modify the `executeRules` method to call `fireAllRules`, then create a blank validation report and populate it with messages fetched by the query we just saw. Finally, the report is returned. The test should now pass without any error. The "phone number required" message will still be present in the knowledge session even though the stateful service hasn't been notified to update the customer object.

The collect conditional element

With the solution just explained, the report creation has been moved outside of the rule engine, which is acceptable. However, with a new `collect` conditional element, we can put it back into the rule engine. The `collect` element can gather multiple objects into one collection. One can use it to gather all the messages in the knowledge session and then put them into the validation report. Only one validation report will be used throughout the lifetime of the stateful knowledge session (even service). This report will be created in the service's constructor. This also means that we'll need a way to clear this validation report between the `executeRules` calls:

```
/**
 * clears this report
 */
public void reset() {
  messagesMap.clear();
}
```

Code listing 17: Method of ValidationReport that clears the report

Add this method to the service implementation (and interface).

The global variable `validationReport` needs to be put back into the `validation-stateful.drl` file. A new rule for creating the validation report will be added:

```
rule createValidationReport
salience -1000 //should be the last rule to fire
  when
    $messages : ArrayList( ) from collect( Message() )
```

```
then
 validationReport.reset();
 for(Message message : (List<Message>) $messages) {
  validationReport.addMessage(message);
 }
end
```

Code listing 18: Rule that collects all messages in the knowledge session and updates the report
(the validation-stateful.drl file)

The condition of this rule is interesting. It matches on the $messages collection, which is created by collecting all facts of the Message type. The collection is then traversed inside the rule consequence and all messages are added into the already cleared validation report. The rule has a negative salience, which ensures that it will be the last one to fire. It only makes sense to create the report after all validation rules are fired. Please note that the java.util.ArrayList and java.util.List types need to be imported in the .drl file.

The executeRules method of the stateful service will then simply call statefulSession.fireAllRules and will return the validationReport local property. Our tests should pass as before.

collect

As we've seen in *Code listing 18*, collect can be used together with from to group facts that meet given constraints. The result can be any object that implements the java.util.Collection interface and provides a public no argument constructor. In our example we were collecting any Messages, but we could have easily collected only warnings by adding a type constraint:

```
$messages : ArrayList( size >= 2 ) from collect( Message( type ==
Message.Type.WARNING ) )
```

Code listing 19: Condition that matches on a collection of at least two warning messages

Variables bound in conditions before collect are visible inside the collect pattern. The collect element can accept the nested from, collect, and accumulate elements, for example:

```
$destinationAccount : Account( )
$transactions : LinkedList( ) from collect ( Transaction(
 to == $destinationAccount, $currency : currency )
 from bankService.getTransactions() )
```

Code listing 20: Nested from a conditional element, which groups all Transactions that have the specified destination
Account, from a service

However, any variables bound inside the `collect` conditional element is not visible outside of it; for example, in this case, `$currency`.

Serialization

Imagine that we have a web application. The stateful service is stored within the HTTP session. A user makes multiple HTTP requests throughout the lifetime of the stateful service. This is all perfect as long as it all happens within one server. However, as soon as we start to talk about scalability and fault tolerance, we need to think about serialization. For example, we may need to serialize all objects in the HTTP session and transfer this session to another server. As it is currently, `StatefulService` fails to serialize. Let's fix it.

 Note: Of course this implies that the rule engine will run in the presentation tier. If you don't like this approach, the stateful service could reside within the service tier. However, with this approach, we would have to maintain its lifecycle (creation, termination). An identifier can be passed from the presentation tier to identify the instance of the stateful service. The service tier would then maintain a map of identifiers and their associated stateful services.

Also note that since stateful service is not thread-safe, only single threaded access is possible. This is something to keep in mind when designing the application. If an object is inside the HTTP session, there is a potential that two threads may access it at the same time. You could, for example, declare all service methods as synchronized. There will still be a possibility of a single user doing multiple requests at the same time, which may cause the validation results to interleave.

Knowledge session recreation

Our first approach will simply recreate the knowledge session upon stateful service deserialization. This approach is fine for sessions with a small number of facts where the facts can be easily reinserted.

The stateful service already implements the `java.io.Serializable` marker interface. All that needs to be done is to implement the `readObject` and `writeObject` methods. The following implementation will serialize just the `KnowledgeBase` object since that is the only state we want to maintain:

```
private void writeObject(ObjectOutputStream out)
    throws IOException {
  out.defaultWriteObject();

  DroolsObjectOutputStream droolsOut =
```

```
        new DroolsObjectOutputStream(out);
    droolsOut.writeObject(knowledgeBase);
}
```

Code listing 21: The writeObject method for serializing the stateful service (the StatefulServiceImpl.java file)

As a good practice, the `defaultWriteObject` object is called first. A special type of `ObjectOutputStream`, such as `DroolsObjectOutputStream`, is needed to serialize the `KnowledgeBase` object. It acts as a wrapper around the `ObjectOutputStream` object.

The following is the `readObject` method, which is mirroring the `writeObject` method:

```
private void readObject(ObjectInputStream in)
    throws IOException, ClassNotFoundException {
  in.defaultReadObject();

  DroolsObjectInputStream droolsIn =
      new DroolsObjectInputStream(in);
  this.knowledgeBase = (KnowledgeBase)droolsIn.readObject();

  this.reportFactory = new DefaultReportFactory();
  statefulSession = createKnowledgeSession(
      new BankingInquiryServiceImpl());
}
```

Code listing 22: The readObject method for de-serializing the stateful service (the StatefulServiceImpl.java file)

The `readObject` method deserializes the `KnowledgeBase` object and creates a new report factory and a banking inquiry service. A better solution would be to use some static service locator to locate them since they are singletons. These objects are used by the `createKnowledgeSession` method to create and initialize a new stateful knowledge session. The `createKnowledgeSession` method also sets a new validation report. Note that the report and the sessions are empty.

Testing

This test will demonstrate that the serialization of the stateful service works:

```
@Test
public void testSerialization() throws Exception {
  Customer customer = createValidCustomer();
  statefulService.insertOrUpdateRecursive(customer);

  ByteArrayOutputStream baos = new ByteArrayOutputStream();
  ObjectOutputStream out = new ObjectOutputStream(baos);
```

```
        out.writeObject(statefulService);
        out.close();

        byte[] bArray = baos.toByteArray();
        ObjectInputStream in = new ObjectInputStream(
            new ByteArrayInputStream(bArray));
        statefulService = (StatefulServiceImpl) in.readObject();
        in.close();
        statefulService.insertOrUpdateRecursive(customer);

        ValidationReport report = statefulService.executeRules();
        assertEquals(0, report.getMessages().size());

        customer.setPhoneNumer(null);
        statefulService.insertOrUpdate(customer);
        report = statefulService.executeRules();
        assertEquals(1, report.getMessages().size());
        assertTrue(report.contains("phoneNumberRequired"));
    }
```

Code listing 23: Test method that exercises the serialization of a stateful service
(the StatefulServiceIntegrationTest.java file)

This test creates a valid customer and adds this customer and all his dependent objects into the stateful service. The stateful service is then serialized into an array of bytes. These bytes can be transferred, for example, to a remote machine. The stateful service is then deserialized from this array. An important thing to note is that after deserializing the statefulService object, it needs to be repopulated by calling the insertOrUpdateRecursive method and passing in the customer. Rules are executed and the test verifies that there are no messages. The customer is then invalidated by clearing his phone number. After updating the stateful session and running the rules, the test verifies that there is exactly one message about the missing phone number.

Session serialization

This section will discuss a complete stateful session serialization (full state including internal memories, agenda, process instances, and so on). A stateful session cannot be serialized out of the box (for example, you cannot just pass it to java.io.ObjectOutputStream). Drools currently supports two modes of stateful session serialization. Each mode is an implementation of the interface org.drools.marshalling.ObjectMarshallingStrategy. It defines methods for writing and reading an object to/from java.io.ObjectOutputStream/ObjectInputStream. An accept method, which returns a Boolean value, can be used to make more complex decisions about which objects to serialize with which strategy. Few implementations of this interface also take ObjectMarshallingStrategyAcceptor as a constructor argument and simply delegate to its `accept` method to do the `accept` logic. `Marshaller` then takes an array of marshaling strategies and can serialize the stateful session.

A class figure of the Drools serialization:

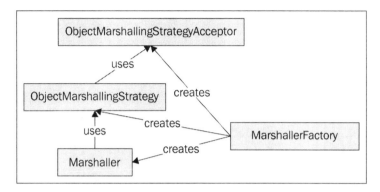

Figure 2: Class diagram of Drools serialization

The following strategies are supported:

- **Identity mode**: It is implemented by the class `IdentityPlaceholderResolverStrategy`. This is a stateful mode, which means that the exact same instance of this strategy is needed at both serialization and deserialization time. Each fact is assigned an ID. These IDs are stored together with their associated facts in a map. It is a map of type `Map<Integer, Object>`. This map is the actual state of this `ObjectMarshallingStrategy` implementation. None of the facts are serialized, only the IDs are. This means that when reconstructing the stateful session from the serialized stream of data, all objects need to be present in memory (that is, the session must be deserialized in the same JVM). This strategy can be used for so-called "session templates", where you prepopulate the session with immutable facts, serialize it, and then simply deserialize it as many times as you want. The session may then be used as usual. This is especially useful if you are creating lot of sessions with the same immutable facts and you're experiencing long fact insertion times (due to a lot of facts, rules, and so on.).

- **Full serialization mode**: This is the default serialization mode. It is implemented by the class `SerializablePlaceholderResolverStrategy`. Everything is serialized, including facts. This strategy can be used for backup and session pause/resume when moving the session to another server. Please keep in mind that upon deserialization of a knowledge session, all facts will have a new identity. Alternatively, you could serialize the fact together with the session in one `ObjectOutputStream`. This way, the object references will be preserved. This is, for example, the case when a HTTP session is serialized.

- **JPA serialization mode**: This is implemented by the class `JPAPlaceholderResolverStrategy`. This strategy can be used if your domain model supports JPA persistence. In this case Drools persists only the entity IDs and entity names as part of the serialized session data. When deserializing, the entities are loaded back via JPA.

In all cases the stateful session's agenda, action queue, process instances, work items, and timers are serialized. Global variables are not serialized, so we need to take care of them.

Full session serialization

We'll now look at serializing the stateful session using the full serialization mode. We'll implement the standard `writeObject` and `readObject` methods. Let's start with the `writeObject` method:

```
private void writeObject(ObjectOutputStream out)
    throws IOException {
  out.defaultWriteObject();

  DroolsObjectOutputStream droolsOut =
      new DroolsObjectOutputStream((OutputStream) out);
  droolsOut.writeObject(knowledgeBase);

  Marshaller marshaller = createSerializableMarshaller(
      knowledgeBase);
  marshaller.marshall(droolsOut, statefulSession);
}
```

Code listing 24: Implementation of the writeObject method of the stateful service (the StatefulServiceImpl.java file)

Firstly, the default object state is serialized followed by the `knowledgeBase` object. A new `Marshaller` object is created by the `createSerializableMarshaller` method. It is then used to serialize the stateful knowledge session into the same output stream.

Please note that currently the stateful serialization mode changes the identities of objects even though they are saved to the same output stream. This should be fixed in future versions of Drools (see `https://jira.jboss.org/jira/browse/JBRULES-2048`).

The `Marshaller` instance will use only one serializable marshaller strategy that will accept all objects `*.*`. The first star represents the package name, and the second star represents the class name. The `createSerializableMarshaller` method is as follows:

```
private Marshaller createSerializableMarshaller(
    KnowledgeBase knowledgeBase) {
  ObjectMarshallingStrategyAcceptor acceptor =
      MarshallerFactory.newClassFilterAcceptor(
      new String[] { "*.*" } );
  ObjectMarshallingStrategy strategy = MarshallerFactory
      .newSerializeMarshallingStrategy( acceptor );
  Marshaller marshaller = MarshallerFactory.newMarshaller(
      knowledgeBase, new ObjectMarshallingStrategy[] {
      strategy } );
  return marshaller;
}
```

Code listing 25: A method for creating a full serialization Marshaller (the StatefulServiceImpl.java file)

Note that in this example, we're using only one pattern for our strategy acceptor; however, many can be defined if needed.

The method that takes care of the deserialization process, the `readObject` method, is shown in *Code listing 26*. It will create a `Marshaller` instance, and it will use it to deserialize the stateful knowledge session. Furthermore, it will initialize its global variables:

```
private void readObject(ObjectInputStream in)
    throws IOException, ClassNotFoundException {
  in.defaultReadObject();

  DroolsObjectInputStream droolsIn =
      new DroolsObjectInputStream((InputStream) in);
  this.knowledgeBase = (KnowledgeBase)droolsIn.readObject();

  Marshaller marshaller = createSerializableMarshaller(
      knowledgeBase);
  statefulSession = marshaller.unmarshall(droolsIn);
```

```
        this.reportFactory = new DefaultReportFactory();
        statefulSession.setGlobal("reportFactory", reportFactory);
        statefulSession.setGlobal("inquiryService",
            new BankingInquiryServiceImpl());
    }
```

Code listing 26: Implementation of the readObject method of the stateful service for deserialization
(the StatefulServiceImpl.java file)

Note that if we used the identity mode serialization, the same `Marshaller` instance would have to be used for both serialization and deserialization, since the identity `Marshaller` instance is stateful.

Summary

In this chapter we've learned about the stateful sessions, what they are used for, and how they keep their state between session invocations. This is especially useful in long, iterative, interaction scenarios. For example, in a web application where a user logs in to the system, makes a couple of changes in multiple HTTP requests, and logs out of the system.

Also, logical assertions were discussed. They are automatically retracted when none of the conditions that inserted them are true. This is useful as it keeps the validation report updated all the time.

Finally, the serialization section discussed two options of serializing a stateful session: identity and serialized. An example was given of how to serialize the stateful service, which contained a stateful session.

7
Complex Event Processing

Rules usually operate on a more or less static set of data (facts). However, for some systems it is necessary to reason over time relationships between facts. This is often called **complex event processing (CEP)** or **event stream processing (ESP)**. JBoss Rules, more specifically Drools Fusion, starting with Version 5.0, provides this support together with sliding windows and temporal operators.

In this chapter we'll look at implementing a banking fraud detection system. It is an ideal candidate for CEP. The volume of events in a banking system is huge and we need to be able to do complex decisions based on these events.

CEP and ESP

CEP and ESP are styles of processing in an **event-driven architecture (EDA)**—a general introduction to EDA can be found at http://www. elementallinks.com/2006/02/06/event-driven-architecture-overview/). One of the core benefits of such an architecture is that it provides a loose coupling of its components. A component simply publishes events about actions that are being performed and other components can subscribe/listen to these events. The producer and subscriber are completely unaware of each other. A subscriber listens for events and doesn't care where they come from. Similarly, a publisher generates events and doesn't know anything about who is listening to those events. Some orchestration layer then deals with the actual wiring of subscribers to publishers.

An event represents a significant change of state. It usually consists of a header and a body. The header contains meta information such as its name, time of occurrence, duration, and so on. The body describes what happened. For example, if a transaction has been processed, the event body would contain transaction ID, the amount transferred, source account number, destination account number, and so on.

CEP deals with complex events. A complex event is a set of simple events. For example, a sequence of large withdrawals may raise a suspicious transaction event. The simple events are considered to infer that a complex event has occurred.

ESP is more about real-time processing of a huge volume of events. For example, calculating the real-time average transaction volume over time.

There are many existing pure CEP/ESP engines, both commercial and open source. Drools Fusion enhances the rule-based programming with event support. It makes use of its Rete algorithm and provides an alternative to existing engines.

Drools Fusion

Drools Fusion is a Drools module that is a part of the Business Logic Integration Platform. It is the Drools event processing engine covering both CEP and ESP (these terms will be used interchangeably in this book). Each event has a type, a time of occurrence, and possibly a duration. Both point-in-time (zero duration) and interval-based events are supported. An event can also contain other data such as any other fact: properties with name and type. All events are facts, but not all facts are events. An event's state should not be changed; however, it should be noted that is valid to populate unpopulated values. Events have clear life cycle windows and may be transparently garbage collected after the life cycle window expires (for example, we may be interested only in transactions that happened in the last 24 hours). Rules can deal with time relationships between events.

Fraud detection

It will be easier to explain these concepts using an example of a fraud detection system. Fraud in banking systems is becoming a major concern. The amount of online transactions are increasing every day. An automatic system for fraud detection is needed. The system should analyze various events happening in a bank, and based on a set of rules, raise an appropriate alarm.

This problem cannot be solved by the standard Drools rule engine. The volume of events is huge and they happen asynchronously. If we simply insert them into the knowledge session, we would soon run out of memory. While the Rete algorithm behind Drools doesn't have any theoretical limitation on the number of objects in a session, we could use the processing power more wisely. Drools Fusion is the right candidate for this kind of task.

Problem description

Let's consider the following set of business requirements for the fraud detection system:

- If a notification is received from a customer about a stolen card, block this account and any withdrawals from this account.

- Check each transaction against a blacklist of account numbers. If the transaction is transferring money from/to such an account, then flag this transaction as suspicious with the maximum severity.

- If there are two large debit transactions from the same account within a 90-second period and each transaction is withdrawing more than 300 percent of the average monthly (30 days) withdrawal amount, flag these transactions as suspicious with minor severity.

- If there is a sequence of three consecutive and increasing debit transactions originating from a same account within a 3-minute period and these transactions are together withdrawing more than 90 percent of the account's average balance over 30 days, then flag those transactions as suspicious with minor severity and suspend the account.

- If the number of withdrawals over a day is 500 percent higher than the average number of withdrawals over a 30-day period and the account is left with less than 10 percent of the average balance over a month (30 days), then flag the account as suspicious with minor severity.

- Perform a duplicate transactions check; if two transactions occur in a time window of 15 seconds that have the same source/destination account number, are of the same amount, and just differ in transaction ID, then flag those transactions as duplicates.

The following are the things that you need to monitor:

- Monitor the average withdrawal amount over all accounts for 30 days
- Monitor the average balance across all accounts

Design and modeling

Looking at the requirements we'll need a way of flagging a transaction as suspicious. This state can be added to the existing `Transaction` type or we can externalize this state to a new event type. We'll do the latter. The following new events will be defined:

- `TransactionCreatedEvent`: This is an event that is triggered when a new transaction is created. It contains a transaction identifier, source account number, destination account number, and actual amount transferred.

- `TransactionCompletedEvent`: This is an event that is triggered when an existing transaction has been processed. It contains the same fields as the `TransactionCreatedEvent` class.

- `AccountUpdatedEvent`: This is an event triggered when an account has been updated. It contains the account number, current balance, and transaction identifier of a transaction that initiated this update.

- `SuspiciousAccount`: This is an event triggered when there is some sort of suspicion around the account. It contains the account number and severity of the suspicion. The severity is an enumeration that can have two values: `MINOR` and `MAJOR`. This event's implementation is shown in the following code listing.

- `SuspiciousTransaction`: Similar to `SuspiciousAccount`, this is an event that flags a transaction as suspicious. It contains a transaction identifier and severity level.

- `LostCardEvent`: This is an event indicating that a card was lost. It contains an account number.

One of the `SuspiciousAccount` events described is as follows. It also defines the `SuspiciousAccountSeverity` enumeration that encapsulates various severity levels that the event can represent. The event will define two properties. One of them is already mentioned severity and the other one, `accountNumber`, will identify the account.

```
/**
 * marks an account as suspicious
 */
public class SuspiciousAccount implements Serializable {
  public enum SuspiciousAccountSeverity {
    MINOR, MAJOR
  }

  private final Long accountNumber;
  private final SuspiciousAccountSeverity severity;

  public SuspiciousAccount(Long accountNumber,
      SuspiciousAccountSeverity severity) {
    this.accountNumber = accountNumber;
    this.severity = severity;
  }

  private transient String toString;
```

```
@Override
public String toString() {
  if (toString == null) {
    toString = new ToStringBuilder(this).appendSuper(
        super.toString()).append("accountNumber",
        accountNumber).append("severity", severity)
        .toString();
  }
  return toString;
}
```

Code listing 1: Implementation of the SuspiciousAccount event

Please note that the equals and hashCode methods in SuspiciousAccount from this code listing are not overridden. This is because an event represents an active entity, which means that each instance is unique. The toString method is implemented using org.apache.commons.lang.builder.ToStringBuilder. All these event classes are lightweight; they have no references to other domain classes (no object reference, only a number, accountNumber, is this case). They are also implementing the Serializable interface. This makes them easier to transfer between JVMs. As a best practice, this event is immutable; the two properties (accountNumber and severity) are marked as final. They can be set only through a constructor (there are no setter methods but only two getter methods). The getter methods were excluded from this code listing.

The events themselves don't carry a time of occurrence, a time stamp (they easily could if we needed it, and we'll see how in the next set of code listings). When the event is inserted into the knowledge session, the rule engine assigns such a time stamp to FactHandle that is returned (do you remember session.insert(..) returns a FactHandle?). In fact there is a special implementation of FactHandle called EventFactHandle. It extends DefaultFactHandle (which is used for normal facts) and adds a few additional fields; for example, startTimestamp and duration. Both contain millisecond values and are of type long.

We now have the event classes and we know that there is a special FactHandle for events. However, it is still unknown how to tell Drools that our class represents an event. Drools type declarations provide this missing link. As was explained in *Chapter 2, Writing Basic Rules*, type declarations can define new types; here we'll see how to enhance existing types. For example, to specify that the class TransactionCreatedEvent is an event, so we have to write:

```
declare TransactionCreatedEvent
  @role( event )
end
```

Code listing 2: Event role declaration (the cep.drl file)

This code can reside inside a normal `.drl` file. If our event had a time stamp property or a duration property, we could map it into `startTimestamp` or `duration` properties of `EventFactHandle` by using the following mapping:

```
@duration( durationProperty )
```

Code listing 3: Duration property mapping

The name in brackets is the actual name of the property of our event that will be mapped to the `duration` property of `EventFactHandle`. This can be done similarly for the `startTimestamp` property.

> Since an event's state should not be changed (only unpopulated values can be populated), think twice before declaring existing beans as events. Modification to a property may result in an unpredictable behavior.

Fraud detection rules

Let's imagine that the system processes thousands of transactions at any given time. It is clear that this is challenging in terms of time and memory consumption. It is simply not possible to keep all data (transactions, accounts, and so on) in memory. A possible solution would be to keep all accounts in memory, since there won't be that many of them (in comparison to transactions) and keep only transactions for a certain period. With Drools Fusion we can do this very easily by declaring that a Transaction is an event.

The transaction will then be inserted into the knowledge session through a custom entry point. As the name suggests it is an entry point into the knowledge session. So far we were always inserting the facts into the session using the default entry point (when calling `session.insert(..)`) The advantage of using a custom entry point is that it applies only to a specific rule(s) (no other rules will see the event). This makes sense, especially if there are large quantities of data and only some rules are interested in them. We'll look at entry points in the following example.

If you are still concerned about the volume of objects in memory, this solution can be easily partitioned, for example, by account number. There might be more servers; each processing only a subset of accounts (a simple routing strategy might be `accountNumber module totalNumberOfServersInCluster`). Then each server would receive only appropriate events.

Notification

The requirement we're going to implement here is essentially to block an account whenever a `LostCardEvent` type is received. This rule will match on two facts. One of type `Account` and one of type `LostCardEvent`. The rule will then set the the status of this account to blocked. The implementation of the rule is as follows:

```
rule notification
  when
    $account : Account( status != Account.Status.BLOCKED )
    LostCardEvent( accountNumber == $account.number )
      from entry-point LostCardStream
  then
    modify($account) {
      setStatus(Account.Status.BLOCKED)
    };
end
```

Code listing 4: Notification rule that blocks an account (the cep.drl file)

As we already know, `Account` is an ordinary fact from the knowledge session. The second fact, `LostCardEvent`, is an event from an entry point called `LostCardStream`. Whenever a new event is created and goes through the custom entry point `LostCardStream`, this rule tries to match (checks if its conditions can be satisfied). If there is an `Account` fact in the knowledge session that didn't match with this event yet, and all conditions are met, the rule is activated. The consequence sets the status of the account to blocked in a modify block.

Since we're updating the account in the consequence and also matching on it in the condition, we have added a constraint that matches only on nonblocked accounts. This not only makes sense but also it is a way to prevent looping (see `status != Account.Status.BLOCKED`).

Test configuration setup

Following the best practice that every code/rule needs to be tested, we'll now set up a class for writing unit tests. All rules will be written in a file called `cep.drl`. When creating this file, just ensure it is on the classpath. The creation of the `knowledgeBase` object won't be shown. It is similar to the previous tests that we've written. We just need to change slightly the default knowledge base configuration:

```
KnowledgeBaseConfiguration config = KnowledgeBaseFactory
    .newKnowledgeBaseConfiguration();
config.setOption( EventProcessingOption.STREAM );
```

Code listing 5: Enabling event processing mode on knowledge base configuration

This will enable the event processing mode. The `KnowledgeBaseConfiguration` event is then used when creating the knowledge base `KnowledgeBaseFactory`. `newKnowledgeBase(config)`.

Part of the setup is also clock initialization. We already know that every event has a time stamp. This time stamp comes from a clock, which is inside the knowledge session. Drools supports several clock types, for example, a real-time clock or a pseudo clock. The real-time clock is the default and should be used in normal circumstances. The pseudo clock is especially useful for testing, as we have complete control over the time. The `initialize` method shown in *Code listing 6* sets up a pseudo clock. This is done by setting the clock type on a `KnowledgeSessionConfiguration` event and passing this object to the `newStatefulKnowledgeSession` method of `knowledgeBase`. The `initialize` method then makes this clock available as a test instance variable called clock when calling `session.getSessionClock()`, as we can see in the following code listing:

```java
public class CepTest {
    static KnowledgeBase knowledgeBase;
    StatefulKnowledgeSession session;
    Account account;
    FactHandle accountHandle;
    SessionPseudoClock clock;
    TrackingAgendaEventListener trackingAgendaEventListener;
    WorkingMemoryEntryPoint entry;

    @Before
    public void initialize() throws Exception {
        KnowledgeSessionConfiguration conf =
            KnowledgeBaseFactory.newKnowledgeSessionConfiguration();
        conf.setOption( ClockTypeOption.get( "pseudo" ) );
        session = knowledgeBase.newStatefulKnowledgeSession(conf,
            null);
        clock = (SessionPseudoClock) session.getSessionClock();

        trackingAgendaEventListener =
            new TrackingAgendaEventListener();
        session.addEventListener(trackingAgendaEventListener);

        account = new Account();
        account.setNumber(1234561);
        account.setBalance(BigDecimal.valueOf(1000.00));
        accountHandle = session.insert(account);
```

Code listing 6: Unit tests setup (the CepTest.java file)

The `initialize` method also creates an event listener and passes it into the session. The event listener is called `TrackingAgendaEventListener`. It simply tracks all rule executions. It is useful for unit testing to verify that a rule is fired or not. Its implementation is as follows:

```
public class TrackingAgendaEventListener extends
    DefaultAgendaEventListener {
  List<String> rulesFiredList = new ArrayList<String>();

  @Override
  public void afterActivationFired(
      AfterActivationFiredEvent event) {
    rulesFiredList.add(event.getActivation().getRule()
        .getName());
  }

  public boolean isRuleFired(String ruleName) {
    for (String firedRuleName : rulesFiredList) {
      if (firedRuleName.equals(ruleName)) {
        return true;
      }
    }
    return false;
  }

  public void reset() {
    rulesFiredList.clear();
  }
}
```

Code listing 7: Agenda Event listener that tracks all rules that have been fired

Please note that the `DefaultAgendaEventListener` event comes from the package `org.drools.event.rule` that is part of the `knowledge-api.jar` file as opposed to coming from the package `org.drools.event` that is part of the old API in `drools-core.jar`.

All Drools agenda event listeners must implement the `AgendaEventListener` interface. Our `TrackingAgendaEventListener` interface extends the `DefaultAgendaEventListener` interface so that we don't have to implement all methods defined in the `AgendaEventListener` interface. Our listener just overrides the `afterActivationFired` method that will be called by Drools every time a rule's consequence has been executed. Our implementation of this method adds the fired rule name into a list of fired rules, `rulesFiredList`. Then the `convenience` method `isRuleFired` takes `ruleName` as a parameter and checks if this rule has been executed/fired. The `reset` method is useful for clearing out the state of this listener; for example, after the `session.fireAllRules` call.

Now, lets get back to the test configuration setup. The last part of the `initialize` method from *Code Listing 6* is the account object creation (`account = new Account(); ...`). This is for convenience so that not every test has to create one. The account balance is set to `1000`. The account is inserted into the knowledge session and its `FactHandle` is stored so that the account object can be easily updated.

Testing the notification rule

The test infrastructure is now fully set up and we can write a test for the notification rule from *Code listing 4*:

```
@Test
public void notification() throws Exception {
    session.fireAllRules();
    assertNotSame(Account.Status.BLOCKED,account.getStatus());

    entry = session
        .getWorkingMemoryEntryPoint("LostCardStream");
    entry.insert(new LostCardEvent(account.getNumber()));
    session.fireAllRules();
    assertSame(Account.Status.BLOCKED, account.getStatus());
}
```

Code listing 8: Notification rule's unit test (the CepTest.java file)

The test verifies that the account is not blocked by accident first. Then it gets the `LostCardStream` entry point from the session by performing `session.getWorking MemoryEntryPoint("LostCardStream")`. Then the code listing demonstrates how an event can be inserted into the knowledge session through an entry point, `entry. insert(new LostCardEvent(...))`.

Note that in a real application you'll probably want to use Drools Pipeline for inserting events into the knowledge session. It can be easily connected to an existing **enterprise service bus (ESB)** or a JMS topic or queue.

Drools entry points are thread-safe, meaning that each entry point can receive facts from a different thread. In this case it makes sense to start the engine in the `fireUntilHalt` mode in a separate thread like this:

```
new Thread(new Runnable() {
  public void run() {
    session.fireUntilHalt();
  }
}).start();
```

Code listing 9: Continuous execution of rules

The engine will then continuously execute activations until the `session.halt()` method is called.

The test then verifies that the status of the account is blocked. If we perform simply `session.insert(new LostCardEvent(..))`, the test would fail, because the rule wouldn't see the event.

Monitoring averageBalanceQuery

In this section we'll look at how to write some monitoring rules/queries over the data that is in the knowledge session. Let's say that we want to know what is the average balance across all accounts. Since all of them are in the knowledge session, we could use `collect` (that was introduced in the *The collect conditional element* section of *Chapter 6, Working with Stateful Session*) to collect all accounts into a collection and then iterate over this collection, sum all balances and then divide it by the number of accounts. Another more preferred solution is to use the neighbor of `collect`, `accumulate`. The following is a query that calculates the average balance across all accounts:

```
query averageBalanceQuery
  accumulate( Account($balance : balance);
    $averageBalance : average($balance) )
end
```

Code listing 10: Query for calculating the average balance over all accounts (the cep.drl file)

Similar to `collect`, `accumulate` iterates over objects in the knowledge session that meet given criteria; however, in the case of `accumulate`, it performs some action on each individual object before returning the result or results. In our example, the action is `average($balance)`. Finally, the result is returned as `$averageBalance` variable. The average balance is updated whenever there is a new account or an existing account is updated or retracted from the knowledge session. Similar to `collect`, you can think of it as a continuous query. Other useful functions that can be used within accumulate are: `count`, which is used for counting objects; `min`/`max`, which is used for finding the minimum/maximum value, `sum`, which is used for calculating the sum of all values, and others. Some of them will be shown in the following examples. We'll also define a new one.

Note that the accumulate function can take any code block (written in the current dialect). This means that it is, for example, valid to write `sum($account.getBalance().multiply($account.getInterestRate()))`.

Furthermore, you can specify constraints on the result of `accumulate`. For example, let's say that we want the `averageBalance` object to be at least `300`. We could write `accumulate( Account($balance : balance); $averageBalance : average($balance); $averageBalance > 300 )`.

The `accumulate` element has many forms; we could have also written `Number( $averageBalance : doubleValue )` from `accumulate( Account($balance : balance), average($balance) )`; however, the use of these other forms is discouraged.

Testing the averageBalanceQuery

The test for this `averageBalanceQuery` query is as follows. First, it will use the default setup, which includes one account in the knowledge session that has a balance of `1000`. Then, it will add another account into the knowledge session and verify that the average balance is correct:

```
@Test
public void averageBalanceQuery() throws Exception {
  session.fireAllRules();
  assertEquals(account.getBalance(), getAverageBalance());

  Account account2 = new Account();
  account2.setBalance(BigDecimal.valueOf(1400));
  session.insert(account2);
  session.fireAllRules();
```

```
    assertEquals(BigDecimal.valueOf(1200.00),
        getAverageBalance());
}

BigDecimal getAverageBalance() {
  QueryResults queryResults = session
      .getQueryResults("averageBalanceQuery");
  return BigDecimal.valueOf((Double) queryResults
      .iterator().next().get("$averageBalance"));
}
```

Code listing 11: Test for the averageBalanceQuery method (the CepTest.java file)

The `getAverageBalance` method gets the query results and extracts the `$averageBalance` variable.

Two large withdrawals

We'll now look at the next requirement. A rule that will flag two transactions as suspicious if they are withdrawing more than 300 percent of the average withdrawn amount over 30 days. The problem is how to find out the average withdrawn amount for an account over 30 days. This is when sliding time windows or sliding length windows come in handy. They allow us to match only those events that originated within the window. In the case of time windows the session clock's time minus the event's time stamp must be within the window time. In the case of length windows only the *n* most recent events are taken into account. Time/Length windows also have another very important reason. They allow Drools to automatically retract events that are no longer needed — those that are outside of the window. This applies to events that were inserted into the knowledge session through a custom entry point.

The average withdrawn amount can be calculated by averaging the amounts of `TransactionCompletedEvents`. We are only interested in transactions that have already been successfully completed. We can now match only those transactions that happened within the last 30 days: `over window:time( 30d ) from entry-point TransactionStream`. If we, for example, wanted the 10 most recent events, we'd write `over window:length( 10 ) from entry-point TransactionStream`.

We know how to calculate the average withdrawn amount. All that remains is to find two transactions happening over 90 seconds that are withdrawing 300 percent or more. `TransactionCreatedEvent` can be used to find those transactions. The implementation is as follows:

```
rule twoLargeWithdrawals
dialect "mvel"
  when
    $account : Account( )
```

```
     accumulate( TransactionCompletedEvent( fromAccountNumber
       == $account.number, $amount : amount ) over
       window:time( 30d ) from entry-point TransactionStream,
       $averageAmount : average( $amount ) )
     $t1 : TransactionCreatedEvent( fromAccountNumber ==
       $account.number, amount > $averageAmount * 3.00 ) over
       window:time(90s) from entry-point TransactionStream
     $t2 : TransactionCreatedEvent( this != $t1,
       fromAccountNumber == $account.number,
       amount > $averageAmount * 3.00 ) over
       window:time(90s) from entry-point TransactionStream
  then
     insert(new SuspiciousAccount($account.number,
       SuspiciousAccountSeverity.MINOR));
     insert(new SuspiciousTransaction($t1.transactionUuid,
       SuspiciousTransactionSeverity.MINOR));
     insert(new SuspiciousTransaction($t2.transactionUuid,
       SuspiciousTransactionSeverity.MINOR));
  end
```

Code listing 12: Implementation of the twoLargeWithdrawals rule (the cep.drl file)

The rule is matching on an `Account` object, calculating the `$averageAmount` variable for this account and finally matching on two different `TransactionCreatedEvents` (we make sure that they are different by performing `!= $t1`). These events represent transactions from this account, which have an amount 300 percent larger than the `$averageAmount` variable; this is enforced with this constraint: `amount > $averageAmount * 3.00`. These events must occur in a time window of 90 seconds as can be seen: `over window:time(90s) from entry-point TransactionStream`. The consequence then inserts three new events into the knowledge session. They flag the account and transactions as suspicious with minor severity.

As you may have noticed, in this rule we've used one stream, `TransactionStream`, for getting two types of events. This is completely valid. If the performance is your primary concern, ideally every event should have its own stream. That way no rule will see events that it is not interested in.

Note that if using a real-time clock, think twice about the length of the time window. Under a heavy load, the CPU might be so busy that the event won't be processed in the expected time window (the event's `startTimestamp` may not be accurate). In that case the sliding length window makes more sense.

Testing the twoLargeWithdrawals rule

As usual, our unit test will exercise some of the corner cases where the rule is most likely to break. It will follow the sequence of events presented in the following timeline figure:

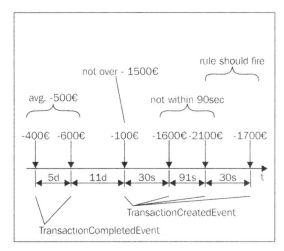

Figure 1: Time diagram – sequence of events

Each event is represented by an arrow pointing down. At the base of the arrow is the amount that is being withdrawn. The first two events are of type `TransactionCompletedEvent` and their task is to build the average amount that was withdrawn. The average will be 500. The following events are of type `TransactionCreatedEvent` and they are the ones we want to keep an eye on. The first two of them meet the time constraint of 90 seconds, but the first isn't three times greater than the average. Therefore, our rule won't be activated. The next event comes after 91 seconds, which doesn't meet the time window constraint. Finally, the last two events meet all constraints, and we can verify that the rule fired and that the account and transactions were marked as suspicious. The test implementation is as follows:

```
@Test
public void twoLargeWithdrawals() throws Exception {
  entry = session
      .getWorkingMemoryEntryPoint("TransactionStream");
  transactionCompletedEvent(400);
  clock.advanceTime(5, TimeUnit.DAYS);
  transactionCompletedEvent(600);
  clock.advanceTime(11, TimeUnit.DAYS);

  transactionCreatedEvent(100);
  clock.advanceTime(30, TimeUnit.SECONDS);
```

```
transactionCreatedEvent(1600);
assertNotFired("twoLargeWithdrawals");

clock.advanceTime(91, TimeUnit.SECONDS);
transactionCreatedEvent(2100);
assertNotFired("twoLargeWithdrawals");

clock.advanceTime(30, TimeUnit.SECONDS);
transactionCreatedEvent(1700);
assertFired("twoLargeWithdrawals");
}
```

Code listing 13: Test for the twoLargeWithdrawals rule (the CepTest.java file)

For brevity, commonly used code snippets have been refactored into helper methods. For example, the creation of `TransactionCompletedEvent` and its insertion into the session has been refactored into the `transactionCompletedEvent` method as shown in the following code listing:

```
private void transactionCompletedEvent(
    double amountTransferred) {
  entry.insert(new TransactionCompletedEvent(BigDecimal
     .valueOf(amountTransferred), account.getNumber())));
}
```

Code listing 14: Helper method that creates TransactionCompletedEvent and inserts it into the knowledge session (the CepTest.java file)

The event is initialized with the transferred amount and source account number, as you may imagine the `transactionCreatedEvent` method from `Code Listing 13` is similar.

Another helper method, `assertFired`, takes a rule name as an argument, fires a rule that matches this name, and verifies that the rule fired using `trackingAgendaEventListener`:

```
private void assertFired(String ruleName) {
  session.fireAllRules(new RuleNameEqualsAgendaFilter(
      ruleName));
  assertTrue(trackingAgendaEventListener
     .isRuleFired(ruleName));
}
```

Code listing 15: Helper method for verifying that a rule with specified name has fired (the CepTest.java file)

The agenda filter `RuleNameEqualsAgendaFilter` was already used in *Chapter 4*, *Transforming Data*. Do not use the deprecated `org.drools.base.RuleNameEqualsAgendaFilter`, otherwise you'll get compilation errors. The logic is the same; however, the deprecated agenda filter doesn't use the new API.

As you may imagine the `assertNotFired` method is similar to the `assertFired` method. If we now run the `twoLargeWithdrawals` test, everything should pass as expected.

Sequence of increasing withdrawals

We'll now focus on the next requirement from the list. Among other things, it talks about an account's average balance over 30 days. We shouldn't have any problem calculating this. Thinking about the implementation of the rule, it seems that more rules are calculating these averages. We should be able to separate this logic into another rule that will calculate this information and store it into some common data structure. Other rules will just match on this data structure and use the calculated averages. We've a plan. Now, let's define this data structure. Drools type declarations can be used for this purpose. The declaration may look as follows:

```
declare AccountInfo
  number : Long
  averageBalance : BigDecimal
  averageAmount : BigDecimal
end
```

Code listing 16: The AccountInfo type declaration (the cep.drl file)

Please note that in this use of the `declare` keyword, we're not modifying existing type (as was the case in *Code listing 2*) but adding a completely new one.

The common data structure is there; we can write the rule that will populate it. Our rule will match on an `Account` object, calculate its average balance over 30 days, and will set this calculated amount into the `AccountInfo` object:

```
rule averageBalanceOver30Days
no-loop true
  when
    $account : Account( )
    accumulate( AccountUpdatedEvent( accountNumber ==
      $account.number, $balance : balance ) over
      window:time( 30d ) from entry-point AccountStream,
      $averageBalance : average($balance) )
    $accountInfo : AccountInfo( number == $account.number )
  then
    modify($accountInfo) {
```

```
        setAverageBalance($averageBalance)
    };
end
```

Code listing 17: Rule that calculates the average balance for an account over 30 days (the cep.drl file)

The `averageBalanceOver30Days` rule accumulates `AccocuntUpdateEvents` in order to calculate the average balance over 30 days. Finally, the consequence sets calculated `$averageBalance` into the `$accountInfo` variable. Note the use of the `no-loop` rule attribute. It is needed, otherwise the rule will loop, because the `AccountInfo` fact is being matched in condition as well as being modified in the consequence. Later, we'll see how to eliminate the `no-loop` attribute.

Average balance test

The `AccountInfo` object needs to be added into the knowledge session before the `averageBalanceOver30Days` rule can be activated. Since it is an internal type, we cannot simply make a new instance of this class (for example, to call new `AccountInfo()`). This type will only be created at runtime, when the knowledge package is compiled. The Drools team thought about this and they have added a method to the `KnowledgeBase` called `getFactType`, which returns an object implementing the `org.drools.definition.type.FactType` interface. This interface encapsulates the type information about an internal type. It allows us to create new instances, get a list of fields, set/get their properties, even get a map of field-value pairs, and set the values from such a map.

The `AccountInfo` bean may be used by many rules, so we'll add it into our unit test `initialize` method that is called before every `test` method execution. First, let's add types to our test class that will be needed:

```
FactType accountInfoFactType;
Object accountInfo;
FactHandle accountInfoHandle;
```

Code listing 18: CepTest unit test class properties (the CepTest.java file)

Now, the following `AccountInfo` setup logic can be added at the end of the `initialize` method. The following code listing will demonstrate how a new instance of an internal type can be created and its properties can be set:

```
accountInfoFactType = knowledgeBase.getFactType(
    "droolsbook.cep", "AccountInfo");
accountInfo = accountInfoFactType.newInstance();
accountInfoFactType.set(accountInfo, "number",
    account.getNumber());
accountInfoFactType.set(accountInfo, "averageBalance",
    BigDecimal.ZERO);
```

```
accountInfoFactType.set(accountInfo, "averageAmount",
  BigDecimal.ZERO);
accountInfoHandle = session.insert(accountInfo);
```

Code listing 19: The AccountInfo internal type setup (the CepTest.java file)

The first line gets the fact type from the knowledge session. The getFactType method takes the .drl file package name and the name of the fact type. Then a new accountInfoFactType.newInstance() instance is created. The accountInfoFactType object is then used to set properties on the accountInfo instance. Finally, accountInfo is inserted into the session and its fact handle is kept.

Similarly, initialization code of AccountInfo might be needed in a real application. When the application starts up, AccountInfo should be preinitialized with some reasonable data.

The unit test of the averagebalanceover30days method is as follows, which will create some AccountUpdatedEvents and verify that they are used to calculate the correct average balance:

```
@Test
public void averageBalanceOver30Days() throws Exception {
  entry = session
      .getWorkingMemoryEntryPoint("AccountStream");

  accountUpdatedEvent(account.getNumber(), 1000.50,1000.50);
  accountUpdatedEvent(account.getNumber(), -700.40, 300.10);
  accountUpdatedEvent(account.getNumber(), 500, 800);
  accountUpdatedEvent(112233441, 700, 1300);

  assertFired("averageBalanceOver30Days");
  assertEquals(BigDecimal.valueOf(700.20).setScale(2),
      accountInfoFactType.get(accountInfo, "averageBalance"));
}
```

Code listing 20: Unit test for the averageBalanceOver30Days rule (the CepTest.java file)

The test first obtains the AccountStream entry point for inserting the events. It uses the accountUpdateEvent helper method to create AccountUpdatedEvents. This method takes the account number, amount transferred, and balance. These parameters are passed directly into the event's constructor as was the case in the previous unit test. The test also creates one unrelated AccountUpdatedEvent to verify that it won't be included in the calculation. Finally, the test verifies that the rule has been fired and the average is of the expected value 700.20 ((1000.50 + 300.10 + 800)/3 = 2100.60 / 3 = 700.20).

However, when we run the test, it fails as soon as it gets to creating the knowledge base with this error:

```
java.lang.RuntimeException: Rule Compilation error : [Rule name='avera
geBalanceOver30Days']
… The method setAverageBalance(BigDecimal) in the type AccountInfo is
not applicable for the arguments (Number)
```

Drools is informing us that there is some problem with the rule's consequence. We're trying to set $averageBalance, which is of type Number (in fact java.lang.Double) into a property that is of type BigDecimal. It seems that the average function does not return BigDecimal as we'd like. Luckily, Drools is open source, so we can look under the hood. As was mentioned in the previous sections, the accumulate element supports pluggable functions (average, sum, count, and so on). These functions are implementations of the org.drools.runtime.rule.AccumulateFunction interface.

If we look at the average function's implementation in class AverageAccumulateFunction, we'll notice that its state consists of two fields: count of type int and total of type double. Here lies the problem. Our domain model uses BigDecimal as a best practice when working with floating point numbers; however, average casts all numbers to primitive doubles. We will now write our own implementation of AccumulateFunction that knows how to work with BigDecimal. This function will be called bigDecimalAverage and will be used as follows (note the last line):

```
accumulate( AccountUpdatedEvent( accountNumber ==
    $account.number, $balance : balance ) over
    window:time( 30d ) from entry-point AccountStream,
    $averageBalance : bigDecimalAverage($balance) )
```

Code listing 21: Part of the averageBalanceOver30Days rule that calculates the average balance using the new bigDecimalAverage accumulate function (the cep.drl file)

The knowledge base setup needs to be modified so that Drools knows about our new accumulate function implementation. A new KnowledgeBuilderConfiguration object will hold this information:

```
KnowledgeBuilderConfiguration builderConf =
    KnowledgeBuilderFactory.newKnowledgeBuilderConfiguration();
builderConf.setOption(AccumulateFunctionOption.get(
    "bigDecimalAverage",
    new BigDecimalAverageAccumulateFunction()));
```

Code listing 22: Section of unit test's setupClass method (the CepTest.java file)

An `AccumulateFunctionOption` is set with the new `accumulate` function, `BigDecimalAverageAccumulateFunction`, on the knowledge builder configuration. This configuration can be passed to the `KnowledgeBuilderFactory.newKnowledgeB uilder(builderConf)` factory method that is used to create the knowledge base.

Let's move to the implementation of the `accumulate` function. We'll first need some value holder for the count and total fields. This value holder will encapsulate all information that the `accumulate` function invocation needs. The function itself must be stateless:

```
/**
 * value holder that stores the total amount and how many
 * numbers were aggregated
 */
public static class AverageData implements Externalizable {
  public int count = 0;
  public BigDecimal total = BigDecimal.ZERO;

  public void readExternal(ObjectInput in)
      throws IOException, ClassNotFoundException {
    count = in.readInt();
    total = (BigDecimal) in.readObject();
  }

  public void writeExternal(ObjectOutput out)
      throws IOException {
    out.writeInt(count);
    out.writeObject(total);
  }

}
```

Code listing 23: The AverageData value holder (the BigDecimalAverageAccumulateFunction.java file)

Note that the `AverageData` holder is a static member class of `BigDecimalAverageAccumulateFunction`. The value holder implements the `Externalizable` interface so that it can be serialized. Finally, the implementation of `BigDecimalAverageAccumulateFunction` that will define the behavior of our custom function:

```
public class BigDecimalAverageAccumulateFunction implements
    AccumulateFunction {

  /**
   * creates and returns a context object
   */
  public Serializable createContext() {
```

```
    return new AverageData();
}

/**
 * initializes this accumulator
 */
public void init(Serializable context) throws Exception {
  AverageData data = (AverageData) context;
  data.count = 0;
  data.total = BigDecimal.ZERO;
}

/**
 * @return true if this accumulator supports reverse
 */
public boolean supportsReverse() {
  return true;
}

/**
 * accumulate the given value, increases count
 */
public void accumulate(Serializable context, Object value) {
  AverageData data = (AverageData) context;
  data.count++;
  data.total = data.total.add((BigDecimal) value);
}

/**
 * retracts accumulated amount, decreases count
 */
public void reverse(Serializable context, Object value)
    throws Exception {
  AverageData data = (AverageData) context;
  data.count++;
  data.total = data.total.subtract((BigDecimal) value);
}

/**
 * @return currently calculated value
 */
public Object getResult(Serializable context)
    throws Exception {
  AverageData data = (AverageData) context;
  return data.count == 0 ? BigDecimal.ZERO : data.total
      .divide(BigDecimal.valueOf(data.count),
          RoundingMode.HALF_UP);
}
```

Code listing 24: Custom accumulate function – BigDecimalAverageAccumulateFunction

The `createContext` method (at the beginning of *Code listing 24*) creates a new instance of the `AverageData` value holder. The `init` method initializes the accumulate function. `supportsReverse` informs the rule engine whether this accumulate function supports the retracting of objects (when a fact is being removed from the knowledge session, `session.retract(..)`, or an existing fact, `session.update(..)-`, is modified). If it doesn't, the rule engine will have to do more work, and if an object is being retracted, the calculation will have to start over. The `accumulate/reverse` methods are there to execute/reverse the `accumulate` action (in this case, the calculation of count and total). The `getResult` method calculates the result. Our implementation uses a hardcoded rounding mode of type `HALF_UP`. This can be easily customized if needed.

Most, if not all, Drools pluggable components implement the `Externalizable` interface. This is also the case with the `AccumulateFunction` interface. We have to implement the two methods that this interface defines. As `BigDecimalAverageAccumulateFunction` is stateless, its `readExternal` and `writeExternal` methods are empty (they are not shown in the code listing).

If we now run the test for the `averageBalanceOver30Days` rule, it now fails with a different error message telling us that `java.lang.Object` cannot be casted to `BigDecimal`. This can be simply fixed by adding a cast into the consequence, `setAverageBalance((BigDecimal)$averageBalance)`. The test should now pass without any errors. Note that instead of defining a custom accumulate function, we could have used a different form of the `accumulate` construct that uses inline custom code. However, this is not recommended. Please look into the Drools documentation for more information.

Looping prevention – property reactive

As promised, when we're looking at *Code listing 17*, we'll look at how to drop the `no-loop` attribute. We'll see another alternative option for how to prevent looping.

Facts can be annotated with the `@propertyReactive` annotation. For example:

```
declare AccountInfo
  @propertyReactive
  number : Long
  averageBalance : BigDecimal
  averageAmount : BigDecimal
end
```

Code listing 25: The AccountInfo property reactive type declaration (the cep.drl file)

What this does is it affects the behavior of the `modify` call. Normally, when we call `modify` with a fact, Drools will simply reevaluate every condition that triggers on this fact. However, facts that are annotated with the `@propertyReactive` annotation behave differently. When such a fact is modified, Drools analyzes which properties have been modified (note that it only works with a `modify` block) and then reevaluates only those conditions that trigger on these properties. For example, the `AccountInfo( number == $account.number )` condition would only be reevaluated if we modify the `number` property of `AccountInfo` and not the `averageBalance` property as is done in the rule from *Code listing 17*. This means that by adding the `@propertyReactive` annotation to the `AccountInfo` fact, we can now drop the `no-loop` attribute from the `averageBalanceOver30Days` rule.

You can also explicitly specify for each rule condition on which properties it should trigger on. For example, `AccountInfo( number == $account.number ) @watch( averageAmount, !averageBalance )`. Here we're telling the condition to trigger on the `number` property (implicitly) and the `averageAmount` property (explicitly) and also not to trigger on the `averageBalance` property. See the documentation for all the possibilities.

Caveat: if you look at the rule in *Code listing 17*, please note that the `Account` fact has no constraints (nothing is inside the brackets); this means that if we declare it with the `@propertyReactive` annotation, it wouldn't trigger on any property modifications. We'd have to explicitly tell it to trigger at least on the number property; in other words, `$account : Account( ) @watch( number )`. Currently, Drools does not automatically recognize that another condition within the same rule is using a property of the `Account` fact (like in this case: `AccountInfo( number == $account.number )`).

After a little side trip, we can now continue with writing the rule `sequenceOfIncreasingWithdrawals`. To refresh our memory; it is about three consecutive increasing debit transactions. With the arsenal of Drools keywords, we've learned so far that it should be no problem to implement this rule. To make it more interesting, we'll use temporal operators. The temporal operators (after and before) are a special type of operator that know how to work with events (their time stamp and duration properties). In our case we'll simply match on three transactions that happened one after another (with no transactions in between):

```
rule sequenceOfIncreasingWithdrawals
  when
    $account:Account($number : number)
    $t1:TransactionCreatedEvent(fromAccountNumber == $number)
      from entry-point TransactionStream
    $t2:TransactionCreatedEvent(amount > $t1.amount,
      fromAccountNumber == $number, this after[0, 3m] $t1)
```

```
      from entry-point TransactionStream
  not (TransactionCreatedEvent(fromAccountNumber == $number,
      this after $t1, this before $t2 )
      from entry-point TransactionStream)
  $t3:TransactionCreatedEvent(amount > $t2.amount,
      fromAccountNumber == $number, this after[0, 3m] $t2 )
      from entry-point TransactionStream
  not (TransactionCreatedEvent(fromAccountNumber == $number,
      this after $t2, this before $t3 )
      from entry-point TransactionStream)
  AccountInfo(number == $number, $t1.amount + $t2.amount
      + $t3.amount > averageBalance * BigDecimal.valueOf(0.9))
then
  insert(new SuspiciousAccount($number,
    SuspiciousAccountSeverity.MAJOR));
  insert(new SuspiciousTransaction($t1.transactionUuid,
    SuspiciousTransactionSeverity.MAJOR));
  insert(new SuspiciousTransaction($t2.transactionUuid,
    SuspiciousTransactionSeverity.MAJOR));
  insert(new SuspiciousTransaction($t3.transactionUuid,
    SuspiciousTransactionSeverity.MAJOR));
end
```

Code listing 26: Implementation of the sequenceOfIncreasingWithdrawals rule (the cep.drl file)

For example, $t2, in the code we have just seen, is TransactionCreatedEvent
that is withdrawing more than $t1; they are from the same account and temporal
operator after; (this after[0, 3m] $t1) ensures that event $t2 occurred after
event $t1, but within 3 minutes. The next line, not (TransactionCreatedEvent(
this after $t1, this before $t2) from ...), is making sure that no event
occurred between events $t1 and $t2.

 Please note that instead of using sliding time windows to check that
two events happened within 3 minutes (over window:time(3m)),
we're using temporal operators (this after[0, 3m] $t1). They
are much cheaper in terms of used resources.

Operators in Drools are pluggable. This means that the temporal operators we've just
seen are simply one of many implementations of the org.drools.runtime.rule.
EvaluatorDefinition interface. Others are, for example, soundslike, matches,
coincides, meets, metby, overlaps, overlappedby, during, includes, starts,
startedby, finishes, or finishedby. Please see *Appendix B, Creating Custom
Operators*, on how to define a custom operator.

As we've seen, operators support parameters that can be specified within the square brackets. Each operator can interpret these parameters differently. It may also depend on an event's time stamp and duration (events we've used in our examples are so-called point in time events and they don't have any duration). For example, `this before[1m30s, 2m] $event2` means that the time when `this` event finished and `$event2` started is between 1 minute, 30 seconds and 2 minutes. Please consult the documentation on Drools Fusion for more details on each operator.

The last line of the `sequenceOfIncreasingWithdrawals` rule's condition tests whether the three matched transactions are withdrawing more than 90 percent of the average balance. The rule's consequence marks these transactions and account as suspicious.

Testing the sequenceOfIncreasingWithdrawals rule

The unit test for the `sequenceOfIncreasingWithdrawals` rule will follow this sequence of events:

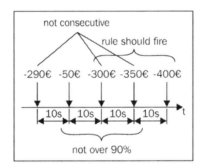

Figure 2: Time diagram – sequence of events

We're using `averageBalance` preinitialized to `1000`. All withdrawals fit into the time window of 3 minutes. The first three withdrawals are not increasing and their sum is not over 90 percent of the average balance. The first, third, and fourth events meet all constraints; they are increasing over 90 percent except one, and they are not consecutive. The second, third, and fourth events are not over 90 percent. Finally, the last three events meet all constraints and the rule should fire. The `test` method implementation is as follows:

```
@Test
public void sequenceOfIncreasingWithdrawals()
    throws Exception {
  entry = session
    .getWorkingMemoryEntryPoint("TransactionStream");
  accountInfoFactType.set(accountInfo, "averageBalance",
    BigDecimal.valueOf(1000));
```

```
session.update(accountInfoHandle, accountInfo);

transactionCreatedEvent(290);
clock.advanceTime(10, TimeUnit.SECONDS);
transactionCreatedEvent(50);
clock.advanceTime(10, TimeUnit.SECONDS);
transactionCreatedEvent(300);
assertNotFired("sequenceOfIncreasingWithdrawals");

clock.advanceTime(10, TimeUnit.SECONDS);
transactionCreatedEvent(350);
assertNotFired("sequenceOfIncreasingWithdrawals");

clock.advanceTime(10, TimeUnit.SECONDS);
transactionCreatedEvent(400);
clock.advanceTime(1, TimeUnit.MICROSECONDS);
assertFired("sequenceOfIncreasingWithdrawals");
}
```

Code listing 27: Unit test for the sequenceOfIncreasingWithdrawals rule (the CepTest.java file)

At the beginning of the test `averageBalance`, the property of `AccountInfo` is set to `1000`. The knowledge session is updated. The test executes successfully.

High activity

The next rule should catch fraudulent activities involving lots of small transactions, especially when the number of transactions over a day is more than 500 percent of the average number of transactions and the account's balance is less than 10 percent of the average balance. Let's pretend that the `AccountInfo` object has all averages that we need to be calculated and ready to be used in other rules. We'll be able to use just the `AccountInfo` object to see if the conditions are met for an `Account` object:

```
rule highActivity
  when
    $account : Account( )
    $accountInfo : AccountInfo( number == $account.number,
      numberOfTransactions1Day > averageNumberOfTransactions *
      BigDecimal.valueOf(5.0), $account.balance <
      averageBalance * BigDecimal.valueOf(0.1) )
  then
    insert(new SuspiciousAccount($account.getNumber(),
      SuspiciousAccountSeverity.MINOR));
end
```

Code listing 28: Implementation of the highActivity rule (the cep.drl file)

The rule looks simple, thanks to decomposition! It will fire if the number of transactions per one day is greater than 500 percent of the average number of transactions per one day over 30 days (numberOfTransactions1Day > averageNumberOfTransactions*500%) and if 10 percent of the average balance over 30 days is greater than the account's balance (averageBalance*10% > account's balance).

Testing the highActivity rule

The test for the highActivity rule is divided into four parts. The first one tests cases with a low number of transactions and a low average balance. The second part tests cases with a low number of transactions, the third part tests cases with a low average balance, and the fourth part tests the successful execution of the rule. The account's balance is set to 1000 by the initialize method. averageNumberOfTransactions of AccountInfo is set to 10. That means for a successful rule execution, averageBalance of accountInfo needs to be over 10,000 and numberOfTransactions1Day needs to be over 50.

```
@Test
public void highActivity() throws Exception {
  accountInfoFactType.set(accountInfo,
      "averageNumberOfTransactions",BigDecimal.valueOf(10));
  accountInfoFactType.set(accountInfo,
      "numberOfTransactions1Day", 401);
  accountInfoFactType.set(accountInfo, "averageBalance",
      BigDecimal.valueOf(9000));
  session.update(accountInfoHandle, accountInfo);
  assertNotFired("highActivity");

  accountInfoFactType.set(accountInfo, "averageBalance",
      BigDecimal.valueOf(11000));
  session.update(accountInfoHandle, accountInfo);
  assertNotFired("highActivity");

  accountInfoFactType.set(accountInfo,
      "numberOfTransactions1Day", 601);
  accountInfoFactType.set(accountInfo, "averageBalance",
      BigDecimal.valueOf(6000));
  session.update(accountInfoHandle, accountInfo);
  assertNotFired("highActivity");

  accountInfoFactType.set(accountInfo, "averageBalance",
      BigDecimal.valueOf(11000));
  session.update(accountInfoHandle, accountInfo);
  assertFired("highActivity");
}
```

Code listing 29: Unit test for the highActivity rule (the CepTest.java file)

While implementing the rules in this chapter, we've seen how to store some intermediate calculation results into an internal type; in our case it is Account Info. This is a common practice. Another alternative would be to extract this calculation into a query and then call this query within our rule. For example, imagine that the Account Info object is missing the numberOfTransactions1Day value and we need to calculate it. The query might look like this:

```
query numberOfTransactions1DayQuery(Long accountNumber,
    Number sum)
  accumulate( TransactionCompletedEvent( accountNumber :=
    fromAccountNumber ) over window:time(1d) from entry-point
    TransactionStream; sum : count(1) )
end
```

Code listing 30: Query that calculates the number of transactions per one day (the cep.drl file)

The query has two arguments, and an account number and a sum. It accumulates all TransactionCompletedEvents that are debiting the given account and happened within the last day. They are simply counted up, and this count is returned as the sum argument. Please note the use of the := symbol. It is a called the unification symbol; it is a special symbol that allows us to use the accountNumber object as input as well as an output argument, depending on how we'll call this query. If we call this query while passing in the account number, this would be the same as writing fromAccountNumber == accountNumber; however, if we call this query without passing in the accountNumber object, this would be the same as writing accountNumber : fromAccountNumber. Note that in our case it does not make sense to use the account number as an output argument, as we're using it in a place where it is scoped to the accumulate construct. It is just for illustration. Using this query, our rule would then become:

```
...
$account : Account( $accountNumber : number )
numberOfTransactions1DayQuery( $accountNumber := accountNumber,
$numberOfTransactions1Day := sum )
$accountInfo : AccountInfo( number == $accountNumber,
    $numberOfTransactions1Day > averageNumberOfTransactions *
    BigDecimal.valueOf(5.0), ...
```

Code listing 31: Excerpt of the highActivity rule using a query (the cep.drl file)

As you can see, the numberOfTransactions1DayQuery object is being called with $accountNumber as an input parameter and $numberOfTransactions1Day as an output parameter (it is an output parameter because it has not been defined yet). In both cases the unification symbol is being used as it is necessary here. It is not possible to use field constraints when calling a query.

Queries are also very useful at removing duplication from rules. If two or more rules share common conditions, they can be sometimes refactored into a common query and the rules can then call this query.

This concludes rule implementations for the fraud detection system. We haven't implemented all rules specified in the requirements section, but they shouldn't be hard to do. I am sure that you can now implement a lot more sophisticated rules.

Summary

In this chapter we've learned about Drools stream mode for CEP. Events in Drools are immutable objects with strong time-related relationships. CEP has great value, especially if we need to make complex decisions over a high number of events. The engine automatically detects when an event is no longer needed and makes sure that it can be garbage collected. We've seen the use of time/length sliding windows and temporal operators.

This chapter also discussed the Drools type declarations, which can define metadata on top of existing types or define new types. As was demonstrated, new types are useful for rule decomposition.

Various examples of rules from a fictive fraud detection system were presented.

Drools is a very extensible tool. The development team try to make almost every feature pluggable and customizable. Custom operators and custom accumulate functions are just a few examples of this pluggability. The usage of some of the temporal operators was demonstrated.

8

Defining Processes with jBPM

Every nontrivial business process needs to make complex decisions. A rule engine is the ideal place for these decisions to happen. However, it is impractical to invoke a rule engine from a standard workflow engine. Instead, if we take a rule engine and add workflow capabilities, we have an ideal tool such as jBPM to model complex business processes.

The basics of jBPM were already covered in the *jBPM* section of *Chapter 5, Creating Human-readable Rules*. We've learned about methods for managing rules execution order; basic components/nodes of a process – start, end, action, ruleflow group, split (diverging gateway), and join (converging gateway).

In this chapter we'll look in more detail at jBPM. We'll build a loan approval process and cover the following advanced concepts of a process: work items, human tasks, faults, subprocesses, events, and others.

Loan approval service

Loan approval is a complex process starting with a customer requesting a loan. This request comes with information such as amount to be borrowed, duration of the loan, and destination account where the borrowed amount will be transferred. Only existing customers can apply for a loan. The process starts with validating the request. Upon successful validation, a customer rating is calculated and only customers with certain rating are allowed to have loans. The loan is processed by a bank employee. As soon as an approved event is received from a supervisor, the loan is approved and money can be transferred to the destination account. An e-mail is sent to inform the customer about the outcome.

Model

If we look at this process from the domain-modeling perspective, in addition to the model that we already have, we'll need a Loan class. An instance of this class will be part of the context of this process.

Figure 1: Java Bean for holding loan-related information

The Loan bean defines three properties: amount, which is of type BigDecimal, destinationAccount, which is of type Account, and durationYears. If the loan is approved, the amount will be transferred to this account. durationYears represents a period that the customer will be repaying this loan.

Loan approval process

We'll now define this process in jBPM. It is shown in the following figure. Try to remember this figure, because we'll be referring back to it throughout this chapter:

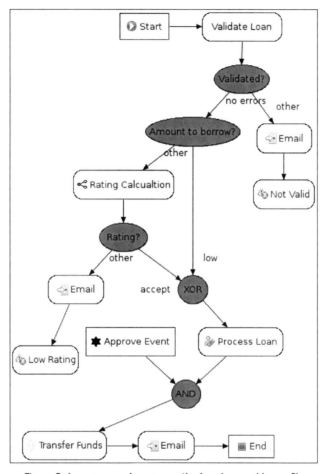

Figure 2: Loan approval process – the loanApproval.bpmn file

You can use the BPMN2 process editor that comes with the Drools Eclipse plugin to create this process. The rest of the chapter will walk you through this process, explaining each node in more detail. The screenshot shown has been taken using the **Default** skin. This skin has been chosen because it shows the node names (the other skins don't), which makes the explanation a lot easier. Normally, you'd use the **BPMN2** process skin. You can change the process skin in Eclipse when you go to **Window** | **Preferences** | **Drools**, then select from the **Preferred process skin** drop-down list.

The process starts with the **Validate Loan** rule task (also called rule flow group). The rules in this group will check the loan for missing required values and do other more complex validation. Similar to what we've done before, each validation rule simply inserts a message into the knowledge session. The next node called **Validated**? is a XOR type split node. The flow will continue through the **no errors** branch if there are no errors or warning messages in the knowledge session; the split node constraint for this branch says:

```
not Message()
```

Code listing 1: The Validated? split node's no errors branch constraint (the loanApproval.bpmn file)

For this to work we need to import the `Message` type into the process. This can be done from the constraint editor; just click on the **Imports...** button. The import statements are common for the whole process. Whenever we use a new type in the process (inside constraints), it needs to be imported.

The **Otherwise** branch is a "catch all" type branch (it is set to **Always true**). It has a higher priority number, which means that it will be checked after the **No errors** branch.

> Note that **Business Process Model and Notation (BPMN)** is a standard that is managed by the **Object Management Group (OMG)**. jBPM implements the latest Version 2.0 of this standard. This means that in theory we could choose any editor that supports this standard and even change the process engine that executes the process.
>
> The `.bpmn` files are pure XML files that conform with a well-formed XSD schema. They can be also edited with any XML editor.

Invalid loan application form

If the validation didn't pass, an e-mail is sent to the customer and the loan approval process finishes as **Not valid**. This can be seen in the **Otherwise** branch. There are two nodes: **Email** and **Not Valid**. **Email** is a special process node called work item.

E-mail work item

Work item is a node that encapsulates some piece of work. This can be an interaction with another system or some logic that is easier to write using standard Java. Each work item represents a piece of logic that can be reused in many systems. We can also look at work items as a process alternative to DSLs.

By default, jBPM comes with various generic work items. For example:

- **Email**: This is used for sending e-mails

- **Log**: This is used for logging messages
- **Finder**: This is used for finding files on a filesystem
- **Archive**: This is used for archiving files
- **Exec**: This is used for executing programs/system commands and several others

 In a real application you'd probably want to use a custom work item rather than a generic one for sending e-mail. For example, a custom work item that inserts a record into your loan repository. Later on we'll see how to define a custom work item.

Each work item can take multiple parameters. In the case of e-mail these are **From**, **To**, **Subject**, **Text**, and others. Values for these parameters can be specified at process creation time or at runtime. By double-clicking on the **Email** node in the process, a custom work editor is opened (see the following figure). Please note that not all work items have a custom editor.

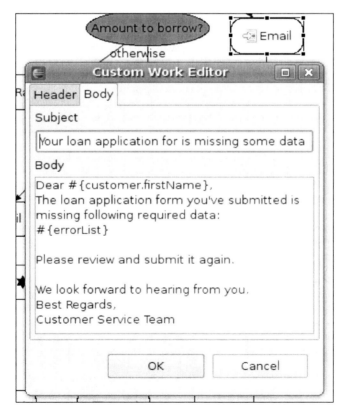

Figure 3: Custom e-mail work item editor (editing the loanApproval.bpmn file)

In the first tab (not visible), we can specify recipients and the source e-mail address. In the second (visible) tab, we can specify the e-mail's subject and body. If you look closer at the body of the e-mail, you'll notice two placeholders. They have the following syntax: #{variable}. A placeholder can contain any mvel code and has access to all process variables (we'll learn more about process variables later on in this chapter). This allows us to customize the work item parameters based on runtime conditions. As can be seen from the screenshot we use two placeholders: customer.firstName and errorList. The customer and the errorList are process variables. The first one represents the current Customer object and the second one is the ValidationReport object. When the process execution reaches this e-mail work item, these placeholders are evaluated and replaced with the actual values (by calling the toString method on the result).

Error event

The second node in the **Otherwise** branch in the process from *Figure 2* is an error event node. This node is similar to an end node. It accepts one incoming connection and has no outgoing connections. When the execution reaches this node, a fault is thrown with a given name (it is a similar concept to Java exceptions). We could, for example, register a fault handler that will generate a record in our reporting database. However, we won't register a fault handler, and in that case, it will simply indicate that this process is finished with an error.

Test setup

We'll now write a test for the **Otherwise** branch. First, let's set up the test environment.

jBPM comes with an abstract test case such as JbpmBpmn2TestCase that we can extend when unit testing processes . It provides some helper assertion methods. This test case can be found in the jbpm-bpmn2 test module (jbpm-bpmn2-5.4.0.Final-tests.jar).

This is similar to what was done in the *jBPM* section of *Chapter 5, Creating Human-readable Rules*. A knowledge base needs to be created from multiple files. For now they are loanApproval.drl and loanApproval.bpmn, and later on we'll add two more: ratingCalculation.drl and ratingCalculation.bpmn.

Then in the setup method a new session is created together with some test data. A valid Customer object with one Account object that is requesting a Loan object. The setup method will create a valid loan configuration and the individual tests can then change this configuration in order to test various exceptional cases:

```
@Before
public void setUp() {
    session = createKnowledgeSession(knowledgeBase);
```

```
trackingProcessEventListener =
  new TrackingProcessEventListener();
session.addEventListener(trackingProcessEventListener);
session.getWorkItemManager().registerWorkItemHandler(
    "Email", new SystemOutWorkItemHandler());

loanSourceAccount = new Account();

customer = new Customer();
customer.setFirstName("Bob");
customer.setLastName("Green");
customer.setEmail("bob.green@mail.com");
Account account = new Account();
account.setNumber(1234567891);
customer.addAccount(account);
account.setOwner(customer);

loan = new Loan();
loan.setDestinationAccount(account);
loan.setAmount(BigDecimal.valueOf(4000.0));
loan.setDurationYears(2);
```

Code listing 2: Test setup method called before every test execution (the DefaulLoanApprovalServiceTest.java file)

A tracking process event listener is created and added to the knowledge session. Similarly to TrackingAgendaEventListener that was used in the previous chapter. This event listener will record the execution path of the process, that is, it will store all executed process nodes in a list. The TrackingProcessEventListener method overrides the beforeNodeTriggered method and gets the node to be executed by calling event.getNodeInstance().

The loanSourceAccount method represents the bank's account for sourcing loans.

The setup method also registers an e-mail work item handler. A work item handler is responsible for the execution of the work item (in this case connecting to the mail server and sending out e-mails). However, the SystemOutWorkItemHandler implementation we've used is only a dummy implementation that writes some information to the console. It is useful for our testing purposes.

Testing the Validated? node's otherwise branch

We'll now test the **otherwise** branch, which sends an e-mail informing the applicant about the missing data and ends with a fault. Our following test will set up a loan request that will fail the validation. It will then verify that the fault node was executed and that the process has been aborted:

```
@Test
public void notValid() {
    session.insert(new DefaultMessage());
    startProcess();

    assertNodeTriggered(processInstance.getId(), "Not Valid");
    assertProcessInstanceAborted(processInstance.getId(),
        session);
}
```

Code listing 3: Test method for testing the Validated? node's otherwise branch (the DefaultLoanApprovalServiceTest.java file)

By inserting a message into the session, we're simulating a validation error. The process should end up in the **otherwise** branch.

Next, the previous test calls the `startProcess` method whose implementation is as follows:

```
private void startProcess() {
    Map<String, Object> parameterMap =
        new HashMap<String, Object>();
    parameterMap.put("loanSourceAccount", loanSourceAccount);
    parameterMap.put("customer", customer);
    parameterMap.put("loan", loan);
    processInstance = session.startProcess(
        PROCESS_LOAN_APPROVAL, parameterMap);
    session.insert(processInstance);
    session.fireAllRules();
}
```

Code listing 4: Utility method for starting the process (the DefaultLoanApprovalServiceTest.java file)

The `startProcess` method starts the loan approval process. It also sets loan and customer as process variables to the `loanSourceAccount` method. The resulting process instance (which is a `test` class property) is in turn inserted into the knowledge session. This will enable our rules to make more sophisticated decisions based on the state of the current process instance. Finally, all rules are fired.

We're already supplying three variables to the process; however, we haven't declared them yet. Let's do it. The process variables can be added through the Eclipse properties editor as can be seen in the following figure (just click anywhere on the process canvas, as this should give the focus to the process itself). Each variable needs a name, type, and optionally a value.

Figure 4: Setting process variables (the loanApproval.bpmn file)

The figure shows how to set the loan process variable. Its **Type** is set to **Object** and **ClassName** set to the full type name `droolsbook.bank.model.Loan`. The other two variables are set similarly.

Now gets back to the test from *Code listing 3*. It verifies that the **Not Valid** node has been triggered and that the process ended in an aborted state.

Note about process unit testing:

jBPM support for unit testing is improving, but it is not ideal. With every test we have to run the full process from start to the end. We'll make it easier with some helper methods that will set up a state that will utilize different parts of the flow. For example, a loan with a high amount to borrow or a customer with a low rating.

Ideally, we should be able to test each node in isolation. Simply start the process in a particular node. Just set the necessary parameters needed for a particular test and then verify that the node is executed as expected.

Drools support for snapshots may resolve some of these issues; however, we'd have to first create all snapshots that we need before executing the individual test methods. Another alternative is to dig deeper into Drools' internal API, but this is not recommended. The internal API can change in the next release without any notice.

The size of the loan

All valid loans continue through the **no errors** branch to the **Amount to borrow?** split node. It is again a XOR type split node. It works based on the amount property of the Loan object. If it is less than 5,000, it continues through the **low** branch, otherwise it takes the **otherwise** branch. The **otherwise** branch is again a "catch all" type branch. Put the following constraint into the split node:

```
Loan( amount <= 5000 )
```

Code listing 5: The Amount to borrow? split node's low branch constraint (the loanApproval.bpmn file)

For all loans that are bigger, a customer rating needs to be calculated.

Test for a small loan

The following method runs a loan with a small amount to borrow through our process. As can be seen in the following code listing, the first line of this test sets up a loan with a low amount. Next, the process is started and the test verifies that the flow continued through the correct branch:

```
@Test
public void amountToBorrowLow() {
  setUpLowAmount();
  startProcess();
```

```
        assertNodeTriggered(processInstance.getId(),
            "Join Rating");
        assertFalse(trackingProcessEventListener
            .isNodeTriggered(PROCESS_LOAN_APPROVAL,
                NODE_SUBFLOW_RATING_CALCULATION));
    }
```

Code listing 6: Test for the Amount to borrow? node's low branch (the DefaultLoanApprovalServiceTest.java file)

The setupLowAmount method inserts a loan with a low amount to borrow into the knowledge session. You could argue that loan could be a global variable instead of a fact. The advantage of having loan as a fact makes it possible to update it later on. Do you remember that global variables shouldn't change when we want to reason over them?

The test expects the next **XOR** node called "Join Rating" on the **low** branch to be executed, and it also expects the next node to be on the **otherwise** branch; **Rating Calculation** isn't executed. To assert that the node has not been executed, we're using trackingProcessEventListener, since JbpmBpmn2TestCase has no support for this.

The isNodeTriggered method takes the process ID, which is stored in a constant called PROCESS_LOAN_APPROVAL. The method also takes the node ID as second argument. This node ID can be found in the properties view after clicking on the fault node. The node ID NODE_SUBFLOW_RATING_CALCULATION is a constant of type long defined as a property of this test class:

```
    final long NODE_SUBFLOW_RATING_CALCULATION = 7;
    final long NODE_WORK_ITEM_TRANSFER = 26;
```

Code listing 7: Constants that hold rating calculation and transfer work item node's IDs
(the DefaultLoanApprovalServiceTest.java file)

By using the node ID we can change the node's name and other properties without breaking this test (node ID is least likely to change). Also, if we're doing bigger refactorings involving node ID changes, we have only one place to update, that is, the test's constants.

Rating Calculation

The first node in the **Amount to borrow** (otherwise) branch is a reusable subprocess node called **Rating Calculation**. This node will calculate the rating of this customer. It will then be used to decide if a loan should be granted or not.

Subprocess

First, some general information about subprocesses. Subprocess is a normal process that can be called from another process. It is effectively a process inside another process. These are the benefits of doing this:

- A complex process can be logically separated into multiple simple processes. The problem can be decomposed into subproblems, as the basic principle says: divide and conquer.

- The new process can be also reused in different contexts. For example, this rating calculation might be used in a mortgage loan approval process. With the help of the on-entry/on-exit actions and parameter mappings, the parent process can supply information to the subprocess and then possibly act on the result. The subprocess remains independent.

- This subprocess can be executed in parallel with the parent process. This means that after reaching the subprocess node, the execution continues in both the parent process and the subprocess (note that this doesn't mean multiple threads). However, this has the disadvantage that we won't be able to use any results from this subprocess in our parent process.

The subprocess is executed in the same knowledge session as the parent subprocess. This means that the subprocess can access facts just as its parent process. The `StatefulKnowledgeSession.getProcessInstances()` method can be used to return the collection of all active process instances associated with a knowledge session.

Furthermore, the subprocess (and also some other process nodes) can define in/out parameter mappings and on-entry/on-exit actions. The parent process will wait on a subprocess if the `Wait For Completion` flag is set to `true`. Only in this case it makes sense to use the out parameter mappings. Another flag that can be set is independent. With this flag set to `true`, the subprocess will continue executing even if the parent process finished executing (it is completed or aborted), otherwise it would be aborted.

Subprocess diagram

The following subprocess represents the rating calculation flow. After it starts, the first thing we do is to insert the subprocess instance into the session, so that we can later write rules reacting to it. We can do this with a script task called `Initialize` with the following body: `insert(context.processInstance);`. Now when this script task executes the subprocess, instance will be inserted into the session.

Next, looking at the diagram, the subprocess continues through a split node. This split node is of type AND, meaning that the execution will continue in all nodes' outgoing branches. On the left-hand side, there's the **Calculate Incomes** rule task and on the right-hand side, there are the **Calculate Monthly Repayments** and **Calculate Expenses** rule tasks. These rule tasks contain rules for accumulating knowledge about customer incomes like salaries of the customer and his/her spouse, type of occupation they have, how long they are employed, how long they were unemployed, how much funds they have in their accounts, information about their properties, or other asserts. The **Calculate Monthly Repayments** rule task calculates how much this loan will cost by month. The **Calculate Expenses** rule task takes into account expenses such as the size of the family, rent, other loans, mortgages, and obligations.

Finally, these two branches are joined together by an AND type join node. This means that the flow won't continue until all its incoming connections are triggered. The next node is a **Calculate Rating** rule task. This is where all the acquired information are translated by a set of rules into one number – rating. This process can be seen in this figure:

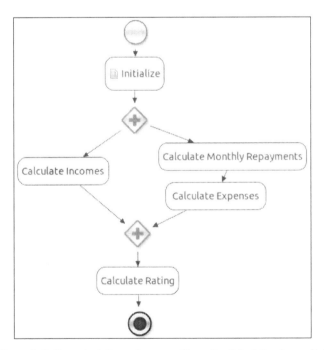

Figure 5: Rating calculation subprocess (the ratingCalculation.bpmn file)

Note that in this screenshot we're using the default **BPMN2** skin. The AND type gateways are shown as a plus symbol. The other gateways, OR and XOR, have symbols of an "x" and "*" respectively. These symbols help as we no longer have to examine the node to see its type.

One important thing when designing the process is to make it simple. The process should describe the core business process. It shouldn't contain every little detail of the process. The rules are ideal for this. They can then fine-tune the business process.

Consider the process from the previous screenshot as an example. It nicely logically separates the individual calculations. By looking at this process diagram, you should immediately get a feeling of what is it trying to achieve.

Now, we know that the process uses rules to calculate a rating. This rating is a fact inside the knowledge session. Next, we'll set this fact as a subprocess variable so that it can be later easily propagated into the parent process. This can be easily achieved with a rule that will match on the Rating fact and the subprocess instance, and it will set the subprocess variable. The rule is as follows:

```
rule updateSubProcess
ruleflow-group "calculateRating"
salience -100
no-loop true
  when
    processInstance : WorkflowProcessInstance(
      processId == "ratingCalculation" )
    $rating : Rating( )
  then
    modify(processInstance) {
      setVariable("rating", $rating);
    }
end
```

Code listing 8: Rule that sets the rating fact as a subprocess variable (the ratingCalculation.drl file)

Next, we want to propagate the calculated rating from the subprocess into the parent process. We'll use **Parameter Out Mapping** as shown here:

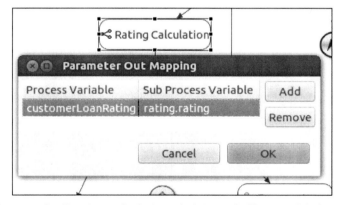

Figure 6: Parameter Out Mapping on the Rating calculation node (the ratingCalculation.bpmn file)

Rating a calculation subprocess test

We'll now write a test which verifies that our subprocess is being called and the variable is set.

```
@Test
public void amountToBorrowHighRatingCalculation() {
  setUpHighAmount();
  startProcess();
  assertNodeTriggered(processInstance.getId(),
      "Rating Calculation");
  assertTrue(trackingProcessEventListener.isNodeTriggered(
      PROCESS_RATING_CALCULATION,
      NODE_GROUP_CALCULATE_RATING));
  assertProcessVarExists(processInstance,
      "customerLoanRating");
  WorkflowProcessInstance process =
      (WorkflowProcessInstance) processInstance;
  assertEquals(1500,
      process.getVariable("customerLoanRating"));
}
```

Code listing 9: Test for the subprocess node (the DefaultLoanApprovalServiceTest.java file)

The test sets up a loan request with a high amount by calling the `setUpHighAmount` method. This method inserts a loan, with the amount set to `19000`, into the knowledge session. Next, the process is started with default parameters, which involve the `customerLoanRating` process variable set to `0`. Next, the test verifies that the subprocess node has been executed together with one node from the subprocess itself – **Calculate Rating**. Finally, the test verifies that the `customerLoanRating` variable has been set to `1500`; it is a customer loan rating calculated for our test loan. The last couple of lines of the `test` method also show us how to get variables from the process instance.

Note that the rules for calculating the rating have been left out. However, for testing purposes you could easily write a rule that inserts a `Rating` fact into the session with its rating property set to `1500`.

Another test for the rating calculation subprocess may check that all its nodes are executed, since the flow contains only `and` type split and join nodes.

Setting the rating using an on-exit action

Another alternative of setting the `customerLoanRating` variable would be to use an on-exit action. The on entry/on exit actions can be defined on various process nodes: subprocess, work item, and human task. Similar to script tasks, which are standalone nodes, the on entry/on exit actions are simply a block of dialect-specific code. We can access `RuleContext` (visible under the `kcontext` variable). In addition to this, we can access a context variable, `org.drools.runtime.process.ProcessContext`.

org.drools.runtime.process.ProcessContext

`ProcessContext` has various methods for working with the current process context. The `getProcessInstance()` method returns the current process instance. If we're in a subprocess, this method will return the subprocess instance.

In general when a process is started, new `ProcessInstance` is created that represents the runtime state of a process. jBPM is based on the **Process Virtual Machine (PVM)** model (more information about this model can be found at `http://docs.jboss.com/jbpm/pvm/article/`).

The `getNodeInstance()` method of `ProcessContext` returns the runtime instance of a currently executing node. The process context can also be used for setting and getting process variables `getVariable/setVariable`. The `getKnowledgeRuntime()` method returns a `KnowledgeRuntime` object that can be used for interaction with the knowledge session.

Nodes that define both entry/exit actions and also in/out parameter mappings use the following order to evaluate them:

- The on-entry actions
- The input parameter mappings
- The node itself
- The output parameter mappings and finally
- The on-exit actions

We'll define an on exit action with the following body:

```
Rating rating = (Rating)kcontext.getKnowledgeRuntime().getObjects(new
ClassObjectFilter(Rating.class)).iterator().next();
context.setVariable("customerLoanRating", rating.getRating());
kcontext.getKnowledgeRuntime().update(kcontext.getKnowledgeRuntime().
getFactHandle(context.getProcessInstance()), context.
getProcessInstance());
```

Code listing 10: Subprocess node's onExit action body (the loanApproval.bpmn file)

First of all, the action retrieves the calculated rating directly from the knowledge session. It simply iterates over all objects in the knowledge session and filters out all objects that are not of type `Rating`. The `Rating` type is a bean that has one property of type `Integer` called `rating`. The code is expecting to find just one `Rating` fact in the knowledge session as can be seen when we call the `next` method.

Next, we set the `customerLoanRating` variable using the `context.setVariable` method, which correctly sets it on the main process context. Finally, we shouldn't forget to update `processInstance` since we've modified it.

Using the on-exit action was not as neat as using the `updateSubProcess` rule together with the out parameter mapping. This was more to show how an on-exit action works.

Decisions on rating

After we've calculated the rating and set it as a process variable, the next process node **Rating?** checks if the customer's loan rating is high enough. It is an XOR type split node with the following `accept` branch constraint:

```
customerLoanRating >= 1000
```

Code listing 11: The Rating? node's accept branch constraint – code type (the loanApproval.bpmn file)

Set the type of this constraint to `code` and the dialect to `mvel`. Code constraints have access to all process variables. As can be seen we're directly referring to the `customerLoanRating` process variable and checking if it is greater or equal than 1,000. If it is, the loan application can continue to the next step of the loan approval process.

If we need to do more complex decisions, we could use a `rule` type constraint like we've done before:

```
processInstance : WorkflowProcessInstance(
    getVariable("customerLoanRating") >= 1000 )
```

Code listing 12: The Rating? node's accept branch constraint – rule type (the loanApproval.bpmn file)

The condition uses a special variable name called `processInstance` of type `WorkflowProcessInstance`. It is special because Drools will match only on the current executing process instance even if there were multiple instances in the knowledge session. Through the `processInstance` type we can access all the process variables. Note that we need to insert the process instance into the knowledge session as we've done in *Code listing 4*. Also, if we're using an out parameter mapping to modify process variables, we need to manually update the process instance (this might be a bug in jBPM) as was done in *Code listing 10*.

Testing the Rating? node

The test will create a loan request for a high amount and for a customer who has a high rating. It will then execute the process and verify that the flow went through the **Rating?** node through the **accept** branch to the XOR join node:

```
@Test
public void ratingSplitNodeAccept() {
    setUpHighAmount();
    setUpHighRating();
    startProcess();

    assertNodeTriggered(processInstance.getId(), "Rating?");
    assertNodeTriggered(processInstance.getId(),
        "Join Rating");
}
```

Code listing 13: The Rating? node's accept branch constraint (the DefaultLoanApprovalServiceTest.java file)

The test executes successfully.

The Transfer Funds work item

We'll now jump almost to the end of our process. After a loan is approved, we need a way of transferring the specified sum of money to the customer's account. This can be done with rules or even better with pure Java, since this task is procedural in nature. We'll create a custom work item so that we can easily reuse this functionality in other processes. Note that if it was a one-off task, it would be probably better suited to a script task node.

The **Transfer Funds** node in *Figure 2* is a custom work item. A new custom work item can be defined in the following four steps (later on we'll see how they are accomplished):

1. Create a work item definition. This will be used by the Eclipse process editor and by the process engine to set and get parameters. For example, the following is an extract from the default `WorkDefinitions.conf` file that comes with Drools. It describes the **Email** work definition. The configuration is written in MVEL. MVEL allows to construct complex object graphs in a very concise format. This file contains a list of maps: `List<Map<String, Object>>`. Each map defines the properties of one work definition. The properties, name and parameters, are the work items that work with `displayName`, `icon`, and `customEditor`, which are used when displaying the work item in the Eclipse process editor. A custom editor is opened after double-clicking on the process node.

    ```
    import org.drools.process.core.datatype.impl.type.StringDataType;
    [
      [
        "name" : "Email",
        "parameters" : [
          "From" : new StringDataType(),
          "To" : new StringDataType(),
          "Subject" : new StringDataType(),
            "Body" : new StringDataType()
        ],
        "displayName" : "Email",
        "icon" : "icons/import_statement.gif",
        "customEditor" : "org.drools.eclipse.flow.common.editor.
    editpart.work.EmailCustomEditor"
      ]
    ]
    ```

    Code listing 14: Excerpt from the default WorkDefinitions.conf file that is part of the drools-core module

    The work item's parameters property is a map of `parameterNames` and their value wrappers. The value wrapper must implement the interface `org.drools.process.core.datatype.DataType`.

2. Register the work definitions with the knowledge base configuration (this will be shown in the next section).

3. Create a work item handler. This handler represents the actual behavior of a work item. It will be invoked whenever the process execution reaches this work item node. All handlers must extend the `org.drools.runtime.process.WorkItemHandler` interface. It defines two methods. One for executing the work item and another for aborting the work item. Drools comes with some default work item handler implementations, for example, a handler for sending e-mails: `org.jbpm.process.workitem.email.EmailWorkItemHandler`. This handler needs a working SMTP server. It must be set through the `setConnection` method before registering the work item handler with the work item manager (next step). Another default work item handler, `SystemOutWorkItemHandler`, was shown in *Code listing 2*.

4. Register the work item handler with the work item manager.

After reading this you may ask why doesn't the work item definition also specify the handler? It is because a work item can have one or more work item handlers that can be used interchangeably. For example, in a test case, we may want to use a different work item handler than in a production environment.

We'll now follow this four-step process and create the **Transfer Funds** custom work item.

The work item definition

Our transfer funds work item will have three input parameters: source account, destination account, and the amount to transfer. Its definition is as follows:

```
import org.drools.process.core.datatype.impl.type.ObjectDataType;
[
  [
    "name" : "Transfer Funds",
    "parameters" : [
        "Source Account" : new ObjectDataType("droolsbook.bank.model.
Account"),
        "Destination Account" : new ObjectDataType("droolsbook.bank.
model.Account"),
        "Amount" : new ObjectDataType("java.math.BigDecimal")
    ],
    "displayName" : "Transfer Funds",
    "icon" : "icons/transfer.gif"
  ]
]
```

Code listing 15: Work item definition from the BankingWorkDefinitions.conf file

The **Transfer Funds** work item definition we just saw declares the usual properties. It doesn't have a custom editor as was the case with the e-mail work item. All the parameters are of type `ObjectDataType`. This is a wrapper that can wrap any type. In our case we are wrapping the `Account` and `BigDecimal` types. We've also specified an icon that will be displayed in the process editor palette and in the process itself. The icon should be of size 16 x 16 pixels.

Work item registration

First, make sure that the `BankingWorkDefinitions.conf` file is on your classpath. We now have to tell Drools about our new work item. This can be done by creating a `drools.rulebase.conf` file with the following contents:

```
drools.workDefinitions = WorkDefinitions.conf BankingWorkDefinitions.
conf
```

Code listing 16: Work item definition from the BankingWorkDefinitions.conf file (all in one one line)

When Drools starts up, it scans the classpath for configuration files. Configuration specified in the `drools.rulebase.conf` file will override the default configuration. In this case only the `drools.workDefinitions` setting is being overridden. We already know that the `WorkDefinitions.conf` file contains the default work items such as e-mail and log. We want to keep those and just add ours. As can be seen from *Code listing 16*, the `drools.workDefinitions` settings accept a list of configurations. They must be separated by a space. When we now open the process editor in Eclipse, the process palette should contain our new **Transfer Funds** work item.

If you want to know more about the file-based configuration resolution process, you can look into the `org.drools.util.ChainedProperties` class.

Work item handler

Next, we'll implement the work item handler. It must implement the `org.drools.runtime.process.WorkItemHandler` interface that defines two methods: `executeWorkItem` and `abortWorkItem`. The implementation is as follows:

```
/**
 * work item handler responsible for transferring amount from
 * one account to another using bankingService.transfer method
 * input parameters: 'Source Account', 'Destination Account'
 * and 'Amount'
 */
public class TransferWorkItemHandler implements
    WorkItemHandler {
```

```
BankingService bankingService;

public void executeWorkItem(WorkItem workItem,
    WorkItemManager manager) {
  Account sourceAccount = (Account) workItem
      .getParameter("Source Account");
  Account destinationAccount = (Account) workItem
      .getParameter("Destination Account");
  BigDecimal sum = (BigDecimal) workItem
      .getParameter("Amount");

  try {
    bankingService.transfer(sourceAccount,
        destinationAccount, sum);
    manager.completeWorkItem(workItem.getId(), null);
  } catch (Exception e) {
    e.printStackTrace();
    manager.abortWorkItem(workItem.getId());
  }
}

/**
 * does nothing as this work item cannot be aborted
 */
public void abortWorkItem(WorkItem workItem,
    WorkItemManager manager) {
}
```

Code listing 17: Work item handler (the TransferWorkItemHandler.java file)

The `executeWorkItem` method retrieves the three declared parameters and calls the `bankingService.transfer` method (the implementation of this method won't be shown). If all went okay, the work item manager is notified that this work item has been completed. It needs the ID of the work item and optionally a result parameter map. In our case it is set to `null`. If an exception happens during the transfer, the manager is told to abort this work item.

The `abortWorkItem` method on our handler doesn't do anything because this work item cannot be aborted.

Please note that the work item handler must be thread-safe. Many process instances may reuse the same work item instance.

Work item handler registration

The transfer work item handler can be registered with a `WorkItemManager` method as follows:

```
TransferWorkItemHandler transferHandler =
    new TransferWorkItemHandler();
transferHandler.setBankingService(bankingService);
session.getWorkItemManager().registerWorkItemHandler(
    "Transfer Funds", transferHandler);
```

Code listing 18: The TransferWorkItemHandler registration (the DefaultLoanApprovalServiceTest.java file)

A new instance of this handler is created and the banking service is set. Then it is registered with the `WorkItemManager` method retrieved from a session.

Next, we need to connect this work item into our process; this means setting its parameters. We need to set the source/destination account and the amount to be transferred. We'll use the **Transfer Funds** in-parameter mappings to set these parameters:

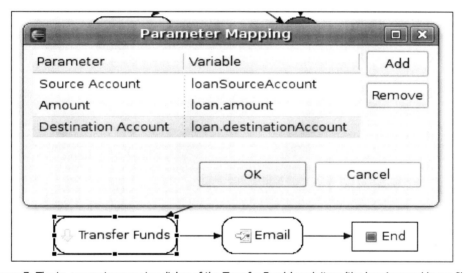

Figure 7: The in–parameter mapping dialog of the Transfer Funds' work item (the loanApproval.bpmn file)

From the previous screenshot, we can see the `Source Account` parameter is mapped to the `loanSourceAccount` process variable. The `Destination Account` process variable is set to the destination account of the `loan`, and the `Amount` process variable is set to the amount of `loan`.

Testing the transfer work item

This test will verify that the **Transfer Funds** work item is correctly executed with all parameters set and that it calls the bankingService.transfer method with correct values. For this test the bankingService service will be mocked with the jMock library, which is a lightweight Mock object library for Java (more information can be found at http://www.jmock.org/). Firstly, we need to set up the banking service mock object:

```
mockery = new JUnit4Mockery();
bankingService = mockery.mock(BankingService.class);
```

Code listing 19: jMock setup of the bankingService mock object (the DefaultLoanApprovalServiceTest.java file)

Next, we can write our test. We are expecting one invocation of the transfer method with loanSourceAccount and loan's destination and amount properties. Then the test will set up the transfer work item as in *Code listing 18*, start the process, and approve the loan (more about this in the next section). The test also verifies that the **Transfer Funds** node has been executed. The test method's implementation is as follows:

```
@Test
public void transferFunds() {
  mockery.checking(new Expectations() {
    {
      one(bankingService).transfer(loanSourceAccount,
          loan.getDestinationAccount(), loan.getAmount());
    }
  });

  setUpTransferWorkItem();
  setUpLowAmount();
  startProcess();
  approveLoan();

  assertNodeTriggered(processInstance.getId(),
      "Transfer Funds");
}
```

Code listing 20: Test for the Transfer Funds work item (the DefaultLoanApprovalServiceTest.java file)

The test should execute successfully.

Human task

Let's go back to the loan approval process. We finished after the **'Rating?'** node. Our next step is to implement the **Process Loan** node. This is where human actors will be involved. We've done what we could with our automated process; now is the time for tasks that a computer can't or shouldn't perform.

jBPM supports human tasks such as the Web Services Human Task specification (WS-HumanTask is an OASIS specification and can be downloaded from `http://download.boulder.ibm.com/ibmdl/pub/software/dw/specs/ws-bpel4people/WS-HumanTask_v1.pdf`). With this specification, we can define human tasks that will be automatically created when the flow reaches this process node. After they are created, they will appear on the ask list screen of designated users who can claim these tasks and start working on them until they are completed. They can also suspend or abort these tasks. Once the task reaches the final state (complete/abort), the process continues execution. Please note that this is a very simplified view; the WS-HumanTask specification defines a more complex life cycle of a task.

From the process perspective, WS-HumanTask is just a special case of a work item. Once it is triggered, the process simply waits for the end result, be it success or failure. jBPM comes with several human task implementations. Some support centralized task management where the task service is accessed remotely; we'll use a more simple implementation that will run as part of our application (synchronously, sharing the same transaction). It should be noted that these implementations are not fully compliant with the WS-HumanTask specification; there may be some features missing.

 Please note that human task support is part of the `jbpm-human-task-XXX.jar` set of modules. We'll be using only the core module, `jbpm-human-task-core.jar`.

The human task process node allow us to specify `actorId`, which is the ID of a person/group that will have the role of `potentialOwner` as defined by WS-HumanTask. Comment, which will become the subject and description of a human task. If priority and option task can be skipped, they can be also defined among other properties.

The core part of the WS-HumanTask specification is a service that manages the tasks. The human task work item handler is kept lightweight. It is a simple client of this service that creates a task based on properties set in the process and registers this task with the service. The process then waits until the task finishes, be it a success or a failure.

Test for the human task

So far it was only theory a test will hopefully make it more clear. In order to write some tests for the **Process Loan** human task, we'll need a human task service that will be managing tasks. Other clients will then use this service to work on these tasks, and when they are completed our process will be able to continue.

Due to its size, the test will be divided into three parts: service setup part, client setup part, and client working on the task part.

We'll start with the service setup (see the following code listing). It will initialize the service, register a human task work item handler, and start the loan approval process:

```
@Test
public void processLoan() throws Exception {
  EntityManagerFactory emf = Persistence
      .createEntityManagerFactory("droolsbook.jbpm");

  TaskService taskService = new TaskService(emf,
      SystemEventListenerFactory.getSystemEventListener());
  LocalTaskService localTaskService = new LocalTaskService(
      taskService);

  MockUserInfo userInfo = new MockUserInfo();
  taskService.setUserinfo(userInfo);

  TaskServiceSession taskSession = taskService
      .createSession();
  taskSession.addUser(new User("Administrator"));
  taskSession.addUser(new User("123"));
  taskSession.addUser(new User("456"));
  taskSession.addUser(new User("789"));

  LocalHTWorkItemHandler htHandler =
      new LocalHTWorkItemHandler( localTaskService, session,
      OnErrorAction.RETHROW);
  htHandler.connect();
  session.getWorkItemManager().registerWorkItemHandler(
      "Human Task", htHandler);
  setUpLowAmount();
  startProcess();
```

Code listing 21: Test for the Process Loan node – set up of service and process startup
(the DefaultLoanApprovalServiceTest.java file)

As part of the service setup, the test creates an `EntityManagerFactory` Java Persistence API (JPA). More information can be found at http://en.wikipedia. org/wiki/Java_Persistence_API). It is used for persisting human tasks that are not currently needed. There may be thousands of human task instances running concurrently and each can take minutes, hours, days, or even months to finish. Persisting them will save us resources, and it may also make the tasks survive a server crash. In the next chapter we'll also see how to persist the whole process. We'll use an in-memory database. The definition of the `droolsbook.jbpm` persistence unit is as follows:

```
<?xml version="1.0" encoding="UTF-8" standalone="yes"?>
<persistence xmlns="http://java.sun.com/xml/ns/persistence"
        xmlns:xsi="http://www.w3.org/2001/XMLSchema-instance"
        xsi:schemaLocation="http://java.sun.com/xml/ns/persistence
http://java.sun.com/xml/ns/persistence/persistence_2_0.xsd"
        version="2.0">
  <persistence-unit name="droolsbook.jbpm"
      transaction-type="RESOURCE_LOCAL">
    <provider>org.hibernate.ejb.HibernatePersistence
    </provider>
    <mapping-file>META-INF/ProcessInstanceInfoMapping-JPA2.xml
    </mapping-file>
    <mapping-file>META-INF/JBPMorm-JPA2.xml</mapping-file>
    <mapping-file>META-INF/Taskorm.xml</mapping-file>
    <class>org.drools.persistence.info.SessionInfo</class>
    <class>org.jbpm.persistence.processinstance.ProcessInstanceInfo</
class>
    <class>org.drools.persistence.info.WorkItemInfo</class>

    <class>org.jbpm.task.Attachment</class>
    <class>org.jbpm.task.Content</class>
    <class>org.jbpm.task.BooleanExpression</class>
    <class>org.jbpm.task.Comment</class>
    <class>org.jbpm.task.Deadline</class>
    <class>org.jbpm.task.Comment</class>
    <class>org.jbpm.task.Deadline</class>
    <class>org.jbpm.task.Delegation</class>
    <class>org.jbpm.task.Escalation</class>
    <class>org.jbpm.task.Group</class>
    <class>org.jbpm.task.I18NText</class>
    <class>org.jbpm.task.Notification</class>
    <class>org.jbpm.task.EmailNotification</class>
    <class>org.jbpm.task.EmailNotificationHeader</class>
    <class>org.jbpm.task.PeopleAssignments</class>
```

```
<class>org.jbpm.task.Reassignment</class>
<class>org.jbpm.task.Status</class>
<class>org.jbpm.task.Task</class>
<class>org.jbpm.task.TaskData</class>
<class>org.jbpm.task.SubTasksStrategy</class>
<class>org.jbpm.task.OnParentAbortAllSubTasksEndStrategy
</class>
<class>org.jbpm.task.OnAllSubTasksEndParentEndStrategy
</class>
<class>org.jbpm.task.User</class>

<properties>
  <property name="hibernate.dialect"
    value="org.hibernate.dialect.H2Dialect"/>
  <property name="hibernate.max_fetch_depth" value="3"/>
  <property name="hibernate.hbm2ddl.auto"
    value="create-drop"/>
  <property name="hibernate.show_sql" value="true"/>

  <property name="hibernate.connection.driver_class"
    value="org.h2.jdbcx.JdbcDataSource"/>
  <property name="hibernate.connection.url"
    value="jdbc:h2:mem:test_droolsbook_jbpm"/>
  <property name="hibernate.connection.username"
    value="sa"/>
  <property name="hibernate.connection.password"
    value=""/>
  <property name="hibernate.connection.pool_size"
    value="3"/>
</properties>
  </persistence-unit>
</persistence>
```

Code listing 22: Human task persistence unit definition (the META-INF/persistence.xml file)

Next, continuing the `test` setup, the `TaskService` object is created. A `UserInfo` object is set to the `TaskService` object. It has methods for retrieving various information about users and groups of users in our organization that the `TaskService` object needs (it is, for example, used when sending notifications). For testing purposes, we're using only a mock implementation – `MockUserInfo`.

The `TaskService` object can be accessed by multiple threads. Next, the `TaskServiceSession` object represents one session of this service. This session can be accessed by only one thread at a time. We use this session to create some test users. Our **Process Loan** task is initially assigned to `actorIds`: `123`, `456`, and `789`. This is defined in the **Process Loan** process node's properties.

Then a default Drools `LocalHTWorkItemHandler` is registered, a new loan application with low amount is created and the process is started. The process will execute all the way down to **Process Loan** human task where `LocalHTWorkItemHandler` takes over. It creates a task from the information specified in the **Process Loan** node and registers this task with the server. It knows how to connect to the server. The process then waits for completion of this task.

The next part of this test represents a client (bank employee) who is viewing his/her task list and getting one task. The client calls service's `getTasksAssignedAsPotentialOwner` method and returns a list of tasks that the client can start working on. The test verifies that the list contains one task and that the status of this task is ready:

```
List<TaskSummary> tasks = localTaskService
    .getTasksAssignedAsPotentialOwner("123", "en-UK");
assertEquals(1, tasks.size());
TaskSummary task = tasks.get(0);
assertEquals("Process Loan", task.getName());
assertEquals(3, task.getPriority());
assertEquals(Status.Ready, task.getStatus());
```

Code listing 23: Test for the Process Loan node – set up of a client and task list retrieval (the DefaultLoanApprovalServiceTest.java file)

The final part of this test represents a client (bank employee) who claims one of the tasks from the task list, starts this task, and finally completes this task:

```
localTaskService.claim(task.getId(), "123");
localTaskService.start(task.getId(), "123");
localTaskService.complete(task.getId(), "123", null);

assertNodeTriggered(processInstance.getId(),
    "Join Process");
}
```

Code listing 24: Test for the Process Loan node – client is claiming, starting, and completing a task (the DefaultLoanApprovalServiceTest.java file)

After the task is completed, the test verifies that the process continues execution through the next join node called **Join Process**.

Final approval

As you may imagine, before any money is paid out to the loan requester, a final check is needed from a supervisor. This is represented in the flow by the **Approve Event** node. It is an event node from the process palette. It allows a process to respond to external events. This node has no incoming connection; in fact the events can be created/signaled through the process instance's `signalEvent` method. The method needs an event type and the event value itself.

The Parameters of the **Event** node include an event type and a variable name that holds this event. The variable must be itself declared as a process variable.

Test for the Approve Event node

A test will show us how this all works. We'll set up a valid loan request. The dummy `SystemOutWorkItemHandler` will be used to get through the **Transfer Funds** and **Process Loan** work items. The execution should then wait for the approve event. Then we'll signal the event using the `processInstance.signalEvent("LoanApprovedEvent", null)` method and verify that the process finished successfully:

```
@Test
public void approveEventJoin() {
  setUpLowAmount();
  startProcess();
  assertProcessInstanceActive(processInstance.getId(),
      session);
  assertFalse(trackingProcessEventListener.isNodeTriggered(
      PROCESS_LOAN_APPROVAL, NODE_WORK_ITEM_TRANSFER));
  approveLoan();
  assertTrue(trackingProcessEventListener.isNodeTriggered(
      PROCESS_LOAN_APPROVAL, NODE_WORK_ITEM_TRANSFER));

  assertProcessInstanceCompleted(processInstance.getId(),
      session);
}
```

Code listing 25: Test for the Approve Event node (the DefaultLoanApprovalServiceTest.java file)

Before sending the approved event, we've verified that the process is in active state and that the **Transfer Funds** work item haven't been called yet.

After sending the approved event, the test verifies that the **Transfer Funds** work item was actually executed and the process reached its final COMPLETED state.

Banking service

The final step is to implement the approveLoan service that represents the interface to our loan approval process. It ties everything that we've done together. The approve loan method takes a Loan object and a Customer object, which is requesting the loan:

```
KnowledgeBase knowledgeBase;
Account loanSourceAccount;

/**
 * runs the loan approval process for a specified
 * customer's loan
 */
public void approveLoan(Loan loan, Customer customer) {
  StatefulKnowledgeSession session = knowledgeBase
      .newStatefulKnowledgeSession();
  try {
    registerWorkItemHandlers(session);
    Map<String, Object> parameterMap =
      new HashMap<String, Object>();
    parameterMap.put("loanSourceAccount",loanSourceAccount);
    parameterMap.put("customer", customer);
    parameterMap.put("loan", loan);
    session.insert(loan);
    session.insert(customer);
    ProcessInstance processInstance =
      session.startProcess("loanApproval", parameterMap);
    session.insert(processInstance);
    session.fireAllRules();
  } finally {
    session.dispose();
  }
}
```

Code listing 26: BankingService's approveLoan service method (the DefaultLoanApprovalService.java file)

The service creates a new session and then registers all the work item handlers that we've implemented. This part is not shown. Normally, it would involve setting up configuration parameters such as the IP address of an SMTP server for the e-mail work item handler and so on.

Next, the `loan` and `customer` objects are inserted into the session; the process is started and the rules are fired. When the process completes, the session is disposed. Please be aware that with this solution, the knowledge session is held in memory from the time when the process starts up to the time when it finishes, which might be a long time. In the next chapter we'll see how to persist this process to avoid wasting memory.

Disadvantages of a process

A process implemented using jBPM may potentially do more work than it should do. This is a direct consequence of how the algorithm behind Drools works. All rule constraints are evaluated at fact insertion time. For example, if we have a process with many nodes and 80 percent of the time, the process finishes at the second node, and most of the computation is wasted. This will be more clear when we get to *Chapter 12, Learning about Performance*.

Another disadvantage is that the business logic is now spread across at least two places. The rules are still in the `.drl` file; however, the process is in the `.bpmn` file. The process file also contains split node conditions and actions. If somebody wants to get the full understanding of a process, he/she has to look back and forth between these files. This may be fixed in future by having better integration in the Eclipse plugin between the Drools' `.drl` file editor and the jBPM's `.bpmn` file editor (for example, it would be nice to see rules that belong to a selected ruleflow group).

Summary

In this chapter we've learned about various jBPM features. It represents an interesting approach to business process representation. The vision of jBPM/Drools is to unify rules and processes into one product. This is a very powerful idea, especially with business processes involving complex decisions, because these complexities can be implemented within rules that are ideal for this.

We've designed a loan approval service that involves validation of the loan request, customer rating calculation, approval events from a supervisor, and finally a custom domain-specific work item for transferring money between accounts.

We've seen jBPM support of human tasks through the WS-Human-Task specification. This allows for greater interoperability between systems from different vendors.

All in all, jBPM represents an interesting approach to rules and processes.

Building a Sample Application

9

This chapter will focus on the usage of Drools in a real application. It connects to previous chapters and should give an overall picture of how it all comes together. We'll look at how Drools can be used in a sample JEE web application covering layered design, persistence, transactions, and others.

This chapter assumes that you have some basic understanding of **Java Persistence API (JPA)**. More information can be found at `http://java.sun.com/javaee/technologies/persistence.jsp`) and the Spring framework.

We'll now look at various aspects of the sample application.

Users

Our application will have three sets of users: normal bank employees, supervisors, and bank customers. Their properties are as follows:

- Normal bank employees will be able to create new customers
- Customers will be able to request loans
- Bank employees will then work on these loans
- Supervisors will issue final loan approvals

Architecture

From bottom to top, this sample application will consist of three layers: persistence, service, and presentation. It can be seen in the next figure. The persistence layer is responsible for storing objects in a database. Transactions guarantee consistency of the database and provide isolation between concurrent requests. The service layer represents the business logic of this application. It consists of the validation service, **complex event processing** (CEP) service, and loan approval service. Finally, the presentation layer uses these services to provide functionality to the users in a user friendly fashion.

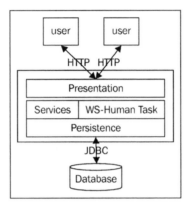

Figure 1: Sample application architecture diagram

Please note that with some minor configuration changes, the service layer and presentation layer may be deployed on different physical servers and communicate over the network. With some more configuration changes, it is even possible to have multiple service or presentation layer deployments. This won't be covered in this book.

Technologies used

The persistence layer will be implemented using JPA 2.0 with Hibernate as the persistence provider. JPA is a standard that makes it easier to switch persistence providers. JPA annotations will be used to map our domain objects into persistent entities (for example, database tables). We'll use local (in other words, not distributed) transactions.

The presentation layer will use the Spring MVC framework to define the behavior of the screens. Spring MVC was chosen because of its simplicity. The actual screens will be implemented as traditional **Java Server Pages (JSP)**. Tomcat servlet container Version 7.X will host our application.

All three layers will be configured with the Spring framework.

Additional Drools projects used

We'll use `drools-spring` for knowledge base construction, `drools-persistence-jpa` and `jbpm-persistence-jpa` for persisting the loan approval process, as well as the `jbpm-human-task-core` module for handling human tasks.

Libraries used

For other third-party libraries needed, please refer to *Appendix C, Dependencies of Sample Application*. It contains a list of libraries and their versions.

Business logic

We'll use our previously implemented services. Created customers will be validated (described in *Chapter 3, Validating*, and *Chapter 6, Working with Stateful Session*) before they are persisted. New loans will go through the loan approval process (described in *Chapter 8, Defining Processes with jBPM*), and if they meet all criteria, a new "process loan" human task will be created. Bank employees will see this task on their task lists and will be able to claim a task, start working on it, and when they are done with it, complete the task. A supervisor will be able to approve a loan. After approval, the process will finish. Various events will be generated and fed into the CEP service (described in *Chapter 7, Complex Event Processing*), running in the background.

Design

Let's now look in more detail at the individual layers. The following figure also give us an overview of what we'll be implementing in this chapter. Again, from bottom to top, we'll have two repositories: one for persisting customers and one for accounts. The services layer will have our three already defined services: validation, loan approval, and CEP service. These services will be hidden behind a public `BankingService`, which will act as a mediator between these services. The presentation tier will use this public service to do all its tasks. There will be various controllers, each responsible for some unit of work; for example, `CustomerSaveFormController` for saving a customer. The presentation tier will also contain a WS-HumanTask client that will be responsible for all communication with the WS-HumanTask server.

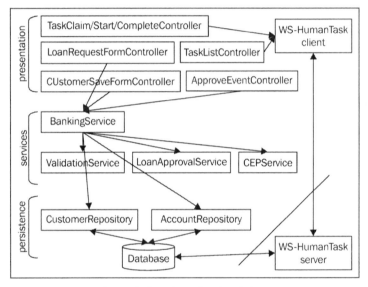

Figure 2: Sample application design

In the persistence layer only the customer repository will be normally used. It will persist the whole object graph (customer object, including address and customer's accounts). An `AccountRepository` repository is also shown. It can be used to persist accounts that have no customers (we won't use this repository in our examples).

Configuration

In the following sections we'll go through some configuration of the various layers. This is necessary before we can write some presentation code and deploy the web application.

JPA annotations for domain objects

We'll start with the persistence layer. All objects that are going to be persisted need to be mapped. This includes the `Customer`, `Address`, `Account`, and `Loan` objects. The validation message objects don't need to be mapped because they are not going to be persisted. Most of the time the default mapping settings will be used. The `@Entity` annotation will be used to declare that a class should be persistent, and we'll also explicitly specify the table name. Every entity needs an ID. A `uuid` field of type `String` will be added to every entity. The `@Id` annotation will declare that this `uuid` field is the ID of an entity. The customer's accounts will be mapped with a `@OneToMany` annotation, which declares that one customer can have many accounts. Let's now look at a mapping of the `Customer` class:

```
@Entity
@Table(name = "app_customer")
public class Customer implements Serializable {
  @Id private String uuid;
  private String firstName;
  private String lastName;
  private Date dateOfBirth;
  private Address address;

  @OneToMany(mappedBy="owner") private Set<Account> accounts;
  private String phoneNumber;
```

Code listing 1: Code extract from the Customer class (the Customer.java file)

Please consult the hibernate manual for advanced mapping (`http://docs.jboss.org/hibernate/orm/4.1/manual/en-US/html/`).

We're using `uuids` as IDs, because they are much easier to work with. We can assign them at object-creation time instead of object-persistence time as is the case with database-assigned IDs. The standard `java.util.UUID` class will be used to generate the `uuid` fields. We can define a factory for creating our domain objects that will automatically assign an `uuid` object to every new object:

```
public class DefaultBankingFactory implements BankingFactory {
  @Override
  public Customer createCustomer() {
    Customer customer = new Customer();
    customer.setUuid(UUID.randomUUID().toString());
    Set<Account> accounts = new HashSet<Account>();
    customer.setAccounts(accounts);
    return customer;
  }
}
```

Code listing 2: The DefaultBankingFactory class that follows the Factory design pattern (the DefaultBankingFactory.java file)

Our factory implements the `BankingFactory` interface, which contains all the factory methods such as `createCustomer`, `createAddress`, `createAccount`, and so on. These methods make sure that all created objects have their references correctly set, for example, the `createAccount` method takes a customer as an argument and adds the newly created account to the collection of the customer's accounts and also sets this customer as the owner of this account. This keeps the referential integrity intact. We can even declare a domain object's constructors as "package private" so that new instances can be created only through this factory.

JPA configuration

Next, we'll work on the JPA 2.0 provider configuration. This configuration also defines the classes that should be made persistent. All this information will be contained in a so-called `persistence-unit`. This configuration is as follows:

```
<?xml version="1.0" encoding="UTF-8" standalone="yes"?>
<persistence xmlns="http://java.sun.com/xml/ns/persistence"
  xmlns:xsi="http://www.w3.org/2001/XMLSchema-instance"
  xsi:schemaLocation="http://java.sun.com/xml/ns/persistence http://
java.sun.com/xml/ns/persistence/persistence_2_0.xsd"
  version="2.0">
  <persistence-unit name="droolsbook.persistence"
    transaction-type="RESOURCE_LOCAL">
    <provider>org.hibernate.ejb.HibernatePersistence</provider>
    <mapping-file>META-INF/Taskorm.xml</mapping-file>
    <mapping-file>META-INF/JBPMorm-JPA2.xml</mapping-file>
    <mapping-file>META-INF/ProcessInstanceInfoMapping-JPA2.xml</
mapping-file>
    <class>droolsbook.bank.model.Customer</class>
    <class>droolsbook.bank.model.Address</class>
    <class>droolsbook.bank.model.Account</class>
    <class>droolsbook.bank.model.LoanApprovalHolder</class>
    <class>org.drools.persistence.info.SessionInfo</class>
    <class>org.drools.persistence.info.WorkItemInfo</class>
    <class>org.jbpm.persistence.processinstance.ProcessInstanceInfo</
class>
    <class>org.jbpm.persistence.processinstance.
ProcessInstanceEventInfo</class>
    <class>org.jbpm.task.Attachment</class>
    <class>org.jbpm.task.Content</class>
    <class>org.jbpm.task.BooleanExpression</class>
```

```
        <class>org.jbpm.task.Comment</class>
        <class>org.jbpm.task.Deadline</class>
        <class>org.jbpm.task.Comment</class>
        <class>org.jbpm.task.Deadline</class>
        <class>org.jbpm.task.Delegation</class>
        <class>org.jbpm.task.Escalation</class>
        <class>org.jbpm.task.Group</class>
        <class>org.jbpm.task.I18NText</class>
        <class>org.jbpm.task.Notification</class>
        <class>org.jbpm.task.EmailNotification</class>
        <class>org.jbpm.task.EmailNotificationHeader</class>
        <class>org.jbpm.task.PeopleAssignments</class>
        <class>org.jbpm.task.Reassignment</class>
        <class>org.jbpm.task.Status</class>
        <class>org.jbpm.task.Task</class>
        <class>org.jbpm.task.TaskData</class>
        <class>org.jbpm.task.SubTasksStrategy</class>
        <class>org.jbpm.task.OnParentAbortAllSubTasksEndStrategy</class>
        <class>org.jbpm.task.OnAllSubTasksEndParentEndStrategy</class>
        <class>org.jbpm.task.User</class>
    </persistence-unit>
</persistence>
```

Code listing 3: JPA 2.0 configuration (the persistence.xml file)

All this information is stored in a file called `persistence.xml`. This file should be stored on the classpath under the `META-INF/` folder. The name of our persistence unit is `droolsbook.persistence`. The transaction type we're using is `RESOURCE_LOCAL`, which is enough since we'll be working with one resource only, that is, database. The `<provider>` element specifies the actual provider; in our case, it is `org.hibernate.ejb.HibernatePersistence`. Next, we load JPA mapping files as we've seen in *Chapter 8, Defining Processes with jBPM*, and tell the hibernate provider what additional files to look into `Customer`, `Address`, `Account`, and `LoanApprovalHolder`, including the standard jBPM classes for JPA annotations. All these classes are declared to be persistent.

Spring framework configuration

We'll configure the Spring framework. This can be done in various ways. XML is the most commonly used. The configuration will reside in three XML files. We'll start with a file called `applicationContext.xml` that will hold configuration related to the service layer (persistence, transactions, knowledge base configuration, and individual services configurations):

```xml
<?xml version="1.0" encoding="UTF-8"?>
<beans xmlns="http://www.springframework.org/schema/beans"
  xmlns:xsi="http://www.w3.org/2001/XMLSchema-instance"
  xmlns:aop="http://www.springframework.org/schema/aop"
  xmlns:tx="http://www.springframework.org/schema/tx"
  xmlns:drools="http://drools.org/schema/drools-spring"
  xsi:schemaLocation="
      http://www.springframework.org/schema/beans http://www.
springframework.org/schema/beans/spring-beans-3.2.xsd
      http://www.springframework.org/schema/tx http://www.
springframework.org/schema/tx/spring-tx-3.2.xsd
      http://www.springframework.org/schema/aop http://www.
springframework.org/schema/aop/spring-aop-3.2.xsd
      http://drools.org/schema/drools-spring http://drools.org/
schema/drools-spring.xsd">
```

Code listing 4: Extract from the Spring configuration (the applicationContext.xml file)

The various Spring configuration files will use more or less the same header (as seen in *Code listing 4*); they will differ only in the XSD namespaces used. The previous file declares four namespaces that will be used: `beans` as the default one, and `aop`, `tx`, and `drools` from the `drools-spring` module. For more information about the Spring namespaces please consult the Spring documentation (`http://static.springsource.org/spring/docs/3.2.x/spring-framework-reference/html/`).

We've already defined the persistence configuration in the `persistence.xml` file. These were just the very basics. We'll now enhance this configuration in Spring. The Spring configuration files will be the ultimate place where everything is configured. The following is the definition of an `entityManagerFactory` interface that will be responsible for creating `EntityManagers`, which will store our objects into the `dataSource` persistent store. The `entityManagerFactory` interface references the persistence-unit configuration named `droolsbook.persistence` defined earlier. It also specifies a bunch of properties that will be simply passed to the persistence provider:

```xml
<bean id="entityManagerFactory"
  class="org.springframework.orm.jpa.
LocalContainerEntityManagerFactoryBean">
```

```xml
    <property name="dataSource" ref="dataSource" />
    <property name="persistenceUnitName"
      value="droolsbook.persistence" />
    <property name="jpaPropertyMap" ref="jpaPropertyMap" />
</bean>

<bean id="jpaPropertyMap" class="org.springframework.beans.factory.
config.MapFactoryBean">
    <property name="sourceMap">
      <map>
        <entry key="hibernate.dialect"
          value="org.hibernate.dialect.H2Dialect" />
        <entry key="hibernate.show_sql" value="true" />
        <entry key="hibernate.format_sql" value="true" />
        <entry key="hibernate.use_sql_comments" value="true"/>
        <entry key="hibernate.hbm2ddl.auto"
          value="create-drop" />
      </map>
    </property>
</bean>

<bean id="dataSource" class="org.springframework.jdbc.datasource.
DriverManagerDataSource">
    <property name="driverClassName" value="org.h2.Driver" />
    <property name="url" value="jdbc:h2:droolsBookDatabaseH2" />
    <property name="username" value="sa" />
    <property name="password" value="sasa" />
</bean>
```

Code listing 5: Extract from the Spring configuration (the applicationContext.xml file),
entityManagerFactory bean definition

The entityManagerFactory interface is an instance of
LocalContainerEntityManagerFactoryBean. It will read the contents of the
persistence.xml file, and based on them and value-pairs in the jpaPropertyMapit
method, it will create the entityManagerFactory interface. The jpaPropertyMap
method is declared as a separate bean so that it can be easily reused later on.

The first JPA property, hibernate.dialect, specifies a class that represents the
dialect of our database. As you can see we'll use the H2 database (http://www.
h2database.com). It can run entirely in memory, which is ideal for our purposes.
The next few properties are self-explanatory. Then, we'll see the hibernate.
hbm2ddl.auto property, whose value is set to create-drop, which specifies that
we want to recreate the database (structure and data) every time we start the
application. Finally, we're also defining the data source itself.

The `applicationContext.xml` file also defines some beans that we'll use later:

```
<bean name="bankingFactory"
  class="droolsbook.bank.model.DefaultBankingFactory" />
<bean name="reportFactory"
  class="droolsbook.bank.service.impl.DefaultReportFactory" />

<bean class="org.springframework.orm.jpa.support.
PersistenceAnnotationBeanPostProcessor" />
<bean name="customerRepository"
  class="droolsbook.sampleApplication.repository.jpa.
JPACustomerRepository" />
```

Code listing 6: Extract from the Spring configuration (the applicationContext.xml file),
which shows various bean definitions

The first two are factories. We've already seen the `DefaultBankingFactory` interface in *Code listing 2* and the `DefaultReportFactory` interface was described in *Chapter 3, Validating*. The next two beans configure a customer repository. The `PersistenceAnnotationBeanPostProcessor` method is responsible for injecting `EntityManagers` into repositories. We'll see how it's done in the next few.

Web application setup

The core components of the persistence and service layers are there. We can start work on the presentation layer. We'll start with the `web.xml` web application configuration file. It is a standard web-app configuration file that defines the basics of a web application such as the name, welcome file list, and some initialization servlets. The initialization servlets will be called when we start the application in a server:

```
<?xml version="1.0" encoding="UTF-8"?>
<web-app xmlns="http://java.sun.com/xml/ns/javaee"
      xmlns:xsi="http://www.w3.org/2001/XMLSchema-instance"
      xsi:schemaLocation="http://java.sun.com/xml/ns/javaee http://
java.sun.com/xml/ns/javaee/web-app_3_0.xsd"
      version="3.0">
  <display-name>sampleApplication</display-name>
  <servlet>
    <servlet-name>sampleApplication</servlet-name>
    <servlet-class>
      org.springframework.web.servlet.DispatcherServlet</servlet-
class>
    <load-on-startup>1</load-on-startup>
  </servlet>
  <servlet-mapping>
```

```
      <servlet-name>sampleApplication</servlet-name>
      <url-pattern>*.htm</url-pattern>
   </servlet-mapping>
   <welcome-file-list>
      <welcome-file>index.jsp</welcome-file>
   </welcome-file-list>
</web-app>
```

Code listing 7: Web application configuration (the web.xml file)

As can be seen from the previous code, Spring's `DispatcherServlet` is loaded on the startup. This servlet by default looks for the `sampleApplication-servlet.xml` configuration file. We'll soon define this file. Just make sure it is placed in the `webRoot/ WEB-INF/` directory. The configuration also defines a servlet mapping for all resources ending with `.htm` to this `DispatcherServlet`. The welcome file is set to `index.jsp`. This file has to be present in the `webRoot/` directory. For testing purposes `index.jsp` will contain a listing of various entry points into the application (list all customers link, add customer link, request loan link, and so on).

As promised, the `sampleApplication-servlet.xml` Spring configuration file is given next. It will import the already defined `applicationContext.xml` configuration file.

Furthermore, the configuration file will define a standard "view resolver". This view resolver will be set to look for views in the `webRoot/WEB-INF/jsp/` directory — view as in **model-view-controller (MVC)** that can be found at `http://en.wikipedia.org/wiki/Model-view-controller`. This will help us to separate our controllers from the view implementations. We'll see how it works in a few sections:

```
<import resource="classpath:applicationContext.xml" />
<context:annotation-config />
<context:component-scan
   base-package="droolsbook.sampleApplication.web"/>
<bean id="viewResolver"
   class="org.springframework.web.servlet.view.
InternalResourceViewResolver">
   <property name="viewClass"
      value="org.springframework.web.servlet.view.JstlView" />
   <property name="prefix" value="/WEB-INF/jsp/" />
   <property name="suffix" value=".jsp" />
</bean>
```

Code listing 8: Extract from the Spring configuration (the sampleApplication-servlet.xml file), which is an initial configuration

The `import resource` elements are simply importing the contents of the resource into one big Spring application context. The `<context:annotation-config />` element activates Spring's annotation support for easier configuration of controllers. For the interface layer we'll use full Spring annotation auto-wiring, because the presentation layer changes more frequently. In the persistence and services layer, reliability is the most important, so we define the wiring ourselves. Then the `<context:component-scan ..>` element tells Springs to scan the given package for various components; in our case it is controllers, so we don't have to define them in the XML file.

Deployment

The deployment involves copying the contents of the `webRoot` directory into Tomcat's `webapps` directory and renaming it to `sampleApplication`. Then create a new lib directory under `webapps/sampleApplication/WEB-INF/` and copy all libraries that are on the classpath into this directory. All other resources on the classpath should go to the `webapps/sampleApplication/WEB-INF/classes` directory. That is all in terms of deployment. Tomcat can be started, and we can access the application at `http://localhost:8080/sampleApplication/`. The `index.jsp` welcome page should be displayed.

The deployment can be even easier if you have installed an Eclipse plugin called **Web Tools Platform (WTP)**. You can then create a dynamic web project; set up a server (Tomcat) and the WTP plugin will do the deployments for you. Note that the WTP plugin is a standard part of Eclipse IDE for Java EE Developers (`http://www.eclipse.org/downloads/`).

Repositories

The infrastructure for the persistence layer is almost set up (only the transaction setup is missing). We can implement the repositories that will be responsible for persistence and lookup of the domain objects. Let's start with the `JPACustomerRepository` interface. The `JPACustomerRepository` interface uses the `EntityManagerto` property to find a customer by the `customerUuid` field, find customers by the first and last name, and also to add a new customer or update an existing one:

```
@Repository
public class JPACustomerRepository implements
    CustomerRepository {

  @PersistenceContext
  private EntityManager em;
```

```
public Customer findCustomerByUuid(String customerUuid) {
  return em.find(Customer.class, customerUuid);
}

public List<Customer> findCustomerByName(String firstName,
    String lastName) {
  return em
      .createQuery(
          "from Customer as c where c.firstName = :first" +
          " and c.lastName = :last")
      .setParameter("first", firstName).setParameter("last",
          lastName).getResultList();
}

/**
 * stores new customer
 */
public void addCustomer(Customer customer) {
  em.persist(customer);
}

/**
 * stores existing customer
 */
public Customer updateCustomer(Customer customer) {
  return em.merge(customer);
}
```

Code listing 9: JPA customer repository implementation (the JPACustomerRepository.java file)

The first thing to note after looking at this code listing is that the
JPACustomerRepository interface has the @Repository annotation. This annotation
clarifies the role of this class. Next, the EntityManager property is declared with the
@PersistenceContext annotation. Thanks to this annotation, the EntityManager
property will be automatically injected by Spring. We neither have to write a setter
method for this property nor have to set the EntityManager property as a required
property in the applicationContext.xml file (see the last two lines of *Code listing 6*).

The methods from *Code listing 9* should be clear; they show a standard usage of
the JPA.

Please note that we won't be writing any unit or integration tests in this chapter due
to the length of this chapter. Normally, every piece of code should be tested.

Validation

In this section we'll describe the validation slice of this application (from bottom to top) that includes a definition of validation knowledge base, validation service, and the user interface.

We already have the validation service implementation. We'll now configure it with Spring. The first step is to build the validation knowledge base that will be used by the validation service. It will be managed by Spring like any other bean. The configuration goes into the `applicationContext.xml` file.

Fortunately, Drools does integrate with Spring out of the box. It provides its own namespace. The validation knowledge base can be defined like this:

```
<drools:kbase id="validationKnowledge">
  <drools:resources>
    <drools:resource type="DRL"
      source="classpath:validation.drl" />
  </drools:resources>
</drools:kbase>
```

Code listing 10: Extract from the Spring configuration (the applicationContext.xml file),
which is a validation knowledge base configuration

The `drools:kbase` element takes a list of resources such as `drools:resource`. Each resource needs at least a type and a source. Based on this it builds the validation knowledge base. Note that the `validation.drl` file needs to be on the classpath.

Next, we can define the validation service itself. The implementation comes from *Chapter 3, Validating* (for simplicity we'll use the stateless validation service `BankingValidationServiceImpl`). The service has two dependencies: `validationKnowledgeBase` and `reportFactory`. Both were defined earlier, so we'll just reference them.

```
<bean name="validationService"
  class="droolsbook.bank.service.impl.BankingValidationServiceImpl">
  <property name="reportFactory" ref="reportFactory" />
  <property name="knowledgeBase" ref="validationKnowledge"/>
</bean>
```

Code listing 11: Extract from the Spring configuration (the applicationContext.xml file),
which is a validationService bean definition

The `validationService` bean definition is straightforward and is one bean with two properties. This service is now ready to be used.

Services

Now that we have defined repositories and validation services, we can implement the first part of our `BankingService` from *Figure 2*; to be more specific, methods for adding a new customer and saving an existing customer will be implemented. These methods will validate the customer with the validation service, and if everything goes well, the customer will be persisted using the repository:

```
/**
 * validates and stores a new customer
 */
public void add(Customer customer) {
  validate(customer);
  customerRepository.addCustomer(customer);
}

/**
 * validates and stores an existing customer
 */
public void save(Customer customer) {
  validate(customer);
  customerRepository.updateCustomer(customer);
}

/**
 * validates customer,
 * @throws ValidationException if there are any errors
 */
private void validate(Customer customer) {
  ValidationReport report = validationService
      .validate(customer);
  if (!report.getMessagesByType(Type.ERROR).isEmpty()) {
    throw new ValidationException(report);
  }
}
```

Code listing 12: Code extract from the BankingServiceImpl.java file

As can be seen in the previous code listing, both the `add` and `save` methods use a `validate` helper method. This method calls the validation service, and if the returned `ValidationReport` definition contains some messages of type `ERROR`, a `ValidationException` exception is thrown. The use of exceptions in this case allows us to deal only with the happy path and worry about the exceptional cases in some exception handler.

If the validation passes, the customer is added/updated with the `customerRepository` interface.

Before we'll be able to use this service in the presentation layer, we have to define it as a Spring bean. The banking service will have several dependencies. We already know that we need the `customerRepository` and `validationService` interfaces. For the additional functionality we'll also need the `aloanApprovalService` and `cepService` interfaces:

```
<bean name="bankingService"
  class="droolsbook.bank.service.impl.BankingServiceImpl">
  <property name="customerRepository"
    ref="customerRepository" />
  <property name="validationService"
    ref="validationService" />
  <property name="loanApprovalService"
    ref="loanApprovalService" />
  <property name="cepService" ref="cepService" />
</bean>
```

Code listing 13: Extract from the Spring configuration (the applicationContext.xml file), which is a bankingService bean definition

Simply add this bean definition to the `applicationContext.xml` file.

Transactions

The persistence of a valid customer is almost complete. The final missing piece from the service layer perspective are transactions. We have to make sure that the system remains consistent under all circumstances (for example, if the server crashes while saving the customer record to the database, the database might get only a partial state).

Luckily with Spring, this can be implemented very easily, and it is just a matter of configuration.

We'll now add the transaction configuration into the `applicationContext.xml` file. It consists of three parts: a transaction manager that manages the transactional resources (in our case the database), then aspect-oriented configuration, which specifies the boundaries of the transaction, and last is the transaction advice, which configures various attributes of a transaction. More information can be found in the Spring documentation:

```
<bean id="transactionManager"
  class="org.springframework.orm.jpa.JpaTransactionManager">
  <property name="entityManagerFactory"
```

```
      ref="entityManagerFactory" />
  </bean>

  <aop:config>
    <aop:pointcut id="bankingServiceMethods"
      expression="execution(*
        droolsbook.bank.service.BankingService.*(..))" />
    <aop:advisor advice-ref="transactionAdvice"
      pointcut-ref="bankingServiceMethods" />
  </aop:config>

  <tx:advice id="transactionAdvice"
    transaction-manager="transactionManager">
    <tx:attributes>
      <tx:method name="*" rollback-for="Exception" />
    </tx:attributes>
  </tx:advice>
```

*Code listing 14: Extract from the Spring configuration (the applicationContext.xml file),
which is a transaction configuration*

We've chosen the `JpaTransactionManager` property as our transaction manager implementation since we'll be using only local transactions. The transactions will automatically begin whenever any method on the `BankingService` interface is executed (`* droolsbook.bank.service.BankingService.*(..)`). Note that we're referring to the `BankingService` interface rather than implementation (this is needed for Spring to correctly create a transactional proxy).

By default the transaction propagation is set to `REQUIRED`. A transaction always needs to be present, whether it is already running one or a new one has to be created. The configuration specifies that all methods will run under a transaction. Whenever an exception is thrown from the banking service methods, the transaction will be automatically rolled back.

Presentation layer

We'll now write a web form for adding new customers into the system. For simplicity, our customers can define just the first name, last name, and a phone number. This form will be stored in a file called `customerSave.jsp`withing in the `webRoot/WEB-INF/jsp/` folder. This JSP will be also capable of displaying any errors and warnings that occurred while the new customer was saved into the system:

```
<%@ taglib prefix="c" uri="http://java.sun.com/jsp/jstl/core"%>
<%@ taglib prefix="fmt" uri="http://java.sun.com/jsp/jstl/fmt"%>
```

```
<%@ taglib prefix="form" uri="http://www.springframework.org/tags/
form"%>
<html><head>
<title><fmt:message key="title" /></title>
<style>
.error {
 color: red;
}
</style></head>
<body><h1><fmt:message key="customerSave.heading" /></h1>
<form:form modelAttribute="customer" method="post">
  <table width="100%" bgcolor="f8f8ff" border="0"
    cellspacing="0" cellpadding="5">
    <c:forEach items="${errors}" var="error">
      <span class="error"><c:out value="${error.type}"/>:
      <c:out value="${error.messageKey}"/></span><br/>
    </c:forEach>
    <c:forEach items="${warnings}" var="warning">
      <c:out value="${warning.type}"/>
      <c:out value="${warning.messageKey}"/><br/>
    </c:forEach>
    <tr>
      <td align="right">First name:</td>
      <td><form:input path="firstName" /></td>
    </tr>
    <tr>
      <td align="right">Last name:</td>
      <td><form:input path="lastName" /></td>
    </tr>
    <tr>
      <td align="right">Phone number:</td>
      <td><form:input path="phoneNumber" /></td>
      </tr>
  </table>
  <br>
  <input type="submit" align="center" value="Execute">
</form:form>
<a href="<c:url value="index.jsp"/>">Home</a>
</body></html>
```

Code listing 15: Customer save form (the customerSave.jsp file)

The first lines of this JSP from the previous code listing are declaring the tag libraries that will be used. It is the standard `core` library, the `fmt` library, and the Spring's `form` tag library.

Next, `customerSave.jsp` defines the `<form:form method="post"
modelAttribute="customer">` form. Please notice the `modelAttribute` property,
which contains the name of the attribute that the controller will be working with. The
next two `forEach` elements display error and warning messages. Next, we can see
the three input fields, namely `firstName`, `lastName`, and `phoneNumber`; they contain
the form body that will be sent when the form is submitted.

Localized messages

The JSP uses localized messages that are displayed by the standard `<fmt:message
key="someKeyName" />` tag. `someKeyName` must be present in a properties file that
will call `messages.properties` that must be on the classpath. Our file might look
like this:

```
title=SampleApplication
customerSave.heading=Save Customer
```

Code listing 16: Localized messages (the messages.properties file)

We have to tell Spring about this file. This can be done with the following
bean configuration. It'll define a `messageSource` bean that will be of type
`ResourceBundleMessageSource`. It's `baseName` property will be set to `messages`,
which is the name of our localized messages file:

```
<bean id="messageSource"
  class="org.springframework.context.support.
ResourceBundleMessageSource">
  <property name="basename" value="messages" />
</bean>
```

*Code listing 17: Extract from the Spring configuration (the sampleApplication-servlet.xml file),
which is the messageSource bean definition*

Customer save form controller

We'll now write a controller for this form. The controller will be accessible under the
`/customerSave.htm` URL. This controller will define a few methods; one that will be
called in case of a `GET HTTP` request (when the form is initially displayed), one for a
`POST HTTP` request (it will be called when the form is submitted), and one method for
creating the model attribute. When the form is submitted and there are no errors, the
controller will use the `bankingService` and `bankingFactory` beans to create a new
customer and add this customer into the system. The user will then be redirected to
the index page. In the case of errors, the user will go back to repair the form:

```
@Controller
@RequestMapping("/customerSave.htm")
```

```
public class CustomerSaveFormController {
  @Autowired
  private BankingService bankingService;
  @Autowired
  private BankingFactory bankingFactory;

  @RequestMapping(method=RequestMethod.POST)
  public String customerSave(
      @ModelAttribute Customer customer, Model model) {
    try {
      bankingService.add(customer);
      return "redirect:index.jsp";
    } catch (ValidationException e) {
      ValidationReport report = e.getValidationReport();
      model.addAttribute("errors", report.getMessagesByType(
          Message.Type.ERROR));
      model.addAttribute("warnings", report
          .getMessagesByType(Message.Type.WARNING));
      return "customerSave";
    }
  }

  @RequestMapping(method=RequestMethod.GET)
  public void newForm() {
  }

  @ModelAttribute("customer")
  public Customer createCustomer() {
    return bankingFactory.createCustomer();
  }
}
```

Code listing 18: Controller for processing the new customer form (the CustomerSaveFormController.java file)

When the user enters the /customerSave.htm URL, Spring will automatically call the newForm method, because it is mapped with RequestMethod.GET; it will then forward the user to the view. After the view translation, this becomes webRoot/WEB-INF/jsp/customerSave.jsp.

Please note that the bankingService and bankingFactory beans are declared with the @Autowired annotations. This means that Spring will automatically set these properties when this controller is created. We also don't have to create setters for these properties.

If the `Customer` object is not valid, a `ValidationException` exception is thrown by the `bankingService` bean. `CustomerSaveFormController` handles this case with a `try-catch` block. The validation report is extracted from the exception and the model (as in MVC) is updated with errors and warnings from the report. The control flow is then forwarded back to the form view return `customerSave`.

The `createCustomer` method will be called when a user displays the customer save form. In our case it creates the `Customer` object itself. This is a shortcut, and in real application we'd create something such as a `CustomerFormdata` transfer object (DTO) that will hold all data needed by the view, and then in the controller we'd create a normal `Customer` object from this `CustomerForm`.

We can now deploy the application and access it on `http://localhost:8080/sampleApplication/customerSave.htm`. After entering a first name and a last name and leaving the phone number field blank, we should get the following response:

Figure 3: Save Customer form with validation messages

The screen is informing us that the phone number is missing (error) and that the address is required (warning). Since we're not dealing with addresses, the warning message is expected. After entering the phone number, the customer will be successfully stored in the database and we'll be redirected to the `index.jsp` page.

As you can see from *Figure 3*, the screen doesn't actually display the messages themselves but only the message key names. This key can now be mapped to the real message and the message can even be localized based on the user's preferred language. To do this we'll now replace the standard output tag `<c:out value="${error.messageKey}"/>` (in *Code listing 15*) with its localized version, `<fmt:message key="${error.messageKey}"/>`. We can do this for both error and warning messages. Then, it is a matter of defining these messages. Add the following to the `messages.properties` file:

```
phoneNumberRequired=Customer phone number is required.
addressRequired=Customer address is required.
```

Code listing 19. Extract from the messages.properties file

If we now reload the screen, full localized messages should be displayed.

The Complex Event Processing service

We'll now integrate the CEP service into the banking service. The CEP service basically needs all kind of events so that it can make complex decisions. One such event is a customer-created event or a customer-updated event. The CEP service has one `notify` method that takes an event. The `add` and `save` methods of `bankingService` can be modified to create these events and send them to the `cepService` interface. By adding `cepService.notify(new CustomerCreatedEvent(customer))` at the end of these methods, we'll create an event referencing the current customer and send it into the `cepService` interface (this is for the `add` method, and the `save` method will create a new instance of `CustomerUpdatedEvent` instead). The CEP service contains a rule session that is maintained throughout the lifetime of this service as we've discussed in *Chapter 7, Complex Event Processing*.

Loan approval

We'll now create screens for the loan approval process (another vertical slice of the application). This consists of a loan request form, task list screen, task manipulation (claim a task, start a task, complete a task), and final supervisor's approval. In this case we'll do a top-down approach starting with the presentation layer.

The Loan Request form

The following screenshot shows the **Loan Request** form:

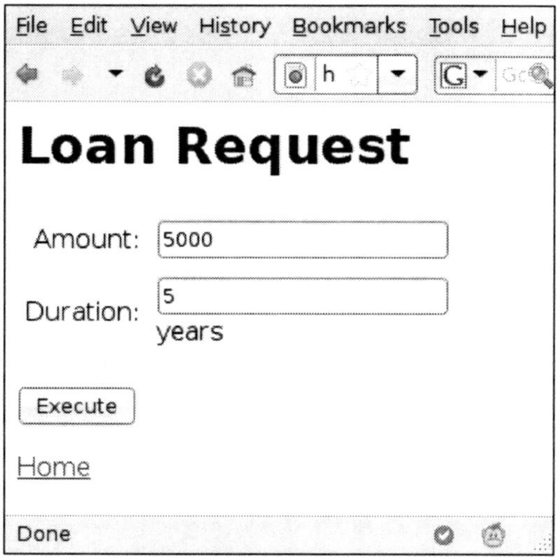

Figure 4: The Loan Request form

Let's start with the implementation of the `loanRequest.jsp` file, which will display the loan request form. We can copy the `customerSave.jsp` file and just replace the form section with the following:

```
<form:form method="post" modelAttribute="loanRequest">
  <table width="100%" bgcolor="f8f8ff" border="0"
    cellspacing="0" cellpadding="5">
    <tr>
      <td align="right">Amount:</td>
      <td><form:input path="amount" /></td>
    </tr>
    <tr>
      <td align="right">Duration:</td>
      <td><form:input path="durationYears" /> years</td>
    </tr>
  </table>
  <br>
  <input type="submit" align="center" value="Execute">
</form:form>
```

Code listing 20: Extract from the loan request form (the loanRequest.jsp file)

This form is very similar to our earlier form. In this case the form body contains the loan amount and loan duration.

Upon submission, `LoanRequestFormController` will be responsible for starting the loan approval process. This controller can be defined like this:

```
@Controller
@RequestMapping("/loanRequest.htm")
public class LoanRequestFormController {
  @Autowired
  private BankingFactory bankingFactory;
  @Autowired
  private BankingService bankingService;
  @Autowired
  private WebSessionUtils webSessionUtils;

  @RequestMapping(method = RequestMethod.POST)
  public String loanRequest(@ModelAttribute Loan loanRequest,
      Model model) {
    bankingService.requestLoan(loanRequest,
        webSessionUtils.getCustomer());
    return "redirect:customerList.htm";
  }

  @RequestMapping(method = RequestMethod.GET)
  public void newForm() {
  }

  @ModelAttribute("loanRequest")
  public Loan createLoanRequest() {
    return bankingFactory.createLoan();
  }
}
```

Code listing 21: Controller for processing the loan request form (the LoanRequestFormController.java file)

When user submits the form, the controller calls the `bankingService.requestLoan(loan, customer)` method. The `loan` object is prepopulated with values entered by the user. The customer represents the currently logged-in user. We won't go into detail of how to get this user. The user is then redirected to the `customerList` view.

The `bankingService.requestLoan` method is shown in the following code listing. It simply delegates to the `loadApprovalService` method:

```
@Override
public void requestLoan(Loan loan, Customer customer) {
  loanApprovalService.requestLoan(loan, customer);
}
```

Code listing 22: Method for requesting a loan (the BankingServiceImpl.java file)

Process persistence

As we already know, the loan approval process can take hours, days, or even months to finish. It is, therefore, important to persist loan approval processes rather than keep them in memory all the time.

We'll use a special persistent knowledge session implementation called `CommandBasedStatefulKnowledgeSession`. It acts like a standard `StatefulKnowledgeSession`; however, with each method call, it persists its state. We just have to remember `sessionId` and we can recreate the session at any stage.

If we look under the hood of this session implementation, we'd see that each of its methods creates a command and executes it with a command service called `org.drools.command.SingleSessionCommandService`.

org.drools.persistence.SingleSessionCommandService

This is a command service implementation that uses JPA to persist the session's state. It is a `comesformdrools-persistence-jpa` module. It has two sets of constructors: one that is used to create a new knowledge session and one for loading an existing persisted knowledge session by `sessionId`. It executes method and then takes a command and executes it on the knowledge session.

This command service needs an `EntityManager` property to do the actual persistence and a transaction manager. This service can work with JTA transactions, as well as local transactions, which we'll use.

Please note that when using the `SingleSessionCommandService` interface, the default implementations of `processInstanceManagerFactory`, `workItemManagerFactory`, and `processSignalManagerFactory` need to be overwritten with their "persistence aware" counterparts (for example, `JPAWorkItemManagerFactory`). For example, imagine a situation when the `workItemManager` property is notified that `workItem` has been completed. Since this `workItemManager` property is different to the one that created this `workItem`, `workItem` may not be in memory and must be loaded first from the persistent storage.

We'll now create a new class that will abstract this session persistence logic. We'll call it JPAKnowledgeSessionTemplate. It will have two methods: one that will deal with new sessions and one that will deal with existing sessions. These methods will take a callback object, which will encapsulate the logic that should be performed with the session. The interface of the KnowledgeSessionCallback callback is as follows:

```
/**
 * callback interface for knowledge session logic. Used with
 * JPAKnowledgeSessionTemplate's doWith* methods.
 */
public interface KnowledgeSessionCallback {

  /**
   * Gets called by the JPAKnowledgeSessionTemplate with a
   * persistable session
   * @param session
   */
  public void execute(StatefulKnowledgeSession session);

}
```

Code listing 23: The KnowledgeSessionCallback interface (the KnowledgeSessionCallback.java file)

This template will allow us to abstract away common code that needs to be performed with the persisted session such as setting the work item handlers and properly disposing the session and the human task handler. We can start with the implementation of JPAKnowledgeSessionTemplate. We will use the JPAKnowledgeService interface, which is a helper class provided by Drools that sets up the CommandBasedStatefulKnowledgeSession knowledge session:

```
/**
 * performs actions with new or persisted knowledge sessions
 */
public class JPAKnowledgeSessionTemplate {
  @PersistenceContext
  private EntityManager em;
  private AbstractPlatformTransactionManager
    transactionManager;

  private KnowledgeBase knowledgeBase;
  private Environment environment;

  private WorkItemHandler emailHandler;
  private WorkItemHandler transferFundsHandler;
  private TaskService localTaskService;
```

```java
public void init() {
  environment = EnvironmentFactory.newEnvironment();
  environment
      .set(EnvironmentName.TRANSACTION_MANAGER,
          new DroolsSpringTransactionManager(
              transactionManager));
  environment.set(
      EnvironmentName.PERSISTENCE_CONTEXT_MANAGER,
      new MapProcessPersistenceContextManager(
          new JpaProcessPersistenceContext(em)));
  environment.set(
      EnvironmentName.OBJECT_MARSHALLING_STRATEGIES,
      new ObjectMarshallingStrategy[] { MarshallerFactory
          .newSerializeMarshallingStrategy() });
}


/**
 * performs action on a new persistable knowledge session
 * @param action to perform
 */
public void doWithNewSession(KnowledgeSessionCallback
    action) {
  StatefulKnowledgeSession session = JPAKnowledgeService
      .newStatefulKnowledgeSession(knowledgeBase, null,
          environment);
  execute(action, session);
}


/**
 * performs action on existing persisted knowledge session
 * @param sessionId primary key of persisted session
 * @param action to perform
 */
public void doWithLoadedSession(int sessionId,
    KnowledgeSessionCallback action) {
  StatefulKnowledgeSession session = JPAKnowledgeService
      .loadStatefulKnowledgeSession(sessionId,
          knowledgeBase, null, environment);
  execute(action, session);
}

private void execute(KnowledgeSessionCallback action,
    StatefulKnowledgeSession session) {
  LocalHTWorkItemHandler hTHandler =
```

```
        new LocalHTWorkItemHandler(localTaskService, session,
            true);
    try {
      registerWorkItemHandlers(session, hTHandler);
      action.execute(session);
    } finally {
      TransactionSynchronizationManager
          .registerSynchronization(new
              SessionCleanupTransactionSynchronisation(
              session, hTHandler));
    }
  }
}

/**
 * helper method for registering work item handlers
 * (they are not persisted)
 */
private void registerWorkItemHandlers(
    StatefulKnowledgeSession session,
    LocalHTWorkItemHandler hTHandler) {
  WorkItemManager manager = session.getWorkItemManager();
  hTHandler.connect();
  manager.registerWorkItemHandler("Human Task", hTHandler);
  manager.registerWorkItemHandler("Email", emailHandler);
  manager.registerWorkItemHandler("Transfer Funds",
      transferFundsHandler);
}
```

*Code listing 24: Template for working with a persistent StatefulKnowledgeSession
(the JPAKnowledgeSessionTemplate.java file)*

The JPAKnowledgeService interface has two methods:
newStatefulKnowledgeSession and loadStatefulKnowledgeSession. They both
take the knowledge base, knowledge session configuration (in our case null), and
environment. The latter method also takes sessionId.

As we can see, the environment is initialized in the init method with:

- **Transaction manager**: We're wrapping our previously defined transaction
  manager into DroolsSpringTransactionManager. It is needed if we want
  to use local transactions.

- **Persistence context manager**: We're wrapping the JPA entity manager into
  jBPM's JpaProcessPersistenceContext, which is then wrapped into
  MapProcessPersistenceContextManager. This is a setup that will work
  with local transactions.

- **Object marshalling strategies**: In our case we use the serialize marshalling
  strategy. We want to do full session serialization.

Both the doWith* methods use the JPAKnowledgeService interface to get the session and then call the execute method, passing in the callback and the session. The execute method does all the work. First, it instantiates the LocalHTWorkItemHandler human task handler. This is an implementation that works with local transactions. The constructor takes a localTaskService interface, session, and a Boolean parameter that indicates that this human task handler cannot be reused for other sessions. Then the execute method calls the registerWorkItemHandlers method, which registers all work item handlers used in our process. Then the execute method performs the logic defined by the callback, and finally, it disposes the session.

As can be seen in the final block, instead of simply calling the session. dispose() method, we're deferring this call after the transaction is completed via SessionCleanupTransactionSynchronisation. This is needed because when the transaction commits (at the end of some BankingServicemethodcall), hibernate tries to write everything to the database and it would deal with a disposed knowledge session, which is illegal:

```
public class SessionCleanupTransactionSynchronisation extends
    TransactionSynchronizationAdapter {
  private StatefulKnowledgeSession session;
  private LocalHTWorkItemHandler hTHandler;

  public SessionCleanupTransactionSynchronisation(
      StatefulKnowledgeSession session, LocalHTWorkItemHandler
hTHandler) {
    this.session = session;
    this.hTHandler = hTHandler;
  }

  @Override
  public void afterCompletion(int status) {
    // note: not interested in rollback
    try {
      hTHandler.dispose();
    } catch (Exception e) {
      e.printStackTrace();
    }
    session.dispose();
  }
}
```

Code listing 25: After transaction completion session disposal (the SessionCleanupTransactionSynchronisation.java file)

Also, please note that we also need to dispose the human task handler, otherwise it might get called with a disposed session, which would cause an error.

Now, we can define the `JPAKnowledgeSessionTemplate` class in Spring as follows:

```
<bean id="knowledgeSessionTemplate" init-method="init"
  class="droolsbook.org.drools.persistence.
JPAKnowledgeSessionTemplate" >
  <property name="knowledgeBase" ref="loanApprovalKnowledge"/>
  <property name="emailHandler" ref="emailWorkItemHandler"/>
  <property name="transferFundsHandler"
    ref="transferFundsWorkItemHandler"/>
  <property name="transactionManager"
    ref="transactionManager" />
  <property name="taskService" ref="localTaskService" />
</bean>
```

Code listing 26: The knowledgeSessionTemplate Spring bean definition (the applicationContext.xml file)

Configurations of the e-mail and transfer funds work item handlers won't be shown. The Spring configuration for the `localTaskService` bean is as follows:

```
<bean id="localTaskService"
  class="org.jbpm.task.service.local.LocalTaskService"
  depends-on="springTaskSessionFactory" >
  <constructor-arg ref="taskService" />
</bean>

<bean id="taskService"
  class="org.jbpm.task.service.TaskService" >
  <property name="systemEventListener" >
    <bean class="org.drools.SystemEventListenerFactory"
      factory-method="getSystemEventListener" />
  </property>
</bean>

<bean id="springTaskSessionFactory" class="org.jbpm.task.service.
persistence.TaskSessionSpringFactoryImpl"
    init-method="initialize" depends-on="taskService" >
  <property name="entityManager" >
    <bean class="org.springframework.orm.jpa.support.
SharedEntityManagerBean">
      <property name="entityManagerFactory"
        ref="entityManagerFactory"/>
    </bean>
```

```
    </property>
    <property name="transactionManager" >
      <bean class="org.drools.container.spring.beans.persistence.
HumanTaskSpringTransactionManager">
        <constructor-arg ref="transactionManager" />
      </bean>
    </property>
    <property name="useJTA" value="false" />
    <property name="taskService" ref="taskService" />
  </bean>
```

Code listing 27: Spring configuration of the jBPM task service (the applicationContext.xml file)

As we already know, the `LocalTaskService` bean is a wrapper around the actual `TaskService` bean that supports local transactions.

Looking at the Spring wiring from the previous code listing, you may have noticed that this time the `TaskService` bean (it was shown in *Chapter 8, Defining Processes with jBPM*) is missing the entity manager property. Actually, this property will be secretly set as part of the `initialize` method of the `springTaskSessionFactory` bean. This is to avoid circular dependency (the `springTaskSessionFactory` bean depends on the `taskService` bean itself).

The `springTaskSessionFactory` bean is responsible for creating all the internal instances in human task that deal with transactions and persistence context management. It needs a transaction manager wrapped in a `HumanTaskSpringTransactionManager` property, the `taskService` bean, and an entity manager. The entity manager is provided by Spring's `SharedEntityManagerBean`.

With this setup done, we can now implement the loan approval service that will be a slightly modified version of what we've done in *Chapter 8, Defining Processes with jBPM*. We'll use the session template to work with a new knowledge session and `LoanApprovalHolder` to keep track of the current request. The `holder` class will contain the customer requesting the loan, `sessionId`, and `processInstanceId`. The `processInstanceId` value will be needed for sending the final loan approval event:

```
    public LoanApprovalHolder requestLoan(final Loan loan,
        final Customer customer) {
      final LoanApprovalHolder holder =new LoanApprovalHolder();
      sessionTemplate
        .doWithNewSession(new KnowledgeSessionCallback() {
          @Override
          public void execute(StatefulKnowledgeSession session){
```

```
            Map<String, Object> parameterMap =
                new HashMap<String, Object>();
            parameterMap.put("loanSourceAccount",
                loanSourceAccount);
            parameterMap.put("customer", customer);
            parameterMap.put("loan", loan);
            session.insert(loan);
            session.insert(customer);
            ProcessInstance processInstance = session
                .startProcess("loanApproval", parameterMap);

            holder.setCustomer(customer);
            holder.setSessionId(session.getId());
            holder.setProcessInstanceId(processInstance
                .getId());
            em.persist(holder);

            session.insert(processInstance);
            session.fireAllRules();
        }
    });
    return holder;
}
```

Code listing 28: Implementation of the requestLoan method (the LoanApprovalServiceImpl.java file)

A new persistent session is created, the `loan` and the customer instances are inserted into the session, the process is started, the `sessionId` and `processInstanceId` values are set, and the rules are fired.

The templating approach guarantees that this logic gets called with a newly created, fully setup persistent knowledge session, which will be properly disposed at the end of this call.

Task list

Once the loan is successfully requested, the bank employees can start to work on the created task. We'll now create a screen that will list all available tasks. The screen will look as follows:

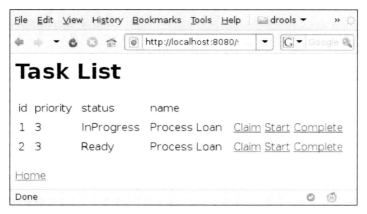

Figure 5: Task list screen

The task list screen displays a table of all available tasks for a user (bank employee). We can see two tasks in the screenshot. Some important properties of the tasks are displayed, such as the task ID, its priority, status, and name. One task is in progress and the other task is ready. The user can claim, start, or complete a task.

One possible improvement is that once the user claims a task, the **Claim** link should be disabled or ideally not shown (this won't be implemented).

This task list screen will be implemented in a file called `taskList.jsp`. The following code extract shows the core of this page, that is, a task list table. This JSP will operate on collection of the `TaskSummary` objects, which will be accessible under bean tasks. The `TaskSummary` object comes from the human task module. Let's now look at the JSP itself:

```
<table width="100%" bgcolor="f8f8ff" border="0"
 cellspacing="0" cellpadding="5">
  <tr>
    <td>id</td><td>priority</td><td>status</td><td>name</td>
  </tr>
  <c:forEach items="${tasks}" var="task">
  <tr>
    <td><c:out value="${task.id}"/></td>
```

```
        <td><c:out value="${task.priority}"/></td>
        <td><c:out value="${task.status}"/> </td>
        <td><c:out value="${task.name}"/></td>
        <td>
           <a href="<c:url value="taskClaim.htm"><c:param
            name="taskId" value="${task.id}"/></c:url>">Claim</a>
           <a href="<c:url value="taskStart.htm"><c:param
            name="taskId" value="${task.id}"/></c:url>">Start</a>
           <a href="<c:url value="taskComplete.htm"><c:param
            name="taskId" value="${task.id}"/></c:url>"
            >Complete</a>
        </td>
      </tr>
      </c:forEach>
   </table>
```

Code listing 29: Extract from the task list JSP (the taskList.jsp file)

As we've discussed, `taskList.jsp` iterates over tasks in the `${tasks}` collection and displays some important information for each task. Worth noting is that the three commands (claim, start, complete) are using `taskId` as an argument. The controllers that these commands will map to will need this ID to identify a task.

The controller implementation is as follows.

```
    @Controller
    public class TaskListController {
       @Autowired
       private TaskService localTaskService;
       @Autowired
       private WebSessionUtils webSessionUtils;

       @RequestMapping("/taskList.htm")
       public String taskList(Model model) {
         User user = webSessionUtils.getUser();
         List<TaskSummary> tasks = localTaskService
             .getTasksAssignedAsPotentialOwner(user.getUserId(),
                 user.getLanguage());
         model.addAttribute("tasks", tasks);
         return "taskList";
       }
    }
```

Code listing 30: Controller for displaying a task list (the TaskListController.java file)

This controller requires two properties: `org.jbpm.task.TaskService` and `WebSessionUtils`. The first one was already shown in *Chapter 8*, *Defining Processes with jBPM*. It can be used to interact with the human tasks. Please note that this is not the `org.jbpm.task.service.TaskService` class; instead, Spring will inject the `localTaskService` bean into this property that we've defined earlier.

The next property, `webSessionUtils`, is a utility class that contains various convenience methods, such as a method for getting the current authenticated user. Implementation of this utility class is out of the scope of this book. We'll use the user's ID and locale for getting the task list. All the controller's logic is contained within the `taskList` method. It uses the `localTaskService` bean to get all available tasks by calling the `getTasksAssignedAsPotentialOwner` method. Finally, a model is updated that contains these tasks and the user is forwarded to the `taskList` view.

Transactions

So far we've only set up transactions around the `BankingService` bean. However, when displaying the task list, we're only using the `TaskService` (the `localTaskService` Spring bean). We'll also need to set up transactions around the `TaskService` bean. Again, this is only a Spring configuration change. Just modify the transaction setup in `applicationContext.xml`. Simply add this to the `aop:config` section:

```
<aop:pointcut id="localTaskServiceMethods"
    expression="execution(*
    org.jbpm.task.TaskService.*(..))" />

<aop:advisor advice-ref="transactionAdvice"
    pointcut-ref="localTaskServiceMethods" />
```

Code listing 31: Extract from the aop:config section (the applicationContext.xml file)

Note that the order is important. Put `pointcut` after our first `pointcut` and `advisor` after our first `advisor`.

Working on a task

By clicking on the **Claim/Start/Complete** link, a user can claim/start/complete a task (for simplicity we're not implementing other actions such as suspend or skip). Let's look in more detail at the claim action. The `taskClaim` method of `TaskClaimController` implementation is as follows. This controller uses the `bankingService` and `webSessionUtils` autowired Spring beans. This controller will read `taskId` from the request as a parameter and will use the `bankingService` bean to claim the task with this ID for the current user, `bankingService.claim(taskId, user.getUserId())`:

```
/**
 * claims specified task for the current user
 */
@RequestMapping("/taskClaim.htm")
public String taskClaim(Long taskId) {
  User user = webSessionUtils.getUser();
  bankingService.claim(taskId, user.getUserId());
  return "redirect:taskList.htm";
}
```

Code listing 32: The taskClaim method of a controller for claiming a task (the TaskClaimController.java file)

Note that the implementation of the `claim` method is not shown, but the `bankingService` bean simply delegates to the `loanApprovalService` bean, which in turn delegates to the `claim` method of `localTaskService`.

Similarly, we can implement controllers for the start and complete actions.

Problem 1 – joinTransaction

After we've implemented all three controllers (start, claim, and complete), we can deploy and run this application. However, if we do it as soon as we submit the loan request form, the application will fail with the following exception:

```
java.lang.IllegalStateException: Not allowed to join transaction on
shared EntityManager - use Spring transactions or EJB CMT instead
```

It seems that Drools is trying call `joinTransaction` on a shared entity manager. Since we're using local transactions, we can simply disregard the `joinTransaction` call. There will always be only one local transaction anyway. By default Drools is designed to work in a JTA environment, which is not our case. To work around this, we'll create our own persistence context manager, `LocalJpaProcessPersistenceContext`, that will extend the one provided by Drools and will ignore the `joinTransaction` calls:

```
private static class LocalJpaProcessPersistenceContext
    extends JpaProcessPersistenceContext {
  public LocalJpaProcessPersistenceContext(EntityManager em) {
    super(em);
  }

  @Override
  public void joinTransaction() {
    // ignore this call for non JTA environment
  }
}
```

Code listing 33: Custom persistence context manager that ignores the joinTransaction calls
(the JPAKnowledgeSessionTemplate.java file)

We'll then modify the `init` method of `JPAKnowledgeSessionTemplate` to use our custom persistence context manager:

```
environment.set(
    EnvironmentName.PERSISTENCE_CONTEXT_MANAGER,
    new MapProcessPersistenceContextManager(
        new LocalJpaProcessPersistenceContext(em)));
```

Code listing 34: Updated init method that shows usage of our custom persistence context manager
(the JPAKnowledgeSessionTemplate.java file)

When we try to submit the loan request form, it should complete successfully. A new issue has been raised with the jBPM team to fix this, so visit `https://issues.jboss.org/browse/JBPM-3926`.

Problem 2 – processing does not continue

However, we're not done yet. We can claim and also start the human task, but if we try to complete our loan approval process, it actually won't continue. You can see this, for example, by adding `DebugProcessEventListener` into the session and watching for the `ProcessNodeTriggeredEvent` events. The issue here is that when the `complete` method of `localTaskService` executes, our knowledge session is not resident in memory and so cannot be notified that a human task has been completed. To fix this we can simply use `JPAKnowledgeSessionTemplate` and perform the task completion inside the callback:

```
@Override
public void complete(final long taskId,final String userId){
   Task task = localTaskService.getTask(taskId);
   sessionTemplate.doWithLoadedSession(task.getTaskData()
     .getProcessSessionId(),
     new KnowledgeSessionCallback() {
       @Override
       public void execute(StatefulKnowledgeSession session){
         localTaskService.complete(taskId, userId, null);
       }
     });
}
```

Code listing 35: Updated complete method with loaded session (the LoanApprovalServiceImpl.java file)

The method first gets the task from the `localTaskService` bean by its primary key. It is needed to get `sessionId`, which is used to load the persisted session.

If we complete the human task now, our session will be notified and the process will correctly continue.

Loan approval event

For a successful loan approval, a supervisor must send an approved event. Normally, we'd create a "loans waiting for approval" screen where the supervisor would pick the loan for approval. This screen would be driven by the persisted `LoanApprovalHolder` instances. We won't be creating this screen, and instead let's pretend that the supervisor knows the `sessionId` value of the process that needs the approval.

Loan approval event will be handled by `ApproveEventController`. The controller will use the `sessionId` value to send the event to the correct session. First, it'll search for `LoanApprovalHolder` by the `sessionId` (note that it is the primary key) value. Then, it'll call the `bankingService.approveLoan` method:

```
/**
 * sends 'loan approved' event to specific process
 */
@PersistenceContext
EntityManager em;

@RequestMapping("/approveEvent.htm")
public String approveEvent(Integer sessionId,
    Model model) {
  LoanApprovalHolder pendingLoanApprovalHolder = em.find(
      LoanApprovalHolder.class, sessionId);
  bankingService.approveLoan(pendingLoanApprovalHolder);
  return "redirect:index.jsp";
}
```

Code listing 36: The approveEvent method of a controller for sending an approval event (the ApproveEventController.java file)

The user is redirected to the `index.jsp` page (note `redirect:index.jsp`).

 As an alternative to `LoanApprovalHolder`, we could use the persisted process data and search for all processes that are waiting for approval. However, in Drools 5.5 the process data is stored as an array of bytes, which makes it impossible to search through the data. Also, there is no easily navigable link between a persisted session state and a persisted process state. This may be improved in future versions of Drools.

The `bankingService` bean delegates to the `loanApproval` service's `approveLoan` method in the following code listing:

```
public void approveLoan(final LoanApprovalHolder holder) {
sessionTemplate.doWithLoadedSession(holder.getSessionId(),
  new KnowledgeSessionCallback() {
    @Override
    public void execute(StatefulKnowledgeSession session){
      SignalEventCommand command=new SignalEventCommand();
      command.setProcessInstanceId(holder
          .getProcessInstanceId());
      command.setEventType("LoanApprovedEvent");
```

```
                command.setEvent(true);
                session.execute(command);
            }
        });
    }
```

Code listing 37: The approveLoan method of the loan approval service (the LoanApprovalServiceImpl.java file)

The method looks up the knowledge session using the `sessionId` value. A new `SignalEventCommand` instance is created and the `processInstanceId` value is set together with the event type and event's value. The command is then executed.

After the bank employee completes the process, loan task and the supervisor sends the approve event, the loan approval process finishes successfully, the money gets transferred, and the customer is informed with an e-mail.

Summary

In this chapter we've learned how to write a basic web application. The application brought together some of the services we've defined in the previous chapters.

The application had layered architecture. All were configured with the Spring framework (data sources, repositories, transactions, knowledge bases, services, view controllers, and others). Spring makes it easy to change the configuration without recompiling the code.

We've learned how to integrate transactions with our services. For example, all new customers are validated, persisted, and all this happens within a transaction. The complex event processing service is notified about all important events within the application.

The loan approval process showed how to deal with a long-running rule sessions. Sessions had to persist during the user "think time", otherwise they will consume resources that could have been used much better. We've defined a session template that abstracts away the session setup logic, as well as the cleanup logic, so this way we won't forget to perform it.

10
Testing

Testing is an important part of the development life cycle. In the earlier chapters we've learned how to write unit and integration tests. This chapter will provide some additional information about testing and troubleshooting rules. It will focus on how to write good unit tests, integration tests, and acceptance tests; it will look at testing support in Guvnor (Business Rules Management System), including some support for static analysis of rules, and finally, some useful advice for rule debugging will be given.

Writing unit tests for rules

By definition a unit in a unit test is the smallest testable part of an application; in our case it's a rule. Writing a unit test for every rule is expensive. It effectively doubles the cost of writing a rule. However, it is worth the effort. To minimize this cost we should focus on each rule in isolation. This includes isolating all external factors such as calls to services, repositories, and so on. Any mocking library can be used for this purpose.

 A mocking library can create a dummy implementation (a mock) of a service that we can use for testing the rules. The mock can record methods that have been called and return predefined values. We can verify that the correct method was executed an expected amount of times with the correct set of arguments. In the previous chapters jMock was used, but easyMock or mockito are also good alternatives.

By isolating all external factors, our unit tests will work even if they change. For example, the implementation of global objects can change, but since the rules use their mocked version, the changes in rule unit tests will be minimized.

Each condition in a rule should be covered in a unit test. When we change a condition, ideally one test should break. This will give us confidence when refactoring rules that the functionality hasn't been changed. This also applies when a new functionality is being added or an existing functionality is being removed. The test should account for cases where there is no fact, one fact, or many facts present in the knowledge session. However, as with everything, always use your common sense while writing tests. For example, it probably doesn't make sense to test every possible scenario in a decision table.

A test for a process can usually be divided into two parts: testing of the process definition and rules (if there are any).

 When testing the process definition, note that the knowledge base can be created just from a `.bpmn` file.

A process definition unit test should ideally test every process node to make sure that every branch of a process works as expected. Focus especially on process nodes with some conditions/actions.

Furthermore, unit tests are sort of living documentation. They are usually updated immediately with the code/rules. Through a unit test, others can understand how this unit works, its API, and how to use this unit.

Rule integration testing

An integration test is a higher level test for the whole knowledge base. It tests rule interactions. Instead of mock objects, it uses fully setup objects (services, repositories, and so on). A process integration test should test the whole process, such as definition and rules together.

An integration test involving rules is no different from a standard integration test. We'll now look at rule acceptance testing.

Rule acceptance testing

By definition, acceptance testing is a black-box testing performed on a system prior to its delivery. Acceptance testing is often performed by the user. There are various tools for implementing acceptance testing. **Framework for Integrated Test (FIT)** is one of them, and more information on FIT can be found at `http://fit.c2.com/`. The FIT tests consist of initial configuration setup, setup of input data, and setup of expectations. All this is stored in a human-readable document (`.doc` or `.rtf`). It can even be part of the system requirements (for example, a table within a document that contains input data and expectations).

Drools adopted FIT-style acceptance testing early on with the FIT for Rules (more information about FIT for Rules can be found at `http://fit-for-rules.sourceforge.net/`). This has been later enhanced in Guvnor.

Guvnor is **Business Rules Management System (BRMS)**. It is a web application for managing rules and processes. It can create, edit, build, and test rules and processes. For more information about Guvnor, please look into Drools documentation. In this book we'll cover only Guvnor's testing support and static analysis of rules.

Download, install, and start Guvnor. There are several builds to choose from. We'll use the build for tomcat server (`guvnor-5.5.0.Final-tomcat-6.0.war`). It can be found in `guvnor-distribution-5.5.0.Final.zip down-loadable`, inside the `binaries` folder. Open your web browser and navigate to `http://localhost:8080/guvnor-5.5.0.Final-tomcat-6.0`. You will be automatically logged in as admin.

We'll now look at testing support in Guvnor. It can be considered as acceptance testing of rules. Its biggest benefit is that it can be performed by a more technically skilled business user. We can define expectations and verify that they were met. When the acceptance test runs, it creates facts from the given input data, inserts them into the knowledge session, fires all rules, and then verifies expectations. All violations are reported.

Guvnor's testing support can be found in the main menu under the heading **QA**. It provides support for running tests and static analysis of rules under the following two subsections: **Test Scenarios in packages** and **Analysis**. In this chapter we'll cover both.

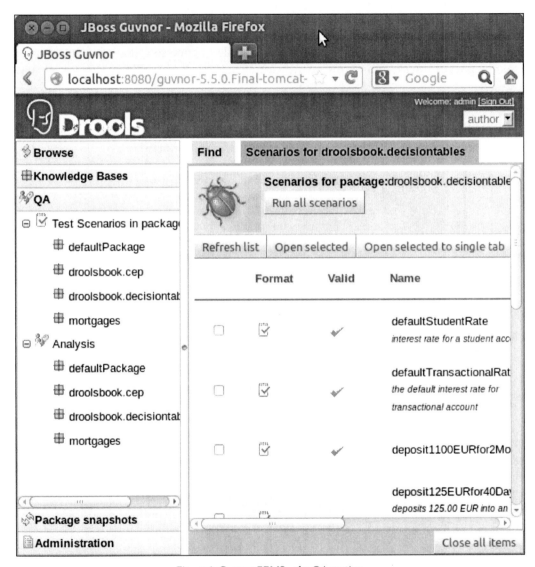

Figure 1: Guvnor BRMS – the QA section

By expanding **Test Scenarios in packages** on the left-hand side, we can see all the configured packages in Guvnor. On the right-hand side of the screenshot, there's a list of already defined tests. Please ignore them for now.

Assume that we've defined rules for calculating interest rates in the `droolsbook.decisiontables` package in Guvnor (again, please consult Drools documentation about how to do it). A quick solution would be to use our existing `.xls` file from the *Calculating the interest rate* section of *Chapter 5, Creating Human-readable Rules*, for converting this file to `.drl`, using `DecisionTableFactory` and importing the resulting `.drl` file into Guvnor. Please note that the model and referencing libraries need to be imported as well. After the package in Guvnor successfully builds, we can start with writing some rule acceptance tests.

Creating a test scenario

Before we can run the tests we have to define them. This is done in the **Knowledge Bases** navigation section. Select **Knowledge Bases** and then **Create New | New Test Scenario**. Give it some name, for example, we can use the same name as we've used for our Java tests, that is, `deposit125EURfor40Days`. A scenario is essentially one JUnit test method. Set the correct package (the one with interest rating calculation: `droolsbook.decisiontables`). Then a new screen for entering the test data should be displayed. Add some input data and some expectations as in the following screenshot:

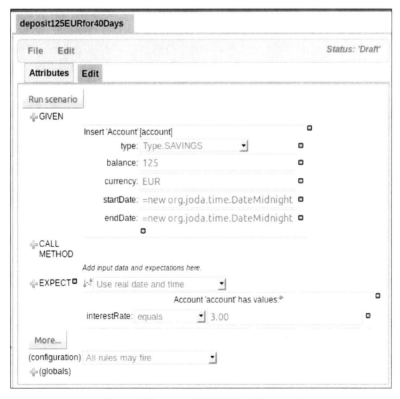

Figure 2: The deposit125EURfor40Days test

The **GIVEN** section defines facts that will be inserted into the knowledge session. In the previous screenshot we're inserting one fact of type `Account`. This fact is bound under the `account` variable name. The following five lines set the account's properties. Depending on the type of the property, we can set them directly as is the case with `currency-String`, `type-enum`, and `balance-BigDecimal`. However, for more complex objects, we can always fall back to an mvel expression as is the case with start and end date that are both of type `DateMidnight`. Each value that starts with the equal (=) symbol is considered as an mvel expression and properly evaluated.

The full value of the `startDate` field is `=new org.joda.time.DateMidnight(2008, 1, 1).minusDays(40)`. In this case we're creating a new instance of an object using mvel expression. The `endDate` field is set to `=new org.joda.time.DateMidnight(2008, 1, 1)`. The duration of the interval defined by `startDate` and `endDate` is exactly 40 days. By selecting the **GIVEN** button, we can add more facts.

The name of the next section, **CALL METHOD**, suggests that we can call a method on an existing fact before rule execution.

The next section, **EXPECT**, defines expectations. Its first line is used for setting `SessionClock` (its purpose was described in *Chapter 7, Complex Event Processing*), which is used mainly when working with CEP. The scenario has one expectation on a fact field. It expects that the `interestRate` property of `account` will be equal to **3.00**. We can add as many expectations like this as we want. Another supported expectation type can verify which rules were fired and how many times.

By clicking on the **More...** button, more input and expectations can be defined. It is something like a round two within this test scenario. The knowledge session will be reused.

A scenario can be further configured to limit the rules that are allowed to fire. This is very useful if we have some rules that have side effects and should be omitted from testing (for example, if they are accessing some external service). Furthermore, simple global objects can be defined. It is similar to defining a fact.

Globals

Our rules often interact with external services that are accessible through global variables. Similar to what we did in rule unit tests, in order to test these rules, stubbed versions of services could be defined. The test could then verify that the service was called *n* times with expected parameters.

We should not forget to add a description for this scenario. It can be added through the **Attributes** tab. It will help with understanding the purpose of this test.

Running a test scenario

After defining a test scenario, it can be executed by clicking on the **Run scenario** button in the top-left corner of *Figure 2*. Guvnor then executes this scenario and displays the results in the top part of the screen as shown in the following screenshot:

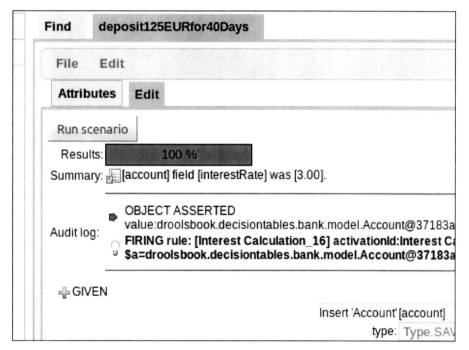

Figure 3: Running the deposit125EURfor40Days test scenario

Results consists of a bar graph representing the success rate of this test scenario. In our case it is 100 percent—one test out of one passed. The **Summary** section summarizes which expectations were met (green tick icon) and which were not (yellow exclamation point). The actual values are also shown. In the previous example the fact `interestRate` field of `account` was set to 3.00, which was expected. If the expectations aren't met, meaning that the actual value is different from the expected one, both values will be shown and the expected value will also be displayed in the **EXPECT** section with a red rectangle around it as shown in the next screenshot:

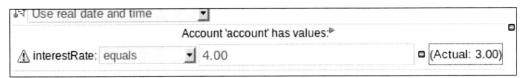

Figure 4: Failing test – expectation isn't met

The **Audit** log from *Figure 3* gives us a detailed view of what happened during the test execution. We can see that an `Account` object has been inserted. Its values can be seen (as represented by the `toString` method of `Account`). The next line shows the **FIRING rule** event, which means that a rule has been executed just after the `Account` fact was inserted. The rule name is `Interest Calculation_16`. The facts that activate this rule are shown as well (note that these rules come from an `.xls` spreadsheet, as the rule names were autogenerated, hence the unusual name `Interest Calculation_16`).

The test can now be saved by clicking on the **Save changes** button in the top part of the screen just below the **Tabs** section. More tests can be defined like this. We can take all tests that were written for interest rate calculation and rewrite them in Guvnor.

As you can see, this interface is targeted more towards technically skilled business users. They can easily write and maintain these tests. However, for developers, it probably makes more sense to use the IDE and Java for writing these tests, as we've done in *Chapter 5, Creating Human-readable Rules*.

Running all test scenarios

After all tests are written, they can be run all at once like a JUnit test suite. In the QA navigation section, click on the `droolsbook.decisiontables` package. All tests within this package can be run by clicking on the **Run all scenarios** button. The results are shown in the following screenshot:

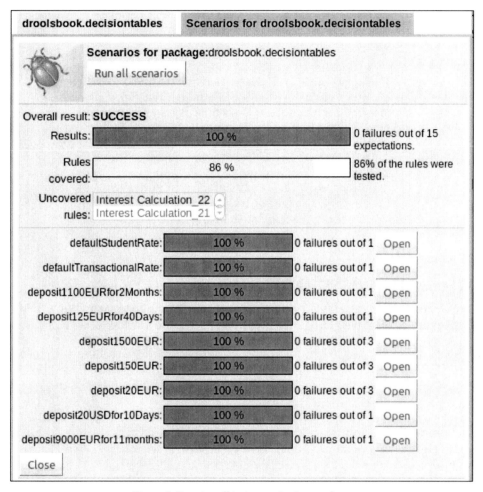

Figure 5: Running all test scenarios in a package

As we can see, the overall result is **SUCCESS**, which means that all tests within this package have successfully passed. There were zero failures out of 15 expectations. The next yellow bar shows the test coverage, that is, it shows what percentage of rules were exercised by the tests. Only 86 percent of the rules in this package were tested. The rules that were not tested are shown in the **Uncovered rules** list box. In a real scenario most of the rules should have at least one to three tests.

The next section displays each executed test scenario in more detail. By clicking on the **Open** button, we can get to the test scenario in question.

These tests can also be called externally through a URL. It is especially useful if we have a continuous integration server that could run these tests every time a package is changed. This URL can be found in the **Knowledge Bases** navigation section. Click on the package you want to test, then on **Edit**, and the URL will be displayed in the bottom-right part of the screen. For example, the URL for running tests:
`http://localhost:8080/guvnor-5.5.0.Final-tomcat-6.0/org.drools.guvnor.Guvnor/package/droolsbook.decisiontables/LATEST/SCENARIOS`.

Static analysis of rules

Testing is useful but it can be very time-consuming. We have to write the test and then maintain them. It would be nice if we also had some automatic way of testing.

Static analysis is what we're looking for. It is another powerful technique that can be used anytime for achieving high quality of rules. The rules are analyzed by a specialized program without actually running it. It can be applied to any rules without any initial investments.

Drools comes with a module called drools-verifier that uses rules to analyze rules. This module can be used standalone (through API or as an ant task) or it is also included in Guvnor under **QA | Analysis**. Analysis can be started by clicking on the **Run analysis** button. The results are shown in the following screenshot:

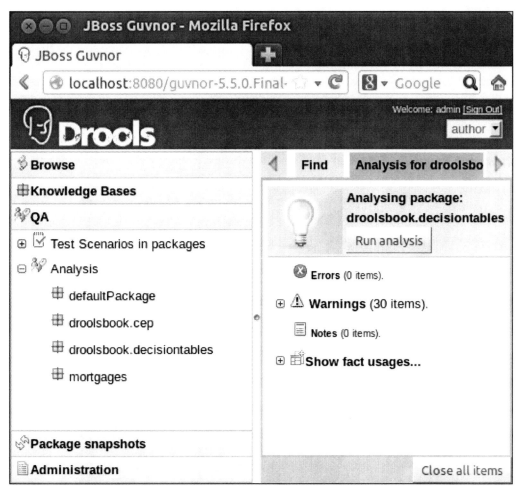

Figure 6: Analyzing a package

Drools-verifier module analyzes rules in a package and creates a report with errors, warnings, and notes. Furthermore, it provides various other information about rules (for example, field usages by fact type and so on). The **errors** section represent significant problems often resulting in the rules not being able to compile. Warnings and notes highlight potential problems with rules (for example, a redundant rule that is already covered by another rule). The Drools-verifier module gives us an interesting tool to look at rules from a different perspective.

Troubleshooting techniques

If we have trouble with writing a new rule or fixing a broken rule, we should first isolate this rule from others. It can be done by commenting out other rules or by extracting this rule to a new file and working there.

The Drools Eclipse plugin has the **Rete Tree** view. The **Rete Tree** view is accessible as the second tab of the DRL editor. It shows the graphical representation of the Rete network (more about it in *Chapter 12, Learning about Performance*). Behind the scenes, it compiles the `.drl` file and so can be used to quickly check if the `.drl` file is valid, and if the file is not valid, an error is displayed.

If the rule compiles, but it still isn't doing what we want, we can use a debug event listeners to see if the expected facts were inserted into the knowledge session, if the rule was actually activated, and if it was fired.

If the rule hasn't been activated, there might be an issue with the rule's conditions. In this case it helps to comment out some conditions and try to make the rule fire without them. This will help us to narrow down the specific rule's condition that is preventing this rule from firing (later in this chapter, we'll also see how to use mvel do to some low-level debugging of rule conditions).

If the rule was fired, but it didn't do what was expected, there is probably an issue with the rule's consequence. The rule's consequence is essentially a block of Java code. We can simply put some `System.out` statements, for example, to print out some variables. If this isn't enough, inside the DRL editor, we can put breakpoints into the rule's consequence. As we already know, Drools, behind the scenes, creates a class from/for each consequence. We can review the source of this class to see any potential problems.

In the following sections we'll look at some of these techniques in more detail.

Event listeners

Event listeners, or in other words callback handlers, have a large variety of uses. They can be used for audit, reporting purposes, debugging, and also for externalizing some functionality from rules. For example, if we look at the validation example in *Chapter 3, Validating*, each rule's consequence is creating a message and adding this message to a report; this can be easily done in the `afterActivationFired` method of `AgendaEventListener`. This way we're abstracting the reporting aspect from the rules. We can easily change the reporting code without touching every rule. Furthermore, more event listeners can be applied at the same time.

Drools supports four types of event listeners. We'll now look at their interfaces:

- `org.drools.event.rule.WorkingMemoryEventListener`: This listens to events on a knowledge session such as fact inserted/updated/retracted events

- `org.drools.event.rule.AgendaEventListener`: This listens to events on the knowledge session's agenda such as activation created/canceled events, before/after activation fired events, and agenda group popped/pushed events

- `org.drools.event.knowledgebase.KnowledgeBaseEventListener`: This listens to events on the knowledge base such as additions/removals of packages, rules, processes, and functions and lock/unlock events on the knowledge base

- `org.drools.event.process.ProcessEventListener`: This listens to events on a process instance such as before/after process started/completed events, process node left/triggered events, and variable changed events

Drools provides various implementation of these listeners. Worth noting is `DebugXXXEventListener` (for example, `org.drools.event.rule.DebugWorkingMemoryEventListener`), which prints everything to the console such as `System.err`. Similar to debug type there is a default type; for example, `org.drools.event.rule.DefaultWorkingMemoryEventListener`, which is designed for extensibility. All its methods are empty so that it can be easily extended and only necessary methods are overwritten.

> Note: Use only event listeners from the knowledge-api module. Event listeners from the drools-core module won't work with the new Drools API and will be removed in a future version of Drools.

Sample Java code for adding an event listener to a knowledge session is as follows:

```
session.addEventListener(new DebugWorkingMemoryEventListener());
```

Code listing 1: Setting a debugging knowledge session event listener that prints all events to the console

> By default `DebugXXXEventListeners` prints out `toString` of the event. This might include lot of unwanted information. You'll probably want to extend the default event listeners and print out only specific information. For example, in the case of the `beforeActivationFired` method of `AgendaEventListener`, you could print out the rule name and possibly facts that caused the activation event.

Debugging

Drools Eclipse plugin provides a powerful environment for debugging rules (please refer to the Drools documentation for instructions on how to install this plugin at `http://www.jboss.org/drools/documentation.html`). Open a `.drl` file in Eclipse and double-click on the left-hand side of the line in the rule consequence, where you want to place a breakpoint:

```
⊖rule "addressRequired"
        when
            Customer( address == null )
        then
            warning(drools);
    end
```

Figure 7: Breakpoint in a rule consequence (see the blue dot on the left-hand side)

The breakpoint will be triggered when the rule fires next. The application needs to be started through a special Drools launcher. The same applies when we want to debug JUnit tests. Right-click on the `Main`/`JUnit` test class, and from the context menu, select **Debug As | Drools Application/Drools JUnit Test**. At the time of this writing, Drools supported only debugging of JUnit tests Version 3.X. We're using JUnit Version 4 in this book. As with standard Java debugging, we can see the current stack trace, access global and local variables, or even execute custom expressions.

When debugging applications that were started with the Drools launcher, various Drools Eclipse Views become available. For example:

- **Agenda**: This can be used to explore activated rules that are placed on the agenda
- **Global Data**: This can be used to explore values of global variables
- **Working Memory**: This can be used to explore facts in the current knowledge session
- **Rules**: This shows all packages and their contents in a tree format

- **Audit**: This shows all events that happened during the rule engine execution, similar to what we've seen when running test scenarios in Guvnor

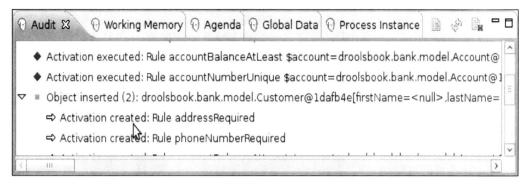

Figure 8: Drools Audit view in Eclipse (tabs represent other views that are available)

The **Audit** view only works offline. It can open a prerecorded knowledge session from a logfile. The following code listing shows how to create such a logfile:

```
KnowledgeRuntimeLogger logger = KnowledgeRuntimeLoggerFactory.
newFileLogger(session, "log_file_name");
...
logger.close();
```

Code listing 2: Audit logger for logging all events in a knowledge session

Please note that the `newFileLogger` method takes a knowledge session as an argument. The logger should be created right after the session and before any objects are inserted into the session or any rules are fired. The output file (in this case called `log_file_name.log`) will be stored in the current JVM working directory. This logfile can then be stored for future analysis. After we finish working with the session, the logger should be closed by calling `logger.close()`.

jBPM

The Eclipse plugin provides additional views for debugging processes. These views are:

- **Process Instances**: This shows all currently running process instances. Each process instance is shown in a tree-like structure and its properties can be examined.

- **Process Instance**: This shows a graphical representation of a process instance with the currently active nodes highlighted.

In order to activate these views a breakpoint can be inserted into the `beforeNodeTriggered` method of `ProcessEventListener` or rule consequence as we've done before. When this breakpoint is triggered, the **Process Instances** view will be populated with the current process instance. After double-clicking on this process instance we can switch to the **Process Instance** view to see the graphical representation of this process with currently active nodes highlighted:

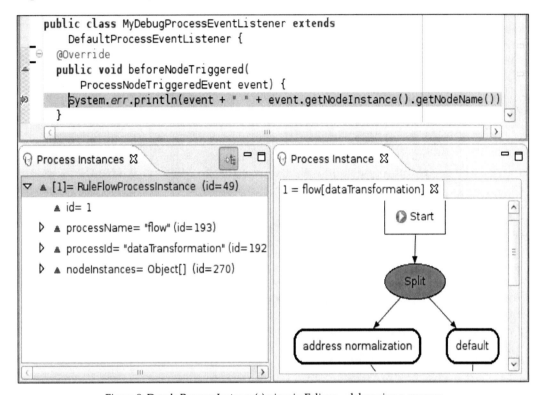

Figure 9: Drools Process Instance(s) view in Eclipse – debugging a process

The screenshot shows a breakpoint that has been triggered in a process event listener's `beforeNodeTriggered` method. The **Process Instances** view shows the currently running process and the **Process Instance** view shows currently active rule tasks.

Debugging rule conditions

As we know we can call any Java method inside a rule conditions. Thanks to free form expression support in Drools. This means we can call a dummy method that always returns true and put a breakpoint into this method:

```
when
    Account ( dummy() )
```

Code listing 3: Some rule condition

Since this is a standard Java code with a standard breakpoint, we can work with it as we are used to:

```
public boolean dummy() {
    return true;
}
```

Code listing 4: Dummy method that returns true

This will allow us to see when exactly Drools evaluates the condition.

Source of generated classes

When the Drools compiler compiles a rule file, it also generates various Java classes. To represent rule consequences and semantic blocks of code (for example, evals, inline evals). For performance reasons, these classes are kept only in memory and they are never stored on disk. However, we can force Drools to dump the source code of these classes to some folder on the disk. There are two ways to accomplish this:

1. From the command line we can start the application as normal and just add the following:

   -Ddrools.dump.dir="target/dumpDir"

   Code listing 5: Specifying the dump directory from the command line

2. Through the API:

   ```
   KnowledgeBuilderConfiguration configuration =
   KnowledgeBuilderFactory.newKnowledgeBuilderConfiguration();
   configuration.setOption(DumpDirOption.get(
       new File("target/dumpDir")));
   ```

   Code listing 6: Specifying the dump directory through the API

KnowledgeBuilderConfiguration can then be used to create KnowledgeBuilder that is used in the knowledge session creation process.

Please note that in both cases the target directory (in our case target/dumpDir) must exist.

This can be useful for getting a deeper understanding of Drools internals, and it can also help while troubleshooting to find out exactly what code is being executed.

Summary

We've learned some principles on how to write rule unit tests, integration tests, and acceptance tests. Unit tests should test each rule in isolation while mocking all other components. Integration tests should test a knowledge base as a whole. The acceptance tests are geared toward more technically skilled business users. With a nice web interface provided by Guvnor, a user can test the rules by setting up input data with expectations. Guvnor then executes these tests and reports results back.

Static analysis of rules was shown as a very easy way of testing rules. Currently it provides only limited value, but as the drools-verifier module evolves, it may be a powerful tool in the future.

We've seen some techniques for rule troubleshooting. Starting with listeners that have lot of other uses, debugging in Eclipse, and to get a deeper understanding of the inner workings of a rule engine, and moreover, we've learned how to view the source of generated classes.

11
Integrating

The focus of this chapter will be on various integration points of the Drools engine with other systems.

We'll start with a discussion of having Drools artifacts change their own life cycle that is independent from the application. We'll see how to build and dynamically load Drools artifacts.

We'll look at how to run rules remotely from a lightweight client. A simple client will be written in Ruby that will be talking to a Drools camel server.

Finally, we'll cover integration with the Spring framework and some rule standards will be discussed.

Dynamic KnowledgeBase loading

In almost all examples in this book the Drools artifacts were packaged together with the application. However, rules, processes, and other Drools artifacts often have different life cycles than applications that use them. These artifacts tend to change more often than the rest of the application. It would be more beneficial if we could build, release, and deploy them separately. In order to achieve this we need to build the KnowledgeBase instance independently from the application. The application should be able to dynamically reload this KnowledgeBase instance at runtime.

Guvnor (Business Rules Management Server) meets our first requirement. It can build, release KnowledgePackages, and make them available through a URL. Later on in this chapter we'll also show how we can use a general build tool such as Ant for this task.

For the second requirement we'll now look at KnowledgeAgent.

KnowedgeAgent

`KnowledgeAgent` allows us to load Drools artifacts dynamically as they change. It is designed to support both poll and push models. However, only the polling model is implemented in Drools (the `KnowledgeAgent` listener periodically scans resources for changes).

 In future the Drools team plans to add implementation for the push model as well. As a result the interfaces are subject to change.

The following figure shows how it works in more detail:

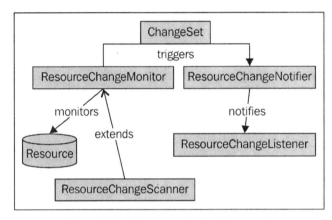

Figure 1: Drools resource loading framework

A resource can represent a single `.drl` file (see `org.drools.builder.ResourceType` enum for all supported resources) or a directory (it can contain multiple resources). `ResourceChangeMonitor` monitors these resources for changes. When a change is detected a `ChangeSet` resource is created that holds all information about this change. The `ChangeSet` resource holds resources that were added, modified, and removed. `ResourceChangeScanner` extends the `ResourceChangeMonitor` interface to provide the "poll type" monitoring. It can be configured to scan for changes in predefined intervals. The default is 60 seconds.

When the monitor detects a change, it triggers the `ResourceChangeNotifier` method, which is responsible for sending notifications to listeners. All listeners must implement the `ResourceChangeListener` interface.

`KnowledgeAgent` is a type of listener that caches one knowledge base. The knowledge base can be accessed through the `getKnowledgeBase` method. The agent keeps this knowledge base up-to-date as the resources change. It can update the knowledge base instance or create a new one (the default behavior). When updating a knowledge base, all associated knowledge sessions will get updated as well, so take care. The following code listing shows how to use the `KnowlegeAgent` listener:

```
ResourceFactory.getResourceChangeScannerService().start();
ResourceFactory.getResourceChangeNotifierService().start();

KnowledgeAgentConfiguration conf = KnowledgeAgentFactory
    .newKnowledgeAgentConfiguration();
conf.setProperty("drools.agent.scanDirectories", "true");

final KnowledgeAgent agent = KnowledgeAgentFactory
    .newKnowledgeAgent("validation agent", knowledgeBase, conf);
```

Code listing 1: KnowledgeAgent usage – creating new knowledge base on every change

The first two lines are starting the monitor and notifier services. They must be started explicitly.

Next, a `KnowledgeAgentConfiguration` listener is created that provides some configuration options for the knowledge agent. It can specify whether the agent should scan resources or whole directories and other settings. *Code listing 1* shows how to enable the `scanDirectories` setting, that is, `aconf.setProperty("drools. agent.scanDirectories", "true");`.

The `KnowledgeAgentFactory` interface is then used to create an instance of the `KnowledgeAgent` listener using our configuration `conf` (see `javadoc` for other ways to create the `KnowledgeAgent` listener). The factory method also takes `knowledgeBase` as an argument. We can create this knowledge base as we normally do.

> Note that the knowledge base retains the locations of its resources. This is possible only when it is created from a file, URL, or a resource on the classpath (as can be seen in the following example). The location information is lost when the knowledge base is created from a byte array, `InpuStream`, or a `Reader` resource.

The agent subscribes for notifications to all resources this knowledge base contains. When a resource is changed, the agent recreates the knowledge base. In our application we have to get this knowledge base by calling `KnowledgeAgent.getKnowledgeBase()` before every stateless/stateful session creation.

In the previous chapter we've mentioned that Drools Guvnor can also build artifacts. Artifacts are grouped into packages. Packages can be built and then accessed via a URL. Our application can then use this URL for creating the `KnowledgeBase` instance. If we'd like to load the validation `KnowledgeBase` from Guvnor, we could add it to the `KnowledgeBuilder` instance like this:

```
kbuilder.add(ResourceFactory.newUrlResource(
"http://localhost:8080/guvnor-5.5.0.Final-tomcat-6.0/org.drools.
guvnor.Guvnor/package/droolsbook.validation/LATEST"),
ResourceType.PKG);
```

Code listing 2: Adding a validation package built by Guvnor

We're specifying the URL where the package is accessible. The package name is `droolsbook.validation`, and we're using the `LATEST` snapshot of this package. With this configuration change we don't even need the `drools-compiler` library on the classpath, because the package is already compiled. The `KnowledgeAgent` listener will periodically poll this URL for changes and will recreate its locally cached `KnowledgeBase` instance.

External artifact building

We already know that we can use Guvnor to build packages externally. In this section we'll look how to do it with a build tool called Ant. We can then easily add an artifact compilation step into our existing build process that we may have.

Note that in future versions the Drools team is planning to add support for Maven as well. If you're running Maven, as a workaround it is possible to call an Ant task from within a Maven build.

Building with Ant

Apache Ant is a general-purpose building tool. More information about Ant can be found at `http://ant.apache.org/`. Module drools-ant, from the `droolsjbpm-tools-distribution-5.5.0.Final.zip` downloadable file contains an Ant task for building Drools artifacts. We'll build the validation knowledge base from *Chapter 3, Validating*, using this Ant task.

All information required by Ant will be stored in a file called `build.xml`. We'll now go step-by-step through this file. It starts with a project definition:

```xml
<?xml version="1.0" encoding="UTF-8" ?>
<project default="compileArtifacts">
  <property name="projectPath" value="" />
  <property name="droolsPath" value="drools_lib" />
```

Code listing 3: The build.xml file – project definition (part 1/4)

As it is usual with Ant build files, the project definition contains a default Ant target that will be called when no target is specified. This default target is called `compileArtifacts`. The next two lines define two properties, `projectPath` and `droolsPath`, that we'll be using. The first property is a path to the current project, and the second is a path to Drools libraries.

The next code listing will define Drools libraries that will be needed:

```xml
<path id="drools.classpath">
  <pathelement location="${droolsPath}/drools-ant.jar" />
  <pathelement location="${droolsPath}/knowledge-api.jar" />
  <pathelement location="${droolsPath}/drools-core.jar" />
  <pathelement location="${droolsPath}/drools-compiler.jar" />
  <pathelement location="${droolsPath}/antlr-runtime.jar" />
  <pathelement location="${droolsPath}/mvel2.jar" />
  <pathelement location="${droolsPath}/ecj.jar" />
  <pathelement location="${droolsPath}/slf4j-api.jar" />
</path>
```

Code listing 4: The build.xml file – Drools classpath definition (part 2/4)

Note that the libraries in the code listing don't have versions. It has been removed to make this code listing more concise. For example, if you're using Version 5.5.0.Final of Drools, `drools-ant.jar` will be `drools-ant-5.5.0.Final.jar`.

The `drools.classpath` classpath references Drools artifacts that are required by validation rules (including their dependencies). You can add more Drools artifacts to this list depending on which features you're using (for example, if you use decision tables, add `drools-decisiontables.jar` and so on). Please note the use of the `droolsPath` variable to locate all Drools libraries.

The `drools-ant.jar` file contains the Drools Ant task. We'll now use the `drools.classpath` classpath to tell Ant about the Ant task.

```xml
<taskdef name="compiler" classpathref="drools.classpath"
  classname="org.drools.contrib.DroolsCompilerAntTask" />
```

Code listing 5: The build.xml file – Drools compiler definition (part 3/4)

The `taskdef` element defines a compiler Ant task. It is implemented by class `DroolsCompilerAntTask`.

Now, we can use this Ant task to compile the validation rules:

```
<path id="model.classpath">
  <pathelement location="${projectPath}lib/banking-model.jar" />
  <pathelement location="${projectPath}lib/joda-time.jar" />
</path>

<target name="compileArtifacts">
  <compiler srcdir="${projectPath}src/main/resources"
    tofile="${projectPath}target/validation.pkg"
    binformat="package" bintype="knowledge"
    classpathref="model.classpath">
    <include name="validation.drl" />
  </compiler>
</target>
</project>
```

Code listing 6: The build.xml file – target for building validation rules (part 4/4)

First, another classpath is defined called `model.classpath`. It contains all model libraries. In our case they are the `banking-model.jar` file and the `joda-time.jar` library. The first JAR file contains all classes used in the model. The second JAR file is a library that our model references.

Finally, the `compileArtifacts` target gathers all information together in order to compile the validation rules. The target's body consists of a compiler target. It defines:

- `srcdir`: This points to the directory with our validation rules.
- `tofile`: This specifies the destination file. In our case it is called `validation.pkg`.
- `binformat`: This specifies that we want to build only a package, and if we didn't specify this, the whole knowledge base would be built.
- `bintype`: This is here just for compatibility purposes. It should be always set to knowledge.
- `classpathref`: This is a reference to our model classpath.

The body of the compiler element is a collection of files that should be compiled. In our case it is only one file called `validation.drl`. Other valid options are artifacts ending with `.brl`, `.xml`, `.dsl`, `.dslr`, `.rf`, `.package`, or `.xls` (note that there is no support for the `.bpmn` files). More files can be imported at once using wild cards (for example, all rule files with `*.drl`).

You can try this build file from a command line. Just navigate to the directory where it resides and type `ant`. Ant will execute the default target, which is in our case set to `compileArtifacts`. After a few seconds you should see a **BUILD SUCCESSFUL** message and the `validation.pkg` file should exist. This package can now be used to create a knowledge base.

Drools Camel server

The Drools Camel server is a module that allows remote knowledge base execution. Camel is an integration framework that is based on known Enterprise Integration Patterns. Drools Camel server supports both, web service (SOAP) and **Representational State Transfer (REST)** protocols (`http://en.wikipedia.org/wiki/Representational_State_Transfer`). The communication with the server can be done in JSON (JSON is a lightweight data-interchange format and can be found at `http://www.json.org/`) or XML formats as well as others.

Interest rate calculation example

The drools-camel module can be found within the `droolsjbpm-integration-distribution-5.5.0.Final.zip` downloadable artifact. It is meant to be integrated with other applications. To demonstrate its usage, we'll build a simple web application for calculating interest rates. We'll use the decision table from *Chapter 5, Creating Human-readable Rules*. We'll then build a lightweight client that will communicate with the server through the REST interface. Thanks to REST the client won't need any Drools libraries for rules execution (not even a JVM). To demonstrate this, we'll build it using Ruby language.

The server

The server will consist of a couple of configuration files and will have few dependencies on other artifacts (see the downloadable source that comes with this book for the complete listing).

The drools-camel server is based on two main projects: Apache Camel for routing requests and Apache CXF that provides various protocol and formats support (it is mainly used for web services).

Let's start with `web.xml`. We'll define a servlet context listener that will initialize the Spring application context on application startup. Next, we'll register a servlet that will handle all requests:

```
<?xml version="1.0" encoding="UTF-8"?>
<web-app xmlns:xsi="http://www.w3.org/2001/XMLSchema-instance"
```

```
 xmlns="http://java.sun.com/xml/ns/javaee"
 xmlns:web="http://java.sun.com/xml/ns/javaee/web-app_2_5.xsd"
 xsi:schemaLocation="http://java.sun.com/xml/ns/javaee http://java.
sun.com/xml/ns/javaee/web-app_3_0.xsd"
 id="WebApp_ID" version="3.0">
  <display-name>camelServer</display-name>
  <context-param>
   <param-name>contextConfigLocation</param-name>
   <param-value>classpath:applicationContext.xml</param-value>
  </context-param>
  <listener>
    <listener-class>
      org.springframework.web.context.ContextLoaderListener
    </listener-class>
  </listener>
  <servlet>
    <display-name>CXF Servlet</display-name>
    <servlet-name>CXFServlet</servlet-name>
    <servlet-class>
      org.apache.cxf.transport.servlet.CXFServlet
    </servlet-class>
    <load-on-startup>1</load-on-startup>
  </servlet>
  <servlet-mapping>
    <servlet-name>CXFServlet</servlet-name>
    <url-pattern>/kservice/*</url-pattern>
  </servlet-mapping>
 </web-app>
```

Code listing 7: The camelServer web application setup (the web.xml file)

As can be seen, all requests will be handled under the /kservice/* URL. Next comes the applicationContext.xml Spring file where we'll define the knowledge base and a session:

```
<drools:grid-node id="node1"/>

<drools:kbase id="interestCalculationKB" node="node1">
  <drools:resources>
    <drools:resource type="DTABLE"
      source="classpath:interest calculation.xls">
      <drools:decisiontable-conf input-type="XLS"
        worksheet-name="Sheet1" />
    </drools:resource>
```

```
    </drools:resources>
</drools:kbase>

<drools:ksession id="interestCalcSession" type="stateless"
  kbase="interestCalculationKB" node="node1"/>

<import resource="classpath:camel-server.xml" />
```

Code listing 8: Excerpt of the Spring setup file – knowledge base setup (the applicationContext.xml file)

We'll ignore the `grid-node` declaration. It is mandatory but it is used for grid deployments that won't be covered here. Note the use of the `drools:decisiontable-conf` element. As we know decision tables require a bit more configuration than other resources, for example, we need to specify the type if it is an XLS-based or CSV-based decision table. In the example we just saw, but we're also specifying the name of the worksheet that we want to use.

The import file `camel-server.xml` defines routes that make `interestCalcSession` available as a REST service:

```
<?xml version="1.0" encoding="UTF-8"?>
<beans xmlns="http://www.springframework.org/schema/beans"
       xmlns:xsi="http://www.w3.org/2001/XMLSchema-instance"
       xmlns:cxf="http://camel.apache.org/schema/cxf"
       xmlns:jaxrs="http://cxf.apache.org/jaxrs"
       xsi:schemaLocation="
       http://www.springframework.org/schema/beans http://www.
springframework.org/schema/beans/spring-beans-2.5.xsd
       http://camel.apache.org/schema/cxf http://camel.apache.org/
schema/cxf/camel-cxf.xsd
       http://cxf.apache.org/jaxrs http://cxf.apache.org/schemas/
jaxrs.xsd
       http://camel.apache.org/schema/spring http://camel.apache.org/
schema/spring/camel-spring.xsd
    ">
  <import resource="classpath:META-INF/cxf/cxf.xml" />
  <import resource="classpath:META-INF/cxf/cxf-servlet.xml" />

  <cxf:rsServer id="rsServer" address="/rest"
     serviceClass="org.drools.jax.rs.CommandExecutorImpl">
       <cxf:providers>
           <bean class="org.drools.jax.rs.CommandMessageBodyReader"/>
       </cxf:providers>
  </cxf:rsServer>
```

```
    <bean id="droolsPolicy"
      class="org.drools.camel.component.DroolsPolicy" />

    <camelContext id="camel"
      xmlns="http://camel.apache.org/schema/spring">
      <route>
        <from uri="cxfrs://bean://rsServer"/>
        <policy ref="droolsPolicy">
          <unmarshal ref="json" />
          <to uri="drools:node1/interestCalcSession" />
          <marshal ref="json" />
        </policy>
      </route>
    </camelContext>
  </beans>
```

Code listing 9: Route setup (the camelServer.xml file)

Firstly, we're importing some standard CXF configuration files that are needed.
Then we set up the server endpoint, `rsServer`, under the `rest` path. The server
is implemented by the `CommandExecutorImpl` class, which is part of the
`drools-camel` module. The `droolsPolicy` bean is there to make Apache Camel
Drools aware. Finally, a route is defined that takes requests from the `rsServer`
endpoint, un-marshals it with `json` un-marsheller, and passes it into the
`interestCalcSession` session; the response is then marshaled with `json` and sent
back as a response to the client.

When we deploy this application and connect to it (`http://localhost:8080/`
`camelServer/kservice/`), we should see a web page like the following screenshot:

Figure 2: Drools camel server running

As you can see in the screenshot, the server is informing us that it is ready to
process requests.

The client

Our client will query for an interest rate on a student account with a balance of 1,000 EUR. Since this client will be very lightweight, a dynamic, interpreted language such as Ruby (for more information about Ruby please refer to http://www.ruby-lang.org/en/) is ideal for this kind of task. Please consult Ruby's manual about how to install this interpreter. We'll also require an additional library for Ruby called json that will allow us to communicate using the JSON protocol.

The full client source code is as follows:

```ruby
require 'net/http'
require 'json'
http = Net::HTTP.new('localhost', 8080)
path = "/camelServer/kservice/rest/execute"
headers = {
  "Content-Type" => "text/plain"
}
post_data = {"batch-execution" => {
  "commands" => [
    {
      "insert" => {
        "out-identifier" => "account",
        "return-object" => true,
        "object" => {
          "droolsbook.decisiontables.bank.model.Account" => {
            "type" => "STUDENT",
            "balance" => "1000",
            "currency" => "EUR"
          }
        }
      }
    },
    {
      "fire-all-rules" => ""
    }
  ]
}}
resp, data = http.post(path, post_data.to_json, headers)
answer = JSON.parse(data)
puts answer["execution-results"]["results"]["result"]["value"]
["droolsbook.decisiontables.bank.model.Account"]["interestRate"]
```

Code listing 10: Ruby client (the interest_request.rb file)

The first few lines until `post_data` ... are straightforward. We'll be connecting to the server at the specified URL and setting some headers. The `post_data` hash data structure holds the request information that we'll be sending. There are two commands. The first is an insert command of a fact named as `account` of class `droolsbook.decisiontables.bank.model.Account`. Its `type` property is set to STUDENT, balance to `1000`, and currency to EUR. Please note that `Account.currency` is of type `String`. The `type` property is an enum and balance is `BigDecimal`. The second command is a `fireAllRules` command. Note that this command is optional since we're dealing with a stateless session.

The next line with .. `http.post` .. sends this request to the server and waits for the response. Note that the data within the `post_data` variable are converted to JSON format by performing `post_data.to_json`. The response is stored within the data variable. Since it is in a JSON format, we have to convert it into a Ruby structure by performing `JSON.parse(data)`. Finally, the client displays calculated `interestRate` by performing `puts answer["execution-results"]["results"]` `["result"]["value"]["droolsbook.decisiontables.bank.model.Account"]` `["interestRate"]`. The response contains `execution-results`, which is an array of `results`; these are our commands that we've sent in that had `out-identifier` set. The structure of these out commands is the same as the structure of input commands. Please see the Drools documentation for the full listing of available commands.

We can run this client with the `ruby interest_request.rb` script. The output should be `1.00`, which is the correct interest rate for this account.

When the server receives the request, it must create facts/global objects from it that can be inserted into the knowledge session. After the rules are executed, it needs to convert these facts/globals into JSON/XML format. Drools Camel server uses the XStream library to perform this marshaling/un-marshaling. As we've seen that it has no problem with types such as `String`, `enum`, or `BigDecimal`. This library can even deal with much more complex custom data structures. Please consult its manual for more information at `http://xstream.codehaus.org/`. For example, if we'd like to set the `startDate` and `endDate` values that are of type `DateMidnight`, for our account fact, we'd have to map them as complex objects together with specifying their type. I've found quite useful the XStream ability to convert ordinary objects to JSON or XML and print the result out. It'll give you an idea about how to represent even more complex objects.

Spring framework integration

Drools, as of Version 5.1, provides out-of-the-box integration with the Spring framework. As we've seen in previous chapters, it comes with a custom drools-spring namespace, which is part of the drools-spring module. This section will be an overview of this namespace.

The drools-spring namespace allows us to define and configure knowledge bases, stateless and stateful sessions, listeners, groups of listeners, and custom accumulate functions including advanced features such as session persistency and others. See the Drools integration documentation for the full listing.

Furthermore, we can work with defined sessions through the command interface. Commands can be entered through the `drools:batch` element. These commands will then be performed on the session. We can set globals, insert facts, issue fire-all-rules call, start a process, or signal events.

An example XML file that uses the drools-spring namespace is explained in *Code listing 11*. It will create a `validationKnowledgeBase` instance using the rule file from *Chapter 3*, *Validating*. Then it will create a stateful knowledge session, set a debug listener, set globals, insert one customer fact, and execute all rules.

```xml
<?xml version="1.0" encoding="UTF-8"?>
<beans xmlns="http://www.springframework.org/schema/beans"
  xmlns:xsi="http://www.w3.org/2001/XMLSchema-instance"
  xmlns:drools="http://drools.org/schema/drools-spring"
  xsi:schemaLocation="
   http://www.springframework.org/schema/beans http://www.
springframework.org/schema/beans/spring-beans-3.2.xsd
   http://drools.org/schema/drools-spring http://drools.org/schema/
drools-spring-1.7.0.xsd">

  <drools:kbase id="validationKnowledgeBase">
    <drools:resources>
      <drools:resource type="DRL"
        source="classpath:validation.drl" />
  </drools:kbase>

  <drools:ksession id="validationSession" type="stateful"
    kbase="validationKnowledgeBase" >
    <drools:agendaEventListener>
      <bean class="org.drools.event.rule.DebugAgendaEventListener" />
    </drools:agendaEventListener>
    <drools:batch>
```

```
        <drools:set-global identifier="reportFactory">
            <bean class="droolsbook.bank.service.impl.
DefaultReportFactory" />
        </drools:set-global>
        <drools:set-global identifier="validationReport">
            <bean class="droolsbook.bank.service.impl.
DefaultValidationReport" />
        </drools:set-global>
        <drools:insert-object ref="customer" />
        <drools:fire-all-rules />
    </drools:batch>
  </drools:ksession>

  <bean id="customer" class="droolsbook.bank.model.Customer"/>
</beans>
```

Code listing 11: Sample Drools configuration in Spring

It is perhaps a little bit unfortunate that it is currently not possible to define the scope of the knowledge session bean. So, for example, you cannot have a new instance of the knowledge session per HTTP request.

Standards

The idea behind standards is to provide better interoperability between rule/process engines to reduce the time required to learn how to use a new rule engine. We should be able to change the rule engine provider without modifying the application.

As we already know, on the process-side jBPM supports the BPMN standard for process definition and the WH-HumanTask for tasks.

On the rule engine side we have a different situation. There have been attempts to make interoperability easier, for example, JSR94 (Java Rule Engine API) that provides guidelines for rule engine administration and runtime. This standard is supported by Drools, but its value is questionable (it neither standardizes the language used to describe rules nor the execution flow or deployment mechanism), and it will be most likely dropped from Drools in future. There are standards for unifying the rule language, for example, **Rule Markup Language (RuleML)**, which is a markup language developed to express rules in XML or **Rule Interchange Format (RIF)**. However, they are not supported by Drools.

Summary

In this chapter we've learned about various integration points available in Drools. The Drools Camel module allows us to build very lightweight, platform-agnostic, and quick-to-write clients that can execute rules remotely. It can be provided as a service for our customers who require more fine-grained integration with our rules. For example, to provide the service with a different UI or add their own services on top of it. Another use case might be if we don't want to share our rules with our customers; we just want to give them the ability to execute them.

We've learned that it is better to give the rules/processes a different life cycle than the rest of the application. The rules and processes tend to change more often. We know how to build a `KnowledgeBase` instance externally and how to dynamically reload it while the application is running.

We've also seen an overview of the Drools Spring integration that allows us not only to define Spring beans but also to work with them through the command interface.

12
Learning about Performance

Performance is an important requirement in most applications. To get the best out of any technology, we need to understand how it works. We can then make better decisions about how to use it, what and where to optimize.

However, performance shouldn't be the most important factor when considering a rule engine. Simply put, a rule engine is a general purpose `if-then` statement executor. It will never achieve performance of a custom-built system. You may also find that with a custom-built system, its performance is excellent at the start, but it degrades as the system grows in complexity. If we don't want to rewrite it over and over, we'll eventually end up with the so-called spaghetti code. The performance of a rule engine in theory does not depend on the amount of rules, and it has the benefits of declarative programming: maintainability, flexibility, and code readability that comes with reasonable performance.

In this chapter we'll look at the Rete algorithm that is behind Drools in more detail. We'll also get a better understanding of what is possible with Drools and what isn't. For example, we'll learn that it doesn't make sense to measure the execution time of a single rule but only the execution time of all rules as a whole. It may clear some questions about rules execution, for example, why are rules evaluated during the insert stage and not the `fireAllRules` stage.

Rete algorithm

If you had to implement a rule engine, you'd probably start with a simple iteration over all rules and checking them one by one if their conditions are true. The Rete algorithm improves this by several orders of magnitude.

From Wikipedia:

> *The Rete algorithm is an efficient pattern matching algorithm for implementing*
> *production rule systems. The Rete algorithm was designed by Dr Charles L. Forgy*
> *of Carnegie Mellon University, first published in a working paper in 1974.*

Pattern matching is the act of checking rules against known facts to determine which
rules can be executed.

The advantage that this algorithm brings is efficiency; however, it comes at a cost
of higher memory usage. The algorithm uses lot of caching to avoid evaluating
conditions multiple times.

The word Rete is taken from Latin where it represents a "net". It is generally
pronounced as ree-tee. This algorithm generates a network from rule conditions.
Each single rule condition is a node in the Rete network. For example:

```
Customer( name != null )
```

Code listing 1: Single rule condition that maps to one node in the Rete network

The Rete network is a rooted, acyclic, and directed graph. You can think of it as a
tree that has some branches joined. In Drools it is represented by the `KnowledgeBase`
class. The network is created when we add knowledge packages into the knowledge
base (note that this is not package-creation time). Rules from a package are
sequentially added to the network and the network is updated as needed. A sample
Rete network is as follows:

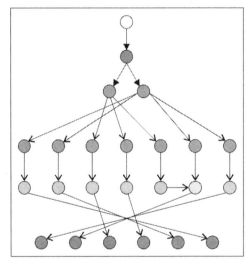

Figure 1: Sample Rete network generated by the Drools Eclipse plugin for rules in the validation.drl file
from Chapter 2, Writing Basic Rules

This is the network for rules from the `validation.drl` file from *Chapter 3, Validating*. The network consists of various node types. Each node type has a different color in *Figure 1*. Please note that for real life `.drl` files with hundreds of rules, the network is much bigger. It is usually very wide with the shape of a flying saucer. Don't be surprised if you see it, it is normal.

The performance of the Rete algorithm is theoretically independent of the number of rules in the knowledge base. If you are curious and want to see some benchmarks, you can find them in the `examples` folder of the `drools-distribution-5.5.0.Final.zip` archive, which is downloadable from the Drools website. There are also some websites that regularly publish benchmarks of various rule engines solving well-known mathematical problems (usually the Miss Manners test and the Waltz), for example: `http://illation.com/tag/drools/`. Performance of Drools is comparable to other open source or even commercial engines.

 Drools uses a version of the Rete algorithm called ReteOO, where OO stands for Object-Oriented. ReteOO is mostly the adaptation of Rete for object-oriented languages.

Node types

We'll now describe each node within the Rete network in more detail. Each node can have one or many input connections, depending on its type, and many output connections. Let's imagine we have the following simple rule:

```
rule "accountBalanceAtLeast"
  when
    $account : Account( balance < 100 )
  then
    warning(drools, $account);
end
```

Code listing 2: Rule that has a constraint on one fact

This rule alone translates into the following Rete network. You can see this network from within the Drools Eclipse `.drl` file editor. Just switch the tab to **Rete Tree** in the bottom-left corner of the editor's screen:

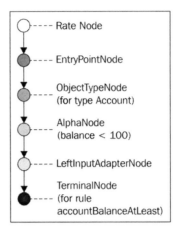

Figure 2: Rete network for the accountBalanceAtLeast rule from Code listing 2

At the top is the Rete node (the white node).

The Rete node

This node is the default entry point into the network. When we insert a fact into the knowledge session (by calling the `session.insert(fact)` method), it enters the Rete network through this node.

 In Eclipse if you open the **Properties** view and then click on a node in the Rete network, you'll see some useful information about a node. For example, its name, type, and depending on node type, various other information.

EntryPointNode

The next node that follows is `EntryPointNode`. This node corresponds to an entry point. As we've seen in *Chapter 7, Complex Event Processing*, we can have many named entry points. In this chapter we'll be dealing only with the default `EntryPointNode` node (our figure will start at this node).

ObjectTypeNode

The inserted fact then continues to a node called `ObjectTypeNode` (the next red node). This node acts as a fact type filter. It passes through only facts with matching type. In our case only objects of type `Account` (or any type that extends `Account`) are allowed to continue. All nodes that descend from this node will deal with constraints on the `Account` type. It is also the case with the next node from *Figure 2* (the blue node).

Each branch descending from the `EntryPointNode` node must start with one `ObjectTypeNode` node.

AlphaNode

Alpha nodes represent the first level of matching. The `AlphaNode` node is responsible for evaluating constraints on single facts. Examples of such tests/constraints are literal (for example, `property1=="someValue"`), variable (for example, `property1 == property2`), inline eval (for example, `eval(someList.isEmpty())`), return value (for example, `property1 == (property2 + 2)`), free form expressions such as `and` and `or`. In our case this constraint is `balance < 100`. If we had multiple constraints on the same fact, they would have been handled by one `AlphaNode` each. For example, this constraint: `balance < 100, currency == "EUR"` would create two `AlphaNodes` one after the other.

> Please note that the order of constraints in a condition is important. In the given example the first `AlphaNode` node will check `balance < 100` and the second `AlphaNode` node will check `currency == "EUR"`. This affects the reusability of the Rete network, as we'll see later on. Often it is a good strategy to put the most shared constraint first in order to help nodes reuse.
>
> Meanwhile, this also means that we should put the most restrictive constraints first; which constraints are the most restrictive depends on our data. The sooner a fact propagation stops, the less work the engine needs to do.

The flow in *Figure 2* continues to the next node (yellow node).

LeftInputAdapterNode

This node acts as an entry point to the second level of matching, beta nodes. It simply creates a tuple out of a single fact. In our case it will be a tuple of size 1 that will contain the `Account` fact. The tuple then propagates to the next node as shown in *Figure 2* (black node). This is the `TerminalNode` node.

TerminalNode

As the name suggests this is the leaf node of the network. It represents the actual rule consequence that should be placed on the agenda (do you remember that all rules with satisfied conditions are placed on the agenda for later execution?). Every rule has at least one TerminalNode node.

Example 1 – inserting a fact

At this point we've described all nodes that are required to represent our rule from *Code listing 2*. To summarize it, if we insert an Account fact that has balance of 50 into the knowledge session. It would enter the Rete network at the Rete node and immediately propagate to the EntryPointNode node. It will then continue through all outgoing connections to ObjectTypeNodes (in our case only one). The ObjectTypeNode node will check that the propagated fact is of type Account and our fact will continue to the next node. The AlphaNode node will evaluate its constraint. Since our fact doesn't satisfy the constraint, the execution will stop at this point (the session.insert(..) method would return). However, if we insert an Account fact with balance of 150, it will successfully satisfy the constraint of the AlphaNode node, and it will continue to the next node. The LeftInputAdapterNode node will wrap our fact into a tuple and it will pass it on to the next node. The TerminalNode node will place a rule that it represents, that is, accountBalanceAtLeast on the agenda.

 As we can see, most of the work that a rule engine has to do happens during the session.insert time, instead of session.fireAllRules time. The latter only executes consequences of rules that were previously activated and placed on the agenda. This is important to keep in mind because it is not something that you'd normally expect.

Another node type that is very common in the Rete network is BetaNode.

BetaNode

This is a node that evaluates constrains on two or more facts. It has two inputs: left and right. The left input is for tuples and the right input is for facts. Each input has associated memory where it stores partial matches.

Let's add another rule to our accountBalanceAtLeast rule:

```
rule studentWithLowAccountBalance
  when
    $account : Account( balance < 100,
      type == Account.Type.STUDENT )
    $customer : Customer( accounts contains $account )
```

```
then
    System.out.println("Customer " + $customer +
    " has student account with low balance");
end
```

Code listing 3: Rule that has a constraint on one multiple facts

The modified Rete network will look like this:

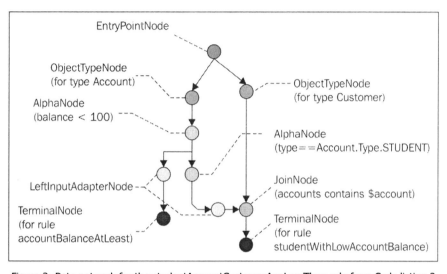

Figure 3: Rete network for the studentAccountCustomerAgeLessThan rule from Code listing 3

We can see that our first network from *Figure 2* is still there (the left-most line from top to bottom). New nodes were added and some of the existing nodes were reused: the `ObjectTypeNode` node for type `Account` and the `AlphaNode` node that checks the `balance` property (the top-left, red node followed by a blue node). You can try to change the order of `Account` constraints like this: `$account : Account(balance < 100, type == Account.Type.STUDENT)`, and you'll see that only the `ObjectTypeNode` node will be reused. We'll look at node sharing later.

The new node (green node) in *Figure 3* is a special type of `BetaNode` called `JoinNode`. As the name suggests, the purpose of this node is to join the tuple with the fact. The result is then tested if it satisfies constraints of this node; in our case it is `accounts contains $account`. The `$account` fact comes from the left input and represents the tuple, and `$customer` is the fact that comes from the right input. If all constraints are satisfied, a new tuple is created from the input tuple and input fact. In our case that will be a tuple of size two that contains the `$account` and `$customer` facts.

Example 2 – inserting a fact

To see how this works we'll go step-by-step through inserting an `Account` fact followed by a `Customer` fact. The `Account` fact will enter the network through the `EntryPointNode` node. It will then propagate through the `ObjectTypeNode` node for type `Account` to the `AlphaNode` node that tests the `balance` property. Let's say the test is successful. As we already know this is the last node that both rules share. The facts then propagate down to two branches: `LeftInputAdapterNode` (where it ends up activating our first rule) and `AlphaNode`. This second `AlphaNode` node contains the following constraint: `type == Account.Type.STUDENT`. If our fact satisfies this constraint, it continues to another `LeftInputAdapterNode`, where it is wrapped into a tuple. This tuple then enters the `JoinNode` node. The tuple is added to the left memory of `JoinNode`. The `JoinNode` node then looks into its right memory if it can create a match. Since the right memory is empty, no match is created and the propagation finishes.

We'll now insert a `Customer` fact into the knowledge session. The fact enters the network and continues through the `ObjectTypeNode` node for type `Customer`. It then propagates into the `JoinNode` node. The `Customer` fact is added to the right memory. The `JoinNode` node then looks into its left memory if it can create a match. It finds the `Account` fact that has been added previously. The `JoinNode` node then evaluates its constraint over the possible match, `accounts contains $account`. If this constraint is satisfied, the `JoinNode` node creates a tuple of size two that contains both the `Account` fact and `Customer` fact. This tuple is then propagated to the next node, which is `TerminalNode`. The `studentWithLowAccountBalance` rule is activated.

There are various types of `BetaNodes`. We've already seen the `JoinNode` node. Others include `NotNode`, `AccumulateNode`, and `ExistsNode`. Their names are self-explanatory. Each node represents one rule construct, for example, the `NotNode` represents the `not` construct.

More complex example

For some more complex rules we also need a node that takes two tuples on its input. For example, imagine we have the following single rule in our knowledge base. This rule will fire if there is no customer with a low account balance, living at a particular address. To implement this rule we'll need `not` with nested `and`, because we need to test the nonexistence of the customers with specific accounts. The rule looks as follows:

```
rule noCustomerWithLowAccountBalance
  when
    $address : Address( addressLine1 == "Rossa Avenue" )
    not (
      $account : Account( balance < 100 ) and
      Customer( accounts contains $account )
```

```
    )
  then
    System.out.println("No customers with low balance in "+
    "their accounts live at Rossa Avenue");
  end
```

Code listing 4: Rule with a complex not constraint

Please note that both `Account` and `Customer` facts are inside one single `not` construct. If we look at the resulting Rete network of this single rule, we'll see the following:

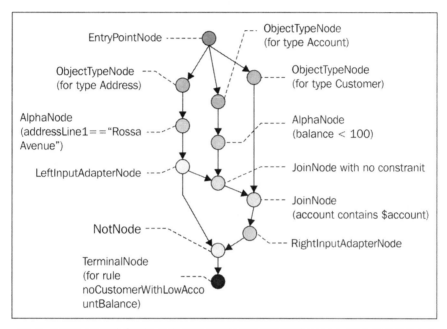

Figure 4: Rete network for the noCustomerWithLowAccountBalance rule from Code listing 4

Note that the `NotNode` node in this case takes two tuples on both its inputs. One comes from the `LeftInputAdapterNode` node, which contains the `Address` fact. The other tuple consists of the `Customer` and `Account` facts. As we already know the `NotNode` node expects a simple fact on its right input. To make this work a `RightInputAdapterNode` node is added to the network. It is the light-brown node.

The `RightInputAdapterNode` node makes the tuple behave like it was a single fact. This allows us to build more complex networks.

EvalConditionNode and FromNode

Similar to TerminalNode these nodes have only one tuple input. The EvalConditionNode node implements the eval construct (not the inline eval). It evaluates its constraints using the propagated tuple as the context. The FromNode node implements the from construct. This node takes facts outside of the Rete network and adds them into the tuple.

Retracting or modifying a fact

We've already seen two examples of what happens when we insert a new fact into the knowledge session. It enters the network through the entry node and propagates down the network to the terminal node. We'll now look at what happens when we retract, modify, or update a fact. Since modify or update is implemented as a half-way retract and then insert, we can focus only on the retract step.

When we insert a fact into the network and it propagates down, it maintains a linked list of tuples it is part of. Each tuple knows which node created it. When we retract this fact, the list of tuples is iterated and the tuple is retracted from the nodes that created it.

This is called asymmetrical Rete because the insert is different to the retract. In symmetrical Rete (pre Drools 5.0), the retract would behave exactly the same as insert. It was done like this because the retract needs to go through the same propagation path as the insert did. However, instead of creating new tuples and adding them into node memories, they would be removed (for this to work the facts couldn't change). In order to follow the same propagation path, the state of the fact had to stay unchanged. This wasn't always possible and so various attempts such as shadow facts were implemented. They didn't solve this problem fully and so Version 5.0 of Drools uses asymmetrical Rete that has none of these problems.

 Performance tip: Facts that are modified often should go at the end of the rule condition section. For example, in the rule from *Code listing 3*, if we modify an Account fact, then both AlphaNodes and JoinNode need to be reevaluated. However, if we modify a Customer fact, then only the JoinNode node needs to be reevaluated.

Initial fact

Imagine that we have a rule that checks if there are no customers in the knowledge session. The rule might look like this:

```
rule noCustomer
  when
    not Customer()
  then
    System.out.println("No customers");
end
```

Code listing 5: A rule with a not constraint as its first condition

As we already know, a not construct is implemented by the NotNode node. This node is of type BetaNode, which means it needs two inputs: right fact input and left tuple input. The right input in our case is a Customer fact. However, since the not Customer() condition is the first in our rule (and also the only one), there is no tuple source to connect the left input to. Let's look at the resulting network:

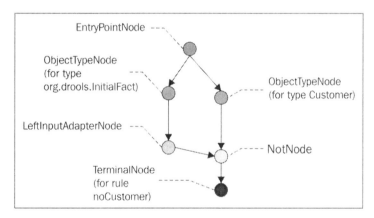

Figure 5: Rete network for the noCustomer rule from Code listing 5

As we can see there is another ObjectType node for a mysterious fact called InitialFact. Its purpose is just for these situations where there is no tuple source to connect with. The InitialFact fact is automatically inserted into the session as the first fact.

Similar to NotNode, other nodes that sometimes need this InitialFact fact are ExistsNode, AccumulateNode, and EvalConditionNode (please note that the EvalConditionNode node needs only one tuple input).

Node sharing

We've already touched on node sharing when we went through the rule from *Code listing 3*. Node sharing is one of the techniques used to minimize the size of the Rete network. The more nodes two rules share, the better. We already know that the order of conditions within a rule and even the order of constraints within a single condition affects the order of nodes within the Rete network and so affects the sharing of nodes.

The node sharing takes place when the network is built, that is, when we're creating a knowledge base out of knowledge packages. The node sharing is implemented very simply by using the `equals` method of the standard `Object` class. When a new rule is added into an existing network, new nodes are created as if the network was empty. These nodes are then inserted into the existing network. When this happens, the algorithm checks if such a node already exists by using the `equals` method. Only the appropriate nodes are being examined at the current level within the network. If a node is found that is equal to the new node, the found node is used instead and the new node is simply discarded.

Example

This may be easiest to explain with an example. We'll build on examples we've seen so far. Let's say that our knowledge base already has the rule `accountBalanceAtLeast` from *Code listing 2* and we want to add the rule `studentWithLowAccountBalance` from *Code listing 3*. We should end up with a network as depicted in *Figure 3*.

The `studentWithLowAccountBalance` rule contains two conditions that are joined by an `and` implicit. The first condition is on a single `Account` fact. It can be handled by two `AlphaNodes`. First, we need to create an `EntryPointNode` node; however, since the network already has such `EntryPointNode`, the existing node is reused instead. The next node that is needed is `ObjectTypeNode` for the `Account` type. Continuing from the `EntryPointNode` node such `ObjectTypeNode` already exists and so it is reused. Next, we continue from this `ObjectTypeNode`. We create an `AlphaNode` node with constraint `balance < 100`. Since there is already such a node, we can reuse it.

The sharing of nodes with the `accountBalanceAtLeast` rule ends here. We create an `AlphaNode` node with constraint `type == Account.Type.STUDENT`. From our current position in the Rete network, we can see that the current node has only one child, an `LeftInputAdapterNode` node. We cannot reuse this node, instead we'll add our `AlphaNode` node to the current node's list of children nodes. Since this is the last `AlphaNode` node, we'll add a `LeftInputAdapterNode` node. At this stage we have a tuple that contains the `Account` fact. The first condition of our rule is implemented. We'll now remember our current position in the network.

The process continues with the second condition of the
`studentWithLowAccountBalance` rule. This condition is on the `Customer` fact.
The `Customer` fact must similarly go through the `EntryPointNode` node that can be
reused. It then continues to `ObjectTypeNode` for the `Customer` type, which must be
added because there is none present. Next ,we need a `JoinNode` because we already
have a tuple that we have to join with, and we also have to implement the `accounts`
`contains $account` constraint. A `JoinNode` node is created that takes the tuple on
its left input and the `Customer` fact on its right input. As before, a check is made if an
equal node, descending from the remembered position, already exists. There is no
such node, so our new `JoinNode` node is simply added to the network. Again, we'll
remember the current position in the network. This is the last condition for this rule,
so a `TerminalNode` node is added and the process has finished.

Node indexing

As the facts propagate through the Rete network, another optimization technique is
to index fact values. We can then evaluate each test more quickly.

The AlphaNode indexing

When a fact meets constraints specified by a node, it is propagated to all its
descending child nodes. This usually means iterating over all child nodes and
propagating the fact. This takes some time, especially if there are many child
nodes. Luckily, we can index some `AlphaNode` node. The `AlphaNode` node with the
`equals` constraints (literal constraints). By default, Drools creates an index (a hash
table) if we are testing a property for more than three different values. The object is
propagated only to nodes, where it makes sense (test will succeed). This means that
we don't have to iterate over those nodes.

Imagine that we have the following types of rules that fire for specific currencies:

```
rule accountEUR
  when
    $account : Account( currency == "EUR" )
  then
    //..
end
```

Code listing 6: A rule with one literal constraint

Let's say there is one rule for different currencies (EUR, USD, GBP, and AUD). Then we may also have one rule that checks if the currency is different from EUR `currency != "EUR"` and one that checks some different property of `Account`, for example, `type == Account.Type.SAVINGS`. These rules will generate the following network (only part of it is shown):

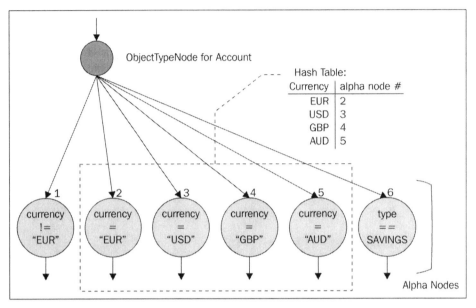

Figure 6: The AlphaNode indexing

From the previous figure, we can see that a fact propagates through the `ObjectTypeNode` node. Let's say that this account has `currency` set to `USD`. This fact will propagate to nodes 1, 3, and 6, completely avoiding nodes 2, 4, and 5.

Computation complexity

We are going to compare this with imperative-programming. Let's say we have the following code:

```
if (account.getCurrency().equals("EUR")) {}
else if (account.getCurrency().equals("USD")) {}
else if (account.getCurrency().equals("GBP")) {}
...
```

Code listing 7: Imperative-style implementation

If we have an `Account` fact where `currency` was set to `GPB`, the program would have to evaluate all three conditions until it finds the correct branch. The complexity is $O(n)$, where n is the number of `if` branches.

However, if we use index, this effectively translates to a lookup in a hashtable, `hashtable.get(account.getCurrency())`, which returns the correct branch/node. This includes calculating the hashcode of `account.getCurrency()` (hashcode of string `GBP`) and a lookup in the hashtable (a quick operation). The complexity is O(1).

The BetaNode indexing

As was the case with the `AlphaNode`s constraints with the `equal` operator indexed, `BetaNode`s have two types of input. Left input for tuples and right input for ordinary facts. By default, `BetaNode` has a left and right memory. Each memory can be indexed. Drools can index up to three constraints (with the `equals` operators).

Since Drools 5.5, comparison operators can be indexed, but only inside `NotNode` or `ExistsNode`.

As we already know:

- When a tuple enters a `BetaNode` node, it is added to the left memory of `BetaNode`. Then a match is attempted. Without an index, we have to iterate over all facts in the right memory, and if they match, a new tuple is propagated.

- This is similar to when a fact enters a `BetaNode` node. It is added to the right memory of `BetaNode`. Then we iterate over all tuples in the left memory, and if a match is found, a new tuple is propagated.

By using an index we don't have to iterate over all facts/tuples in the opposite memory. We will be iterating only over facts/tuples that meet the indexed constraints. For each object found we have to test the rest of the constraints (ones that weren't indexed).

Example

Let's consider the following single rule that matches customer with its account:

```
rule accountWithCustomerLastName
  when
    Customer( $lastName : lastName )
    $account : Account( name == $lastName )
  then
    //..
end
```

Code listing 8: A rule that matches on two facts that are joined on Account.name == Customer.lastName

This rule will be represented by a network of one Rete node, one `EntryPointNode` node, two `ObjectTypeNode` nodes, one `LeftInputAdapterNode` node (for `Customer`), one `JoinNode` node, and finally one `TerminalNode` node.

Next, we'll insert the following objects:

- `new Customer(..)` with `lastName` set to `Edwards`: This fact will be added to the left memory (as a tuple of size 1).

- `new Customer(..)` with `lastName` set to `Parker`: This fact will be added to the left memory (as a tuple of size 1).

- `new Customer(..)` with `lastName` set to `Douglas`: This fact will be added to the left memory (as a tuple of size 1).

- `new Customer(..)` with `lastName` set again to `Douglas`: This fact will be added to the left memory (as a tuple of size 1).

- `new Account(..)` with `name` set to `Morris`: This fact will be added to the right memory and a match will be attempted, since `leftMemory.get("Morris") == null`, it won't succeed. No tuple will be propagated.

- `new Account(..)` with `name` set to `Parker`: This fact will be added to the right memory and a match will be attempted; however, this time `leftMemory.get("Parker")` returns one object (`ID = 2`). Since our `BetaNode` node has only one constraint, there is no need to do further tests. The new tuple that will be propagated will be of size 2, consisting of objects 2 and 6.

This result is illustrated in the following figure. Please note the contents of the two indexes/hashtables:

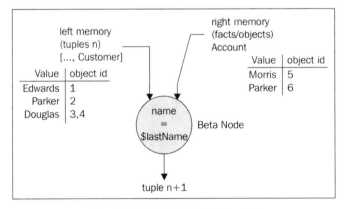

Figure 7: JoinNode with its memories

Many of the options described in this section are configurable through the `KnowledgeBaseConfiguration` interface or in the file `drools.default.rulebase.conf` that can be found in the `drools-core.jar/META-INF` directory.

Left and right unlinking

This is another feature of Drools that helps to reduce the amount of memory, especially for large knowledge bases with lots of rules. Its principle is simple. As we know, beta nodes have left and right memory, every time a fact propagates, it is added to the right memory, and every time a tuple propagates, it is added to the left memory. However, if a fact/tuple is being propagated and the opposite left/right memory is empty, there can't be any match. The fact/tuple would normally enter the right/left memory and it would wait there until the opposite memory gets filled, so a match can be attempted. What Drools can do instead is that it can unlink the current (left or right) memory. This will save us unnecessary node memory population. Then, in case the opposite memory gets populated, the unlinked side gets linked back and receives all the propagations that were left out.

Note that this feature is turned off by default and you have to explicitly enable it by setting LRUnlinkingOption to ENABLED on the knowledge base configuration.

The KnowledgeBase partitioning

Drools supports parallel execution mode. One session can be executed by multiple threads.

Note that this feature is not supported in Drools 5.5.0.Final. It might be reintroduced in future; for now, keep this in mind and take this information as a curiosity.

The Rete network is split into multiple partitions. Each partition is handled by a PartitionTaskManager object. It manages a list of suspended propagations and makes sure that only one of them is being executed at a time over this partition. When a fact is propagated through the network, it may go through one or more partitions. Once a propagation reaches the boundary between two partitions, the other partition's PartitionTaskManager is notified and the current propagation is transferred to its list of propagations. The suspended propagation then waits in this list until the other partition manager is ready to take it further.

Each knowledge session has a unique set of its own PartitionTaskManager.

How are partitions formed? When we have an empty network and we want to add a new rule, first we have to add the Rete node, `EntryPoinNode`, and `ObjectTypeNode`. These types of nodes are always within the partition called MAIN. The other nodes that are added for our rule form a new partition 0. We now have a network representing one rule that has two partitions. If this rule was the `accountBalanceAtLeast` rule from *Code listing 2*, the partitions would look as follows:

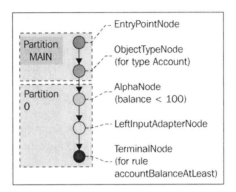

Figure 8: Rete network for the `accountBalanceAtLeast` rule from Code Listing 2 with partitions.

If we now continue to add more rules into this network, they may reuse existing nodes as we've learned in the section about node sharing. If a node is reused, its partition is reused as well. If not, a new partition is created and all remaining nodes for this rule are added to this new partition.

After adding the rule `noCustomerWithLowAccountBalance` from *Code listing 3*, the partitions will look as follows:

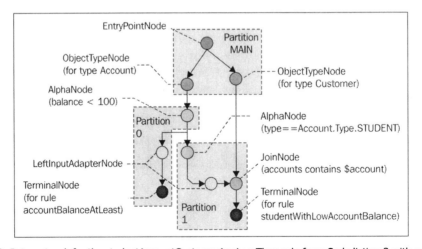

Figure 9: Rete network for the studentAccountCustomerAgeLessThan rule from Code listing 3 with partitions

If we want to add more rules, this process repeats until we've added all.

Please note that only the fact propagations are executed in parallel. Rule consequences are still executed sequentially when you call fireAllRules.

If you start the session in the fireUntilHalt mode, the rule consequences will be executed immediately (as soon as the rule becomes activated).

Parallel execution

The following code snippet shows how to configure the Drools for parallel execution. It is done through the KnowledgeBaseConfiguration. It provides two options: MultithreadEvaluationOption that simply turns this feature on (it is disabled by default) and MaxThreadsOption that sets the maximum number of threads across all partitions:

```
KnowledgeBaseConfiguration configuration = KnowledgeBaseFactory
  .newKnowledgeBaseConfiguration();
configuration.setOption(MultithreadEvaluationOption.YES );
configuration.setOption(MaxThreadsOption.get(2) );
KnowledgeBasekbase = KnowledgeBaseFactory
  .newKnowledgeBase(configuration);
```

Code listing 9: Enabling multithread evaluation

This knowledge base can be then used as normal. If we don't specify the maximum number of threads, it will be defaulted to the number of partitions we have.

Summary

In this chapter we've learned about the Rete algorithm and mainly about how it uses the Rete network to represent our rules. We've explored various types of nodes that are within the Rete network: Alpha nodes that can apply a constraint on a single fact and Beta nodes that can apply a constraint on multiple facts. We've seen various rules and their corresponding Rete networks.

We've learned about various optimizations used within Drools. One of them was node sharing. By sharing the nodes we can greatly reduce the amount of work a computer must do in order to execute our rules. After all, there is no point in evaluating the same conditions multiple times.

We've seen that the order of the conditions within a rule and even the order of the constraints within a condition is crucial when it comes to node sharing. Drools currently doesn't implement any node-rearranging strategy to achieve the best node sharing. When designing your rules, try to put the most restrictive conditions and constraints first. Try to keep the same order for them. By doing this the advantage that you can get from node sharing will be maximized.

The Rete node indexing section described how the Alpha and Beta node indexing works. Keep in mind that it applies only to constraints with an equal operator. However, there are plans to extend this support also for relational operators (greater than, less than, and so on).

This chapter showed the power of declarative programming. We just declare what should be done and the engine can then decide how to do it, as effectively as possible depending on the runtime conditions.

A
Setting Up the Development Environment

This section describes the setup of the local development environment for working with Drools.

Environment setup

Java Version 1.5+ is required to run examples in this book. Drools can be downloaded from `http://www.jboss.org/drools/downloads.html`. You'll need the Drools (`drools-distribution-5.5.0.Final.zip`) and Drools and jBPM tools (`droolsjbpm-tools-distribution-5.5.0.Final.zip`) downloads. The former is the rule engine itself, that is, the binaries. The latter is the Drools Eclipse plugin. It greatly helps at writing rules. The Drools new project wizard in Eclipse can create a simple Drools project that is ready to run. When setting it up, you need to tell it the location of `Drools Runtime` (where you extracted the Drools binaries).

Next, you'll also need to download jBPM. Go to `http://www.jboss.org/jbpm/` and select the **Downloads** link. From there go to **jBPM 5 | jbpm-5.4.0.Final** and download the `jbpm-5.4.0.Final-bin.zip` file. Similar to setting up the Drools runtime, we'll set up jBPM Runtime inside Eclipse.

If for some reason the Eclipse plugin is not an option, Drools can be set up by maven or manually. When using maven, add at least the following dependencies to your project's `pom.xml` file:

```
<dependencies>
  <dependency>
    <groupId>org.drools</groupId>
    <artifactId>knowledge-api</artifactId>
    <version>${drools.version}</version>
```

```
      </dependency>
      <dependency>
        <groupId>org.drools</groupId>
        <artifactId>drools-core</artifactId>
        <version>${drools.version}</version>
      </dependency>
      <dependency>
        <groupId>org.drools</groupId>
        <artifactId>drools-compiler</artifactId>
        <version>${drools.version}</version>
      </dependency>
      <dependency>
        <groupId>org.jbpm</groupId>
        <artifactId>jbpm-flow</artifactId>
        <version>${jbpm.version}</version>
      </dependency>
      <dependency>
        <groupId>org.jbpm</groupId>
        <artifactId>jbpm-flow-builder</artifactId>
        <version>${jbpm.version}</version>
      </dependency>
      <dependency>
        <groupId>org.jbpm</groupId>
        <artifactId>jbpm-bpmn2</artifactId>
        <version>${jbpm.version}</version>
      </dependency>
    </dependencies>
    <properties>
      <drools.version>5.5.0.Final</drools.version>
      <jbpm.version>5.4.0.Final</jbpm.version>
    </properties>
```

Code listing 1: Drools and jBPM dependencies in a maven's pom.xml file

By adding these dependencies into the project's pom file, we're declaring that our project depends on the Drools libraries such as knowledge-api, drools-code, and drools-compiler and the jBPM libraries such as jbpm-flow, jbpm-flow-builder, and jbpm-bpmn2. Depending on the features used, we may need to add or remove other Drools/jBPM libraries. Please note the drools.version property that is set to Version **5.5.0.Final**. You may need to change it depending on the latest release available. The same applies to the jBPM version property.

If you are not sure about which Drools version is compatible with which jBPM version, just Google for `Drools compatibility matrix`. This information is part of the Drools Introduction documentation.

We may also need to tell maven where to get these libraries. They can be downloaded from the official JBoss maven repository, which is located at `https://repository.jboss.org/nexus/content/repositories/releases/`. The following code snippet does the trick:

```
<repositories>
  <repository>
    <id>JBoss Repository</id>
    <url>https://repository.jboss.org/nexus/content/repositories/
releases/</url>
    <snapshots>
      <enabled>false</enabled>
    </snapshots>
    <releases>
      <enabled>true</enabled>
    </releases>
  </repository>
</repositories>
```

Code listing 2: JBoss maven repository in a maven's pom.xml file

Note that the latest snapshot releases can be downloaded from `https://repository.jboss.org/nexus/content/repositories/snapshots/`.

Let's now look at libraries that are needed in more detail.

Dependencies and their licenses

Drools is licensed under Apache License, Version 2.0 (ASL is a free software license that allows us to develop free, open source, as well as proprietary software, and its contents can be found at `http://www.apache.org/licenses/LICENSE-2.0.html`). In order to run the examples in this book, at least the following libraries will be needed on the Java classpath:

- `antlr-runtime-3.3.jar`: This is a parser generator and helps with parsing rule files (licensed under ANTLR 3 License, which is based on the BSD license)

- `ecj-3.5.1.jar`: This is a generic eclipse Java compiler and part of Eclipse Java Development Tools (licensed under the Eclipse Public License v1.0)

- `knowledge-api-5.5.0.Final.jar`: This is a Drools and jBPM user API or also known as the public API, and most of the classes we'll be dealing with are located here (licensed under ASL)

- `knowledge-internal-api-5.5.0.Final.jar`: This is a Drools and jBPM internal user API (licensed under ASL)

- `drools-compiler-5.5.0.Final.jar`: This is a knowledge compiler, understands rule syntax, and compiles rules into Java classes (licensed under ASL)

- `mvel2-2.1.3.jar`: mvel is property extraction and expression language for Java; some core Drools features are implemented using mvel, and it is also used as a dialect in the rule language (licensed under ASL)

- `drools-core-5.5.0.Final.jar`: This is a Drools engine itself (licensed under ASL)

- `slf4j-api-1.6.4.jar`: This is a logging library (licensed under MIT license)

- `protobuf-java-2.4.1.jar`: This is a serialization library (licensed under BSD 3 license)

In order to build and run processes, we'll also need the following jBPM libraries:

- `jbpm-flow-5.4.0.Final.jar`: This is a library for process execution (licensed under ASL)

- `jbpm-flow-builder-5.4.0.Final.jar`: This is a library for building processes (licensed under ASL)

- `jbpm-bpmn2-5.4.0.Final`: This is used to build processes in the BPMN2 format (licensed under ASL)

These libraries are valid for Drools Version 5.5.0.Final and jBPM Version 5.4.0.Final. Please note that you may need different versions of these libraries, depending on your version of Drools/jBPM.

B

Creating Custom Operators

We've already seen various operators that can be used within rule conditions. These include == and !=; relational operators such as >, <, and >= ; temporal operators such as after, during, and finishes; or others such as matches, which does regular expression matching. In this section we'll define our own custom operator.

The == operators uses the Object.equals or hashCode methods for comparing objects. However, sometimes we need to test if two objects are actually referring to the same instance. This is slightly faster than Object.equals or hashCode comparison (only slightly faster, because the hash code is calculated once for object and then it is cached).

Imagine that we have a rule, which matches on an Account fact and a Customer fact. We want to test if the owner property of Account contains the same instance of a Customer fact as the Customer fact that was matched. The rule might look like this:

```
rule accountHasCustomer
  when
    $customer : Customer( )
    Account( owner instanceEquals $customer )
  then
    //..
end
```

Code listing 1: Rule with a custom operator such as instanceEquals in the custom_operator.drl file

From the previous rule we can see the use of a custom operator named instanceEquals. Most, if not all, Drools operators support a negated version with not:

```
Account( owner not instanceEquals $customer )
```

Code listing 2: Condition that uses the negated version of the custom operator

This condition will match on the `Account` fact whose `owner` property is of a different instance than the fact bound under the `$customer` binding.

Some operators support parameters. They can be passed within the angle brackets as we've already seen in *Chapter 7, Complex Event Processing*, when we were discussing temporal operators.

Based on our requirements we can now write the following unit test for our new `instanceEquals` operator:

```
@Test
public void instancesEqualsBeta() throws Exception {
    Customer customer = new Customer();
    Account account = new Account();

    session.execute(Arrays.asList(customer, account));
    assertNotFired("accountHasCustomer");

    account.setOwner(new Customer());
    session.execute(Arrays.asList(customer, account));
    assertNotFired("accountHasCustomer");

    account.setOwner(customer);
    session.execute(Arrays.asList(customer, account));
    assertFired("accountHasCustomer");
}
```

Code listing 3: Unit test for the accountHasCustomer rule

It tests three use cases. The first one is an account with no customer. The test verifies that the rule didn't fire. In the second use case, the `owner` property of `Account` is set to a different customer than what is in the rule session. The rule isn't fired either. Finally, in the last use case, the `owner` property of `Account` is set to the right `Customer` object and the rule fires.

Before we can successfully execute this test, we have to implement our operator and tell Drools about it. We can tell Drools through the `PackageBuilderConfiguration` method. This configuration is fed into the familiar `PackageBuilder` instance. The following code listing, which is in fact the unit test setup method, shows how to do it:

```
@BeforeClass
public static void setUpClass() throws Exception {
    KnowledgeBuilderConfiguration builderConf =
    KnowledgeBuilderFactory.newKnowledgeBuilderConfiguration();
```

```
    builderConf.setOption(EvaluatorOption.get(
        "instanceEquals",
        new InstanceEqualsEvaluatorDefinition()));

    knowledgeBase = DroolsHelper.createKnowledgeBase(null,
        builderConf, "custom_operator.drl");
}
```

Code listing 4: Unit test setup for custom operator test

A new instance of the `PackageBuilderConfiguration` method is created and a new evaluator definition is added. It represents our new `instanceEquals` operator, `InstanceEqualsEvaluatorDefinition`. This configuration is then used to create a `KnowledgeBase` object.

We can now implement our operator. This will be done in two steps:

1. Create `EvaluatorDefinition`, which will be responsible for creating evaluators based on actual rules.

2. Create the actual evaluator (please note that the implementation should be stateless).

The evaluator definition will be used at rule compile time and the evaluator at rule runtime.

All evaluator definitions must implement the `org.drools.base.evaluators.EvaluatorDefinition` interface. It contains all methods that Drools needs to work with our operator. We'll now look at the `InstanceEqualsEvaluatorDefinition` interface. The contents of this class is as follows:

```
public class InstanceEqualsEvaluatorDefinition implements
    EvaluatorDefinition {
  public static final Operator INSTANCE_EQUALS = Operator
      .addOperatorToRegistry("instanceEquals", false);
  public static final Operator NOT_INSTANCE_EQUALS = Operator
      .addOperatorToRegistry("instanceEquals", true);

  private static final String[] SUPPORTED_IDS = {
      INSTANCE_EQUALS.getOperatorString() };

  private Evaluator[] evaluator;

  @Override
  public Evaluator getEvaluator(ValueType type,
      Operator operator) {
    return this.getEvaluator(type, operator
```

```
            .getOperatorString(), operator.isNegated(), null);
   }

   @Override
   public Evaluator getEvaluator(ValueType type,
       Operator operator, String parameterText) {
     return this.getEvaluator(type, operator
         .getOperatorString(), operator.isNegated(),
         parameterText);
   }

   @Override
   public Evaluator getEvaluator(ValueType type,
       String operatorId, boolean isNegated,
       String parameterText) {
     return getEvaluator(type, operatorId, isNegated,
         parameterText, Target.FACT, Target.FACT);
   }

   @Override
   public Evaluator getEvaluator(ValueType type,
       String operatorId, boolean isNegated,
       String parameterText, Target leftTarget,
       Target rightTarget) {
     if (evaluator == null) {
       evaluator = new Evaluator[2];
     }
     int index = isNegated ? 0 : 1;
     if (evaluator[index] == null) {
       evaluator[index] = new InstanceEqualsEvaluator(type,
           isNegated);
     }
     return evaluator[index];
   }

   @Override
   public String[] getEvaluatorIds() {
     return SUPPORTED_IDS;
   }

   @Override
   public boolean isNegatable() {
     return true;
   }
```

```
@Override
public Target getTarget() {
  return Target.FACT;
}

@Override
public boolean supportsType(ValueType type) {
  return true;
}

@Override
public void readExternal(ObjectInput in)
    throws IOException, ClassNotFoundException {
  evaluator = (Evaluator[]) in.readObject();
}

@Override
public void writeExternal(ObjectOutput out)
    throws IOException {
  out.writeObject(evaluator);
}
```

Code listing 5: Implementation of custom EvaluatorDefinition

The `InstanceEqualsEvaluatorDefinition` instance contains various information that Drools requires, for example, the operator's ID—whether this operator can be negated and what types it supports.

At the beginning two operators are registered using the `Operator.addOperatorToRegistry` static method. The method takes two arguments: `operatorId` and a flag indicating whether this operator can be negated.

Then there are few `getEvaluator` methods. Drools will call these methods during the rule compilation step. The last `getEvaluator` method gets passed in the following arguments:

- `type`: This is the type of operator's operands.
- `operatorId`: This is the identifier of the operator (one evaluator definition can handle multiple IDs).
- `isNegated`: This specifies whether this operator can be used with `not`
- `parameterText`: This is essentially the text in angle brackets; the evaluator definition is responsible for parsing this text. In our case it is simply ignored.
- `leftTarget` and `rightTarget`: These specify whether this operator operates on facts, fact handles, or both.

Then the method lazily initializes two implementations of the operator itself, InstanceEqualsEvaluator. Since our operator will operate only on facts and we don't care about the parameter text, we need to cater only for two cases: non-negated operations and negated operations. These evaluators are then cached for another use.

It is worth noting the supportsType method always returns true, since we want to compare any facts regardless of their type.

All Drools evaluators must extend the org.drools.spi.Evaluator interface. Drools provides an BaseEvaluator abstract that we can extend to simplify our implementation. Now we have to implement few evaluate methods for executing the operator under various circumstances. Using the operator with a literal (for example, Account(owner instanceEquals "some literal value")) or variable (for example, Account(owner instanceEquals $customer)). The implementation of InstanceEqualsEvaluatoroperator is as follows (please note that it is implemented as a static inner class):

```java
public static class InstanceEqualsEvaluator extends
    BaseEvaluator {

public InstanceEqualsEvaluator(final ValueType type,
    final boolean isNegated) {
  super(type, isNegated ? NOT_INSTANCE_EQUALS
      : INSTANCE_EQUALS);
}


@Override
public boolean evaluate(
    InternalWorkingMemory workingMemory,
    InternalReadAccessor extractor, Object object,
    FieldValue value) {
  final Object objectValue = extractor.getValue(
      workingMemory, object);
  return this.getOperator().isNegated()
      ^ (objectValue == value.getValue());
}


@Override
public boolean evaluate(
    InternalWorkingMemory workingMemory,
    InternalReadAccessor leftExtractor, Object left,
    InternalReadAccessor rightExtractor, Object right) {
  final Object value1 = leftExtractor.getValue(
      workingMemory, left);
  final Object value2 = rightExtractor.getValue(
      workingMemory, right);
```

```java
        return this.getOperator().isNegated()
            ^ (value1 == value2);
    }

    @Override
    public boolean evaluateCachedLeft(
        InternalWorkingMemory workingMemory,
        VariableContextEntry context, Object right) {
      return this.getOperator().isNegated()
          ^ (right == ((ObjectVariableContextEntry)
          context).left);
    }

    @Override
    public boolean evaluateCachedRight(
        InternalWorkingMemory workingMemory,
        VariableContextEntry context, Object left) {
      return this.getOperator().isNegated()
          ^ (left == ((ObjectVariableContextEntry)
          context).right);
    }

    @Override
    public String toString() {
      return "InstanceEquals instanceEquals";
    }
  }
}
```

Code listing 6: Implementation of a custom Evaluator

The operator's implementation just defines various versions of the evaluate method. The first one is executed when evaluating alpha nodes with literal constraints. The extractor is used to extract the field from a fact and the value represents the actual literal. The ^ operator is the standard bitwise exclusive or a Java operator.

The second evaluate method is used when evaluating alpha nodes with variable bindings. In this case the input parameters include left/right extractor and left/right fact (please note that the left and right facts represent the same fact instance).

The third one, evaluateCachedLeft, and the fourth one, evaluateCachedRight, will be executed when evaluating beta node constraints.

For more information please refer to the API and parent class org.drools.base. BaseEvaluator.

Both the evaluator definition and the evaluator should be serializable.

Summary

This shows us the power of Drools expressiveness. Custom operators can be useful in various situations. For example, if we find ourselves repeating the same conditions over and over again, or if we want get rid of some ugly-looking free form expression or inline `eval`. All this can be done by writing a custom, domain-specific operator. The rule becomes much easier to read and write.

C
Dependencies of Sample Application

The following is a listing of third-party dependencies and their versions as needed by the sample application implemented in *Chapter 9, Building a Sample Application*. The dependencies are given in a Maven POM format (Maven is a build tool, and for more information, please visit http://maven.apache.org/). Drools and jBPM dependencies are given in the following code listing:

```xml
<dependency>
  <groupId>org.drools</groupId>
  <artifactId>drools-core</artifactId>
  <version>${drools.ver}</version>
</dependency>
<dependency>
  <groupId>org.drools</groupId>
  <artifactId>drools-compiler</artifactId>
  <version>${drools.ver}</version>
</dependency>
<dependency>
  <groupId>org.drools</groupId>
  <artifactId>drools-spring</artifactId>
  <version>${drools.ver}</version>
</dependency>
<dependency>
  <groupId>org.drools</groupId>
  <artifactId>drools-persistence-jpa</artifactId>
  <version>${drools.ver}</version>
</dependency>
<dependency>
  <groupId>org.jbpm</groupId>
```

```
    <artifactId>jbpm-flow-builder</artifactId>
    <version>${jbpm.version}</version>
</dependency>
<dependency>
  <groupId>org.jbpm</groupId>
  <artifactId>jbpm-persistence-jpa</artifactId>
  <version>${jbpm.version}</version>
</dependency>
```

Code listing 1: Extract from the sample application pom.xml file (part 1)

Next, other third-party dependencies are given in the following code listing:

```
<dependency>
  <groupId>commons-lang</groupId>
  <artifactId>commons-lang</artifactId>
  <version>2.6</version>
</dependency>

<dependency>
  <groupId>org.slf4j</groupId>
  <artifactId>slf4j-log4j12</artifactId>
  <version>1.6.4</version>
</dependency>
<dependency>
  <groupId>org.slf4j</groupId>
  <artifactId>slf4j-api</artifactId>
  <version>1.6.4</version>
</dependency>
<dependency>
  <groupId>org.slf4j</groupId>
  <artifactId>jcl-over-slf4j</artifactId>
  <version>1.6.4</version>
</dependency>

<!-- Spring -->
<dependency>
  <groupId>org.springframework</groupId>
  <artifactId>spring-core</artifactId>
  <version>${spring.ver}</version>
</dependency>
<dependency>
  <groupId>org.springframework</groupId>
  <artifactId>spring-beans</artifactId>
  <version>${spring.ver}</version>
</dependency>
```

```
</dependency>
<dependency>
  <groupId>org.springframework</groupId>
  <artifactId>spring-orm</artifactId>
  <version>${spring.ver}</version>
</dependency>
<dependency>
  <groupId>org.springframework</groupId>
  <artifactId>spring-context</artifactId>
  <version>${spring.ver}</version>
</dependency>
<dependency>
  <groupId>org.springframework</groupId>
  <artifactId>spring-tx</artifactId>
  <version>${spring.ver}</version>
</dependency>
<dependency>
  <groupId>org.springframework</groupId>
  <artifactId>spring-webmvc</artifactId>
  <version>${spring.ver}</version>
</dependency>
<dependency>
  <groupId>org.springframework</groupId>
  <artifactId>spring-web</artifactId>
  <version>${spring.ver}</version>
</dependency>
<dependency>
  <groupId>org.springframework</groupId>
  <artifactId>spring-jdbc</artifactId>
  <version>${spring.ver}</version>
</dependency>
<dependency>
  <groupId>org.aspectj</groupId>
  <artifactId>aspectjrt</artifactId>
  <version>1.7.1</version>
</dependency>
<dependency>
  <groupId>org.aspectj</groupId>
  <artifactId>aspectjweaver</artifactId>
  <version>1.7.1</version>
</dependency>
<dependency>
  <groupId>org.springframework</groupId>
  <artifactId>spring-test</artifactId>
```

```
      <scope>test</scope>
      <version>${spring.ver}</version>
    </dependency>

    <!-- Hibernate -->
    <dependency>
      <groupId>org.hibernate</groupId>
      <artifactId>hibernate-entitymanager</artifactId>
      <version>4.1.9.Final</version>
    </dependency>
    <dependency>
      <groupId>org.hibernate</groupId>
      <artifactId>hibernate-core</artifactId>
      <version>4.1.9.Final</version>
    </dependency>

    <!-- HSQLDB -->
    <dependency>
      <groupId>com.h2database</groupId>
      <artifactId>h2</artifactId>
      <version>1.3.170</version>
    </dependency>
```

Code listing 2: Extract from the sample application pom.xml file (part 2)

Finally, we'll define properties that have been used earlier:

```
<properties>
    <drools.ver>5.5.0.Final</drools.ver>
    <jbpm.version>5.4.0.Final</jbpm.version>
    <spring.ver>3.2.1.RELEASE</spring.ver>
</properties>
```

Code listing 3: Extract from the sample application pom.xml file (part 3)

Index

E

Eclipse plugin 253
EDA 137
enterprise service bus (ESB) 147
EntryPointNode 276
equals method 17
error event
  about 172
  otherwise branch, testing 174-176
  test setup 172, 173
ESP 137, 138
ETL 81
EvalConditionNode 282
eval element 30
evaluate method 303
event-driven architecture. *See* EDA
Event node 196
event stream processing. *See* ESP
executeRules method 118, 129
exists element 29
external artifact
  building 260
  building, Apache Ant used 260-262
Extract, Transform, Load. *See* ETL

F

file formats
  DRL file format 90
  DSL file format 89
  DSLR file format 90
final approval
  about 196
  Approve Event node test 196
findAddress rule 68
fireAllRules method 19
FIT 241
Framework for Integrated Test. *See* FIT
fraud detection
  about 138
  business requirements 139
  design 139-141
  modeling 139-142
  rules 142
fraud detection rules
  averageBalanceQuery, monitoring 147

high activity 163
increasing withdrawal sequence 153, 154
notification 143
two large withdrawals 149, 150
twoLargeWithdrawals rule, testing
  with 151, 153
FromNode 282
From operator 33
full serialization mode 134
functions 25

G

getAge() method 30
getAverageBalance method 149
getConversionToEurFrom function 72
getEvaluator method 301
getFactHandle method 117
getKnowledgeRuntime() method 182
getNodeInstance() method 182
getTasksAssignedAsPotentialOwner
  method 195
global variables 24

H

hashCode method 17, 297
helper method 123
high activity
  about 163, 164
  testing 164-166
human task
  about 191
  test 192-195

I

iBatis configuration 79, 80
identity mode 133
imports 23
increasing withdrawal sequence
  about 153, 154
  average balance test 154-159
  looping, prevention 159-162
  @propertyReactive annotation 160
  sequenceOfIncreasingWithdrawals rule,
    testing 162, 163
initialize method 164

validation report
   conditional element, collecting 128, 129
   serialization 130
   updating 127
validation service 57, 58

W

Web Tools Platform. *See* **WTP**
WTP 210

X

XOR 109

Thank you for buying
Drools JBoss Rules 5.X Developer's Guide

About Packt Publishing

Packt, pronounced 'packed', published its first book "*Mastering phpMyAdmin for Effective MySQL Management*" in April 2004 and subsequently continued to specialize in publishing highly focused books on specific technologies and solutions.

Our books and publications share the experiences of your fellow IT professionals in adapting and customizing today's systems, applications, and frameworks. Our solution based books give you the knowledge and power to customize the software and technologies you're using to get the job done. Packt books are more specific and less general than the IT books you have seen in the past. Our unique business model allows us to bring you more focused information, giving you more of what you need to know, and less of what you don't.

Packt is a modern, yet unique publishing company, which focuses on producing quality, cutting-edge books for communities of developers, administrators, and newbies alike. For more information, please visit our website: www.packtpub.com.

About Packt Open Source

In 2010, Packt launched two new brands, Packt Open Source and Packt Enterprise, in order to continue its focus on specialization. This book is part of the Packt Open Source brand, home to books published on software built around Open Source licences, and offering information to anybody from advanced developers to budding web designers. The Open Source brand also runs Packt's Open Source Royalty Scheme, by which Packt gives a royalty to each Open Source project about whose software a book is sold.

Writing for Packt

We welcome all inquiries from people who are interested in authoring. Book proposals should be sent to author@packtpub.com. If your book idea is still at an early stage and you would like to discuss it first before writing a formal book proposal, contact us; one of our commissioning editors will get in touch with you.

We're not just looking for published authors; if you have strong technical skills but no writing experience, our experienced editors can help you develop a writing career, or simply get some additional reward for your expertise.

Drools Developer's Cookbook

ISBN: 978-1-84951-196-4   Paperback: 310 pages

Over 40 recipes for creating a robust business rules implementation by using JBoss Drools rules

1. Master the newest Drools Expert, Fusion, Guvnor, Planner and jBPM5 features

2. Integrate Drools by using popular Java Frameworks

3. Part of Packt's Cookbook series: each recipe is independent and contains practical, step-by-step instructions to help you achieve your goal.

jBPM Developer Guide

ISBN: 978-1-84719-568-5   Paperback: 372 pages

A Java developer's guide to the JBoss Business Process Management framework

1. Thoroughly understand how the jBPM framework works

2. Build custom Java Enterprise solutions using the jBPM framework

3. No experience with jBPM required

4. Helpful guidance on converting a business analyst's spec into complete, working software

Please check **www.PacktPub.com** for information on our titles

PUBLISHING

community experience distilled

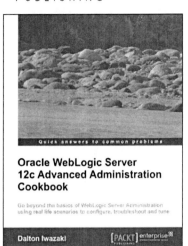

**Oracle WebLogic Server
12c Advanced Administration
Cookbook**

Go beyond the basics of WebLogic Server Administration
using real life scenarios to configure, troubleshoot and tune

Dalton Iwazaki

Oracle WebLogic Server 12c Advanced Administration Cookbook

ISBN: 978-1-84968-684-6   Paperback: 300 pages

Go beyond the basics of WebLogic Server
Administration Using real life scenarios to configure,
troubleshoot and tune

1. Learn how to set a WebLogic environment with
   stability, high availability and performance

2. Premature optmization is the root of all evil.
   Configure and tune only what really matters.

3. Understand what are you doing and why. Every
   recipe covers the theory behind the practice.

Oracle BPM Suite 11g:
Advanced BPMN Topics

Master advanced BPMN for Oracle BPM Suite including
inter-process communication, handling arrays,
and exception management

Mark Nelson   Tanya Williams

Oracle BPM Suite 11g: Advanced BPMN Topics

ISBN: 978-1-84968-756-0   Paperback: 114 pages

Master advanced BPMN for Oracle BPM Suite
including inter-process communication, handling
arrays, and exception management

1. Cover some of the most commonly
   misunderstood areas of BPMN

2. Gain the knowledge to write professional
   BPMN processes

3. A practical and concise tutorial packed with
   advanced topics which until now had received
   little or no documentation for BPM Suite
   developers and architects

Please check **www.PacktPub.com** for information on our titles

CPSIA information can be obtained at www.ICGtesting.com
Printed in the USA
BVOW001650300613

324594BV00005B/33/P